city kid
new york

The Ultimate Guide for NYC Parents
with Kids Ages 4–12

Alison Lowenstein

universe publishing

Dedication

For Lucy and Max, my city kids, and Peter, their city dad

First published in the United States of America in 2010 by
UNIVERSE PUBLISHING
A Division of Rizzoli International Publications, Inc.
300 Park Avenue South
New York, NY 10010
www.rizzoliusa.com

© 2010 by Alison Lowenstein
Cover Illustration by Sujean Rim
Design by Headcase Design

2010 2011 2012 2013 / 10 9 8 7 6 5 4 3 2 1

First Edition
Printed in the United States of America

ISBN-13: 978-0-7893-1878-7
Library of Congress Catalog Control Number: 2009938674

contents

acknowledgments

I'd like to give a special thanks to the following people for their support in writing this book: My amazing husband, Peter, who is truly the best father and husband, and who helped me tremendously. My children, Lucy and Max, who accompanied me all around the city, testing out everything for the book, and who are now experts on all the family programs and kid-friendly restaurants throughout the city. My parents, Michael and Eileen Lowenstein, who brought me up with a never-ending love and appreciation for the city and are always supportive of all my endeavors. My in-laws, Fred and Melinda Isaacs, who take time out to watch my kids each week and are always willing to help me out at a moment's notice. Without all of you, this book wouldn't be possible.

I'd also like to thank Debbie, Peter, Avery and Kyra Johnsen; Brogan Ganley; Alison Burke Griffiths; Teri Cunningham; Dina Kutcher; Robin Muskin; Emma Starr; Aimee Nadler; Allison Prete; Leslie Kaufman; Vivian Manning-Schaffel; Amy Sirot; Valerie Walsh; and Amy Widman. A big thanks to the many city parents who took time out to tell me about their favorite places and parenting tips, which were an invaluable addition to the book. A very special thanks to all the friends I made while parenting in the city and with whom I bonded as we watched our children grow from babies to kids.

I'd like to give a special thanks to Caitlin Leffel for signing the book up and always standing behind the project, and to my editor, Claire L. Gierczak, for another amazing editing job and also for her patience and enthusiasm. I'd like to thank Elizabeth Smith for her fine copyediting. A thanks goes to Brisa Robinson for her support for the book. And a special thanks to my agent, Kirsten Manges, who was also a city kid.

introduction: raising a city kid

A few years ago I wrote an essay for the Bad Parent column of a popular online parenting magazine detailing how I've made the decision to have my two children share a room and otherwise sacrifice space that they would have had to run around in the suburbs in order to live in New York City. In the essay I stated that although I had the opportunity to sell my apartment and buy a suburban home, I opted out because I wanted my kids to grow up in an urban environment. Although I admitted some of the main reasons I lived in New York was for the first-rate sushi and the lively playgrounds, there were a slew of other reasons, such as being steps away from some of the most amazing cultural centers in the city and exposing my kids to theater, dance, and musical performances at some the city's most historic venues.

As someone who grew up in Queens, I know the benefits of having the city at your fingertips. In addition to its unique cultural diversity, the city is one large classroom for kids filled with museums, theaters, and unique experiences that wouldn't be available on a daily basis unless your family lived in the city itself. This is one of the reasons why an increasing number of parents are forgoing the move to the suburbs and bringing up their children here. And so with the influx of families, New York City is becoming more kid friendly than ever before. Over the past few years, the city has become home to various children's theater companies, film festivals, kids' clothing boutiques, and even spas that are specialized for kids. You can't even walk down the

streets of the Upper East and West Sides, TriBeCa, or all over Brooklyn, along with many other parts of the city, without seeing an enormous number of families. There are a ton of magazines geared toward city parents alongside an entire community of NYC parent bloggers with thousands of daily readers. More and more people are deciding that they don't have to give up their urban lifestyles once kids enter the equation and are finding new ways and resources to provide their kids with stimulating and memorable childhoods in the big city.

Yes, there are many sacrifices that parents and kids have to make by living in the city, but they are heavily outweighed by the benefits. You know that a city is great when people give up their dining room in their "convertible two-bedroom apartment" to transform the space into their kids' room or live in a fourth-floor walk-up with two kids when they could have easily bought a house in the suburbs with a driveway and two-car garage. NYC families make these sacrifices for both the community and joys of city life.

City kids may go without a backyard with a swing set and a pool, but they have Central Park and a floating pool on a barge that docks at different locations each summer, opening up a whole new neighborhood of the city to explore. The city is the backyard for many city kids and you see them everywhere—the playgrounds are filled to the brim. All of these young New Yorkers have breathed new life into the city. The only downside to having all of these kids living in the city is that after-school programs, classes, and camps fill up quickly. In fact the *New York Times* ran an article about Brooklyn parents lining up at 4 a.m. on the registration day for Carmello the Science Fellow's summer camp, just as they probably did for concert tickets when they were teenagers. The positive side is that because parents and kids are so interested in all of these various camps and classes, many unique programs can succeed here.

I remember one Columbus Day my daughter was off from school, and we went to Central Park to have a boat race at the Conservatory Water with the radio-controlled boats. As we walked from the subway, we passed a renowned museum and tons of eclectic restaurants and shops. Our biggest obstacle was making our way through the Columbus Day parade to enter Central Park. While enjoying our boat race, we could hear the music and sounds of the parade booming behind us, and all I could think was "This is New York City." In many towns the parade would have been the biggest event of the week, but here the parade is just one of many activities taking place outside your door.

There is so much to do in the city, and the biggest enemy facing New Yorkers is time. Between work and other responsibilities it's hard to keep up. I wrote *City Kid New York* to provide parents with a resource that will make parenting in the city a bit easier. In a fast-paced city like New York, people don't have the time to research the best museums to visit with kids or an inexpensive place to throw a cool birthday party or who to call when their kid is sent home from school with lice. I've filled the book with NYC families' favorite things to do and places to shop. I've spoken with NYC parents from all over the five boroughs to find out what kids' shops, classes, toys, and more they couldn't live without and have included all their recommendations in the book. I've also taken my kids all over the city, testing out almost everything I've suggested in the book. (Luckily we didn't have to test out the lice experts, but they all came highly recommended.) We've had a great time traveling around all of the boroughs, and I truly hope your family does, too!

Chapter One

City Parents:

411 on City Parenting—from School to Sitters

The diapers are gone and you are no longer spending your Saturday mornings in Mommy and Me music classes or following your toddler around the playground. Welcome to the next step of city parenting. Although you've been a parent for years and you've been able to navigate your way through a period of sleepless nights, weaning, and potty training, the truth is it has only just begun. Get the 411 on getting your child into kindergarten, where to find the best night-sitter so the two of you can finally get out to the movies, how to keep your house lice-free, and where to find yummy antibiotics for fussy kids, and find answers to New York City–centric questions like what age do kids have to start paying for a ride on the subway.

Public or Private:
Getting Schooled in the City

Congratulations, you've made it through the NYC preschool admissions process. I'm sure you have some battle scars and many tales to share, like waking up extra early the day after Labor Day to call for an application, or braving the insanely crowded school tours and open houses. I bet your head is still swimming with terms like "gross motor play," with wondering what the Bank Street teaching philosophy really means, and tuition prices that cost more than a small car. Yes, you're an expert on school admissions and yet the battle is not over. Now we've reached the point where the real competition starts: the coveted kindergarten spot. With the recent surge of parents forgoing the suburbs, getting into a kindergarten isn't as simple as signing up for your local public school or writing a check to the private school of your choice.

Public School

New York City public schools have vastly improved since the days when I attended an overcrowded Queen's public school. There are many options throughout the city, from your zoned school to many excellent charter schools.

Registering for a public school kindergarten

If you aren't sure what school district you are zoned for, you can either call 311 or visit the extremely user-friendly Web site of the New York City Department of Education (www.schools.nyc.gov) for a searchable zone finder and map. This is important to do before you think of buying or renting an apartment with the hope of it being zoned for a specific school.

Pre-registration for pre-K and kindergarten is announced on the Department of Education (DOE) Web site and usually happens early in the year between the months of February and April. My neighborhood school posts signs around the area as a reminder to parents that registration is in process, but it's also listed on each school's Web site. The cut-off for the birth date of students enrolling in New York City public schools is December 31 of each year, which means that if your child turns five in December of the year that he or she enters kindergarten, you may apply for admission. When you arrive at registration you must bring either your child's birth certificate or his or her passport, as well as two documents that prove your residency. There are several documents you can choose from to show proof of residency. The list below is taken directly from the New York City Department of Education's Web site:

❖ A residential utility bill (gas or electric) in the resident's name that is dated within the last sixty days

❖ Documentation or letter on letterhead from a federal, state, or local government agency indicating the resident's name and address that is dated within the last sixty days

❖ An original lease agreement, deed, or mortgage statement for the residence

❖ A current property tax bill for the residence

❖ A water bill for the residence that is dated within the last sixty days

❖ Official payroll documentation from an employer that is dated within the last sixty days, such as a form submitted for tax withholding purposes or payroll receipt (please note that a letter on the employer's letterhead will not be accepted)

You will need to apply at your zoned school. In addition, if your child is enrolled in a Pre-K program at your local zoned school, you must still apply for Kindergarten. However due to the fact that city public schools have become so popular with families, and to avoid overcrowding, schools are capped at a certain number of students. If the amount of applications exceeds the number of seats in the grade, students will be chosen by a lottery. Priority is given to children in the school's zone, but spots are granted first to children who have a sibling already enlisted in their zoned school. If there isn't a spot available in your zoned school, the DOE will work with you to place your child at another school in the district for the remainder of the year, and they will be able to enter the zoned school at any time when a spot opens up or they can chose to stay at the other school.

In addition to your local zoned school, there are also many charter schools that you can apply to for your child throughout the city, just check the DOE Web site. The charter schools available often have limited seats, and students are chosen through a lottery.

If you want the inside scoop on your local public school, charter school, or Gifted and Talented school, head to the unbelievably useful Web site, **Inside Schools** (www.insideschools.org), which both walks parents through the process and also offers overviews of all the schools in New York City, with comments by parents who have children enrolled in their respective school. In recent years the Department of Education has been rating city public schools with letter grades, so you can see if your zoned school made the grade by looking at the school's progress report, also on their Web site.

Gifted and Talented Public Schools

If you feel that your city kid needs an additional academic challenge, then have him take the test for the gifted and talented program. The Otis-Lennon School Ability Test (OLSAT) and the Bracken School Readiness Assessment (BSRA) are tests you must take in order to be admitted to a gifted and talented school. Your child will be graded according to her abilities in a percentile. If your child is enrolled in public school, you will receive further information on the admissions tests and programs from your child's school. You can also go on to the Department of Education's Web site and download an application. The application process usually begins around October and closes in mid-November. Once you receive your child's scores, you will be notified of what schools she qualifies to apply for, and you can start applying to various schools with gifted and talented programs or that are entirely self-contained gifted schools. There is a list of all participating schools on the Department of Education Web site ,and you can contact each school for its open house and tour dates as well as submit your applications electronically. Just to note, spaces are limited for kids

who are in the second grade and subsequent grades at the elementary level, and it's best to apply for either a kindergarten or first grade spot.

Books

To read up on the application process, be sure to pick up a copy of these helpful books:

❊ *New York City's Best Public Elementary Schools: A Parent's Guide*
by Clara Hemphill

❊ *New York City's Best Public Middle Schools: A Parent's Guide*
by Clara Hemphill

❊ *A Parent's Guide to Special Education in New York City*
by Laurie Dubos and Jana Fromer

Private Schools

The competition is tough for a spot at New York City's private schools, but this shouldn't discourage you from applying. Making the decision to send your child to a private school is a personal and family choice since tuition for most private schools in Manhattan averages more than $30,000 per year, and is increasing. However many NYC parents find the idea of their child attending the same school from kindergarten through twelfth grade quite appealing, and they tend to start their children at the desired school in a nursery/pre-K program if available.

If you want to have your child attend a private school, you should sign your child up to take the Early Childhood Assessment Test through the Educational

Records Bureau (220 East 42nd Street, 800-989-3721). The test is usually referred to as the "ERB," and is a one-on-one test with an instructor that can be taken at your child's preschool. If the preschool your child is enrolled in doesn't permit ERB testing, you can have your child tested at the ERB offices. There is a detailed description of the testing process on the ERB Web site (www.erbtest.org). There are a few schools, like Saint Ann's School in Brooklyn Heights, that don't require their applicants to take the ERB, so be sure to check if your desired schools require the test. Once you've made a list of the schools to which you'd like your child to apply, you must get applications from the schools (most can be downloaded from the school's Web sites). Many of the schools ask the parents of the applicant to write essays for the application, and you must also attend an interview at the school. The process is quite intimidating, competitive, and somewhat complicated; you might consider hiring an educational consultant or taking a workshop to find out more about the process from experts.

Consultants and Workshops

If you'd like to get some help with the application process, I've listed some educational consultants below:

Abacus Guide Educational Consulting
212-712-2228
www.abacusguide.com
Emily Glickman, who runs Abacus, has been specializing in educational consulting for over ten years.

She works with families to help them find the right school and leads them through the application process. From helping parents understand the ins and outs of applying to schools to discussing the right time to take the ERB, Abacus covers the entire process. They offer three programs: Preschooler's Prep, which introduces parents to the process of kindergarten admissions and the ERB by explaining what skills are being tested and providing toys and workbooks for exam preparation. This program costs $950. The School Selection Program helps families understand the private school process as well as the timeline and costs $850. The Private School Admission Report is a program where Emily works with families for a full year from the spring before the application to the fall when they apply. She helps with all aspects of the process from editing essays to reviewing thank-you cards and offering mock interviews. The program involves two in-person meetings with Emily as well as unlimited phone calls (she can be reached on weekends and evenings). This program costs $2,850. The Abacus Web site has detailed descriptions of the programs and offers tons of helpful information.

Aristotle Circle
212-360-2301
www.aristotlecircle.com
Aristotle Circle offers families advice on the private school process. They also have a workbook that parents can purchase to help their child prepare for the ERB. The consulting rates start at $150 an hour and include assistance on every aspect of the application process. Aristotle Circle consultants help parents choose the right school and provide essay optimization, ERB preparation, parent-and-child

interview preparation, guidance for twins, wait-list strategies, and other strategies to ensure that your child gets into the right school.

Cherry Tree Consultants
917-886-0005

www.cherrytreeconsultant.com

This group works with families to help them "navigate through the [private school application] process and come up with a plan that will help put the 'pieces of the puzzle' together as easily and seamlessly as possible."

Manhattan Private School Advisors
212-280-7777

www.privateschooladvisors.com

Founded by Amanda Uhry, this school advisory firm works with parents from all over the world who have kids from pre-K all the way up to the eleventh grade. This team helps parents find the right school so that each individual child realizes his or her future. They guide parents and kids through the application process, interviews, and testing. Parents pay a set fee of $18,000, and if your child doesn't get into your first-, second-, or third-choice school, they will repeat the process the following year at no charge—something that they have never had to do.

The Parents League of New York
115 East 82nd Street bet. Park and Lexington avenues

212-737-7385

www.parentsleague.org

The Parents League is a helpful resource to navigate your way through the NYC school admissions process. The Parents League offers informative workshops on school admissions and also lists school resources for a wide variety of both public and private schools including boarding schools. The league is affiliated with approximately three hundred schools. Members of the league can make an appointment for a meeting with an advisor to discuss the application process. Joining the league has many other benefits in addition to the school advisory services. The membership also includes city guides, workshops, and resources for finding babysitters, traveling with the family, and other amenities.

Books and Web Sites

If you want to do the legwork on your own, you can search the books and Web sites below for information. You can also check out your desired school's Web site for extensive admission information as well as a list of frequently asked questions.

Books:

These guides provide a list of private schools in NYC and will give you a rundown of the application process.

❖ *The Manhattan Family Guide to Private Schools and Selective Public Schools*, 5th ed. by Victoria Goldman

❖ *Applying to Private Schools in NYC: A Guide* by School Choice International

❖ *Everything You Need to Know (and More!) About Getting Your Child into Private School* by Jeanine Jenks Farley

Web sites:

Peruse these Web sites that range from reviews of the schools by parents to information on the private school process.

Independent School Admission Association
www.isaagny.org

The Web site for the Independent School Admission Association Program of Greater New York offers helpful information on independent schools in the area.

NYC Private Schools Blog
www.nycprivateschoolsblog.com

This blog is parent focused and covers approximately eight hundred New York City private schools, with information and postings on the world of NYC private school life. It's very informative and worth a visit.

Private School Review
www.privateschoolreview.com

This Web site reviews various private schools throughout the country and gives you a rundown of statistical information about each school.

Top NYC Kid Questions

When does my child have to pay for the bus and subway?
According to the Metropolitan Transportation Authority's Web site (www.mta.info), children under 44 inches tall can ride free of charge on New York City Transit subways and on local Transit buses and Long Island Bus services. No more than three children per adult may ride for free. On NYC Transit express buses, children ages two and under may ride for free if they sit on an adult's lap.

When can my child be legally left alone in NYC?
In New York State, there is no law specifying an age when kids can be left alone in their home. The State has left it up to the parent's discretion. That said, a very young child should not be left alone at home. You must figure out if your child is responsible enough to be left at home, because if anything happens to him or her, it will be your responsibility, as parent. Years ago, before I was a mom, I met someone who, to see if her ten-year-old daughter was ready to be left alone, actually made her daughter pass a test she had written up. I thought that this idea was so great that I am thinking of making up a test with multiple-choice questions to see if my child knows how to react in certain situations when she wants to be left alone in the house. Many child safety programs state that the ideal age is twelve years old, but again it's up to you.

There is also no New York State law that dictates a minimum age when a child can babysit another child. Again, you must assess your own child's maturity level and how much responsibility they can have for the younger child.

When can my children ride the subway by themselves or go to the store alone?
Again, this is up to the parent. Metro North states on their Web site that, "Riders should also have the maturity to be able to react to unexpected situations that may arise in any

transportation system, such as train delays, cancellations, or other service disruptions. For these reasons, MTA Metro-North Railroad recommends that children under the age of eight be accompanied by an adult or a responsible youth (at least twelve years old) when riding its trains."

Obviously, very young children shouldn't ride the subway alone. In fact there was a huge uproar when writer and NYC mom Lenore Skenazy wrote a newspaper column about how she left her nine-year-old son at Bloomingdale's with a MetroCard and told him to find his way home. She has since written a book called *Free-Range Kids: Giving Our Children the Freedom We Had Without Going Nuts with Worry* that details the uproar and her belief that we should give our kids more freedom.

It's up to parents to determine when children are allowed to head to the store. At P.S. 321 in Park Slope, school officials let the fourth- and fifth-grade classes leave the school grounds for lunch (pending parent's permission). The Department of Education allows children to head to local restaurants for lunch, but it's up to parents to decide if their children are ready.

From Lice to Coughs:
The NYC Parents' Guide to Health

It doesn't matter whether your child goes to public or private school, there is no way to avoid receiving the dreaded letter in your child's backpack informing you that a student in the school has contracted lice. Once the word is out, parents start to panic, but there is no need to worry. Here are some ways to both prevent lice and rid lice from your child's hair.

Lice Prevention:

If you want to be proactive about avoiding lice infestation, check out these various hair care products and services that will keep lice out of your home:

Shampoos:
Rosemary and tea tree oils seem to repel lice. Try stocking up on shampoos that are formulated with these ingredients to ward off these unwanted pests.

Boo!
www.cozyscutsforkids.com
Cozy Cuts For Kids, the popular Manhattan kid's salon has created Boo!, an anti-lice shampoo and conditioner. The owner, Cozy Friedman, suggested that we spray the leave-in conditioner throughout our kids' hair before they leave for school each morning and so far we've never had a problem. You can pick up Boo! at area salons and also at C. O. Bigelow in NYC (www.bigelowchemists.com).

California Baby
www.californiababy.com
This line of organic hair care products includes California Baby Tea Tree and Lavender Shampoo & Bodywash, which prevents lice. We love to bring these products on vacation since the shampoo doubles as a body wash. You can find California Baby products all over the city at Ricky's NYC (www.rickysnyc.com). You can also order the shampoo on the Web.

Rosemary Repel hair care by Fairy Tale Hair Care

www.fairytaleshaircare.com

You can pick up Fairy Tale Hair Care products at Kidville (www.kidville.com) and Lulu's Cuts & Toys (www.luluscuts.com) in Brooklyn. You can order them on the Web as well. They have bed bug spray that is nontoxic and made with all-safe materials for children and pets.

Hire a lice removal service:

If you have lice in the house, call on these NYC lice experts.

Abigail F. Rosenfeld

718-435-2592 or 917-968-0627

Abigail Rosenfeld is also known as "the Lice Lady" and she specializes in lice checks, with prices varying by location. She works out of her house in the Kensington section of Brooklyn, and the vibe in this home salon is very friendly and cozy. Rosenfeld uses a Nisska comb, Pantene conditioner, and baking soda to remove the lice; she doesn't use any chemicals. Abigail advises parents to keep a fine-tooth comb handy to check if your child has lice once you've heard that lice are going around school; it's best to catch them early. She charges $15 to check for lice, and between $75 and $200 for lice removal in her home. There's an additional charge if she travels to your home.

Lice Busters NYC

718-360-1830

www.licebustersnyc.com

Dalya Harel will remove lice from your child's hair at her salon in Brooklyn or at your home. She charges $20 to check for lice and from $100 to $200 for lice removal.

For home visits, she charges $250 a person. Dalya doesn't use chemicals, instead removing the lice only by methodically combing the scalp. She also offers advice on how to clean the house once you have lice. When I spoke to her, she offered advice, noting that lice are attracted to clean hair, so don't wash your child's hair every day. You can also try putting garlic extract in your child's hair as a preventative measure.

Head Lice Hero

888-966-5423

www.headlicehero.com

Head Lice Hero doesn't pick nits or lice, but uses the safe brand of products to remove the lice. The entire lice-removal process of one application takes a half an hour to forty-five minutes. Lice specialists are available throughout the metro area and cost $229 for the home visit and $90 for the treatment. The lice specialist will leave you with a printout on how to clean your house and rid it of lice.

Rx—Pharmacies for Kids

Of course you can head to your local pharmacy when your child is sick, but these cool kid-centric pharmacies offer kids the choice of many flavors for their prescription medicine and cater to their needs.

Cherry's Pharmacy

207 East 66th Street at Third Avenue

212-717-7797

www.cherryspharmacy.com

For years this beloved East Side pharmacy for kids has been mixing up a variety of flavored medicine. The staff is extremely friendly and helpful and their well-stocked shop also sells bath products and other staples for kids.

Younger kids will be drawn to their train table, which will occupy them as you wait for their prescription to be filled. An added plus is that they offer free delivery throughout Manhattan and will ship products.

KidsRx Children's Health Pharmacy

523 Hudson Street at West 10th Street
212-741-7111

189 Seventh Avenue at 2nd Street
Brooklyn
718-369-6100
www.kidsrx.com
KidsRx offers kids a choice of flavored medicine. The West Village location has a train overhead and a train table on-site, so kids can hang out while their parents shop. The pharmacy is stocked with vitamins, bath products, and other necessities for kids.

Thérapie New York

309 Columbus Avenue bet. 74th and 75th streets
www.therapieny.com
212-877-3307
In addition to having a well-stocked toy section that can distract any sick child, this popular Upper West Side store/pharmacy offers a variety of flavored prescription medicines for your child. They also have an extensive line of various shampoos, soaps, lotions, and sunscreen.

A Night Out:
Getting a Sitter

So you want a night out? A great way to find a sitter is by word of mouth. I'm lucky to be from the NYC area, with family nearby, but if we need to find a night-sitter, we ask our friends with full-time sitters for recommendations. Honestly, there are good and reliable babysitters everywhere in the city. For example, you can ask the childcare workers at the local gym daycare, or the teachers if you have a younger child in preschool or daycare, or you can call your local church or synagogue.

The Internet is a great place to look for a sitter, although you will need to be careful and check references because anyone can respond to something like a Craigslist ad. The Internet offers a whole range of other options, like posting an ad on a local parenting board to see if other folks in your neighborhood know of good babysitters. You could also head to www.urbanbaby.com to look for reputable childcare.

An inexpensive way to find reliable babysitting is to create a babysitting co-op, where each parent takes a turn watching another's child. The community co-op can create its own structure for keeping track of the babysitting dates within the group. You can also do a babysitting exchange with another friend. The exchange concept is much easier to work out now that your children are older and easier to put to bed and sleep through the night (of course, this varies by child).

I've listed the sitting services that I've heard good things about below, and although I can't personally endorse them, they are a great place to start when searching for an occasional sitter. Most of the childcare agencies charge a small fee to join, and provide an outline of how much a sitter should be paid. You can get all the information by calling or checking the Web sites of the agencies below.

Absolute Best Care Nanny Agency

274 Madison Avenue, Suite 503, at West 38th Street
212-481-5705
www.absolutebestcare.com

Rated "Best of NY" in *New York* magazine, this sitter service provides families with both sitters and house-keepers. You can sign up online for the babysitting club where fees range from $50 to $250, plus an hourly rate for the babysitter. Sitters set their own salaries with rates starting at $15 an hour. Sitters usually need twenty-four hours notice when scheduling.

The Baby Sitters' Guild

60 East 42nd Street bet. Park and Madison avenues
212-682-0227
www.babysittersguild.com

For almost sixty years this babysitting service has been finding sitters for New York City families. They can find bilingual sitters in over sixteen languages. Sitters start at $25 per hour for one child and $5 per hour for each additional child. You can call the same day to arrange an evening sitter.

Barnard College Babysitting Agency

Eliot Hall
49 Claremont Avenue at 119th Street
212-854-2035
www.eclipse.barnard.columbia.edu/~bbsitter

There is a $25 fee to sign up for this service that places parents with sitters from Barnard College, an undergraduate liberal arts college for women in Manhattan. Rates for sitters start at $7.50 per hour.

Metropolitan Sitters

321 West 82nd Street bet. West End Avenue and Riverside Drive
917-575-7370
www.metropolitansitters.com

For a monthly fee of $25, this sitter service will pro-vide parents with access to college-educated sitters and nannies. They also offer sitters that can stay overnight as well as sitters that will travel with your family. Rates start at $16 per hour for two children.

New York City Explorers

388 Atlantic Avenue at Bond Street
Brooklyn
718-625-6923

186 Underhill Avenue bet. St. John and Sterling streets
Brooklyn
718-399-6923
www.nycityexplorers.com

New York Kids Club offers "Bag of Tricks" babysit-ting—an educational babysitting service where sitters arrive with a bag of tricks, including books and arts and crafts projects. Rates range from $15 to $25 an hour. The more notice you give them, the less expensive it is, so be sure to call in advance. This service also offers a popular drop-off program; check their Web site for dates for both "Sleep in Saturdays," from 8 a.m. until 1 p.m. on scheduled dates, and "Movie Night," from 5 p.m. until 10 p.m. on scheduled weekends.

Sittercity

888-211-9749
www.sittercity.com

This online service places college-educated babysit-ters with families throughout the country. There is a fee to join and the sitters' rates vary. They also offer tutors and dog walkers through this service. If you type in your zip code, you can see a list of babysit-ters available in your neighborhood.

Chapter Two

After-School Activities:

From Sports to Volunteering

City kids have the advantage of taking after-school dance classes at Lincoln Center and acting classes at the renowned Atlantic Center Theater. In this great city, kids have the unique opportunity to learn how to master the trapeze or create artistic works at the city's finest museums. Signing your child up for an after-school activity or a weekend class is a great way to expose them to a world outside of their class-rooms. Taking extracurricular classes enhances their education from the world around them and can actually shape their future. So sign your child up for a filmmaking class or a chess lesson, and then enjoy watching student films or playing a smart game of chess with your child.

One word of advice, don't overbook your child with classes. Beyond the fact that you don't want your child stressing about practicing three different dance routines for end-of-year recitals while rehearsing for a play, you must also take into account all of the travel time you will need to spend carting them around for multiple classes. Remember also that many schools partner with popular after-school classes to host activities in the schools after hours (and so don't need parents escorting kids to class). In my local public school my kids can take classes straight after school, ranging from Super Soccer Stars in the schoolyard to Gymstars Gymnastics hosted in the gymnasium. The school also offers piano lessons, science workshops, and art instruction. Just to note, with looming budget cuts, many after-school activities may face cuts, so try and support your school's after-school programs by getting involved (if you have the time) in your school's PTA as well as any committees that help your school. Since many people utilize after-school classes as activity-driven childcare, you should sign up as soon as possible, even inquiring with your child's school the summer before school starts.

In addition to taking classes, kids can also give back and volunteer. Many of the charity organiza-tions in the NYC area offer parent and child volun-teering—a rewarding way to spend time together. I know that once my kids were too old for the Mommy and Me playgroup, I missed taking classes with them and found that volunteering was a way that we could spend time together and also give back to the city we love dearly.

One-Stop Shopping:
Places that Offer a Host of Classes and After-school Programs

There are plenty of classes that your city kids can take. Here are a few places that offer a one-stop venue for educational classes that range from cooking and dance to swimming and music. Many of these centers offer pickup for children who attend nearby local schools, and I've starred these venues for easy finding.

*Abrons Art Center at the Henry Street Settlement

466 Grand Street at Montgomery Street
212-598-0400
www.henrystreet.org
The Abron Arts Center offers kids ages three and up the opportunity to take dance, art, theater, voice, and music classes, and also offer Suzuki method music classes (they offer adult classes, too). Located on the Lower East Side, they also offer fun family workshops on Sundays where kids and their parents try everything from cartooning workshops to making "green" art projects. They host an art camp. In addition to the classes in the arts The Henry Street Settlement also has an after-school program through their Youth Services division and pick students up from area schools offering kids classes in sports, fashion design and the arts.

Brooklyn Arts Exchange

421 Fifth Avenue at 8th Street
Brooklyn
718-832-0018
www.bax.org

Kids can take classes in drama, musical theater, dance, tumbling, and yoga at this nonprofit arts center in Park Slope, Brooklyn. They also offer a popular full-time summer arts program as well as birthday parties where kids can enjoy partaking in dance and drama.

*The Children's Aid Society

105 East 22nd Street at Park Avenue South
212-940-4800
www.childrensaidsociety.org
With locations throughout the city, including the East Side Rhinelander Children's Center and the Philip Coltoff Center in the West Village, the Children's Aid Society offers a host of classes including acting, animation, arts, and sports. The classes vary location to location and some branches offer an after-school program with pickup from local schools. Check their Web site to see the schedule and programs offered as well as to find a location near you.

Creative Arts Studio

310 Atlantic Avenue at Smith Street
Brooklyn
718-797-5600

119 Union Street at Columbia Street
Brooklyn
718-243-0658
www.creativeartsstudio.com
Kids can enjoy a wide range of classes at this Brooklyn art studio, including drama, hip-hop dancing, tap dancing, filmmaking, creative writing, musical theater, musical composition, along with many others. The Creative Arts Studio has two locations in Brooklyn. The location on Atlantic Avenue is centrally located near all subway lines. Creative Arts Studio hosts a

popular summerlong camp with extended hours. My daughter, Lucy, went to camp here and loved it. Each week has a different theme and kids get to swim and go on field trips .

*14th Street Y of the Educational Alliance

344 East 14th Street bet. 1st and 2nd avenues
212-780-0800
www.14streety.org

The 14th Street Y of the Educational Alliance offers an after-school program with pickup from area schools. Classes are also offered on weekends when kids can take swimming instruction and families can enjoy open swim. The after-school classes offered include a host of sports classes from baseball, basketball, soccer leagues, flag football, and gymnastics. They also have parenting workshops for single parents and other informative parenting classes and support groups.

*Jewish Community Center in Manhattan

334 Amsterdam Avenue at West 76th Street
646-505-4444
www.jccmanhattan.org

The spacious Jewish Community Center located on the Upper West Side has an after-school program where they pick kids up from local schools and provide them with a long list of classes, including art, dance, science, swimming, gymnastics, and cooking. The JCC has a separate program for tweens and also offers many family programs. The JCC offers a day camp and serves as a great asset to the community.

There are Jewish Community Centers in the other boroughs that offer similar programs. The JCC programs are open to people of all backgrounds.

LaGuardia Community College

31-10 Thomson Avenue at Van Dam Street
Queens
718-482-7244
www.lagcc.cuny.edu

Located just minutes from Manhattan in Long Island City, this community college has a continuing education department that offers kids ages six and up the chance to take a variety of classes that won't break the bank, including creative writing, guitar, French, Mandarin theater, math, cooking, keyboard, chorus.

*92nd Street Y

1395 Lexington Avenue at East 92nd Street
212-415-5500

92YTribeca
200 Hudson Street at Desbrosses Street
212-601-1000
www.92y.org

The 92nd Street Y's Noar Program is an after-school program that runs from 3 p.m. until 6 p.m., for children of kindergarten age through sixth grade. The Y offers a staff-led pickup from local schools as well as buses that pick children up from schools around the city. In addition to the after-school program, kids can also sign up for classes in art, music, science, dance, and sports activities. The Y can also host your child's next birthday party, with a range of activities from gymnastics to pool parties. The 92nd Street Y has a new location in TriBeCa at an arts and entertainment venue, which hosts many family-friendly concerts and has a space for kids' birthday parties as well as a cool kid-friendly café.

New York Kid's Club

Check Web site for locations throughout New York City

212-721-4100

www.nykidsclub.com

With locations in Manhattan and Brooklyn, the New York Kids Club offers gymnastics, cooking, rock climbing, dance, science, and other classes, which vary by location.

*YMCA

Check the Web site for locations throughout New York City

www.ymcanyc.org

Join one of the branches of the YMCA and enjoy the full use of their facilities, which can include everything from swimming classes to gymnastics. Most offer after-school programs or inexpensive day camps for which the Y branch's staff will provide pickup from local schools for afternoon care. Many Ys also host birthday parties for kids. Just to note, each branch offers different programs, so check the Web site of the location nearest you for its schedule of activities and programs.

Arts and Crafts

From painting classes at art colleges to learning how to knit a sweater, there are many options for your budding artist in New York City.

Visual Arts

The Artful Place

171 Fifth Avenue at Lincoln Place

Brooklyn

718-399-8199

www.theartfulplace.com

From bookmaking to sand art, this art studio in Park Slope hosts various workshops for kids ages five through twelve.

The Art Students League of New York

215 West 57th Street bet. Seventh and Eighth avenues

212-247-4510

www.theartstudentsleague.org

This West Side art league offers inexpensive classes with professional artists on Saturdays for kids ages eight through twelve. During the summer, they also offer weekday classes for kids. Children can study sculpture, drawing, portraits, mixed media, design, and other art forms. Classes run for three and a half hours.

Bronx River Art Center

1087 East Tremont Avenue at Devoe Avenue

Bronx

718-589-5819

www.bronxriverart.org

Kids can take art classes in computer graphics, printmaking, ceramics, drawing, and other arts for free at this Bronx art center. Every June they have an end-of-year show, open to the public, that is filled with students' work.

Church Street School for Music and Art

74 Warren Street bet. Greenwich Street and West Broadway

212-571-7290

www.churchstreetschool.org

This TriBeCa school for art and music offers a large variety of art classes, including painting, sculpture, digital media, and a drawing class that develops portfolios for high school admissions.

Educational Alliance

197 East Broadway bet. Clinton and Jefferson streets

212-780-2300

www.edalliance.org

The Young Artists Program at the Educational Alliance offers kids ages ten through nineteen art classes in cartooning, clay pottery, drawing, painting, photography, and portrait drawing. There is limited enrollment, due to small class sizes.

Hi Art!

Check Web site for a list of participating museums

212-757-7565

www.hiartkids.com

Have your kids explore the world of art at these popular art classes hosted around the city. Hi Art! offers highly rated classes for toddlers to preteens. The interesting aspect to these art classes is that they are taught by working artists, not art educators, and involve trips to many NYC museums for artistic inspiration. Kids can study everything from manga to painting.

Kids at Art at the Little Shops of Crafts

431 East 73rd Street bet. First and York avenues

212-410-9780

www.kidsatartnyc.com

Kids can take one-hour weekly classes at this Upper East Side art studio to explore watercolors, collage, pottery, and other artistic media. The studio offers a summer program as well as fun art-themed birthday parties where kids can make everything from pajamas to flowerpots. They have classes during school breaks.

The Painted Cloud

168 Marcy Avenue at South 5th Street

Brooklyn

www.thepaintedcloud.blogspot.com

Too cold for the playground after school? Do not fret; sign up for an art class at the Painted Cloud, an art space in Williamsburg for kids ages ten and under. Along with afternoon art classes for kids, the Painted Cloud also offers interesting drop-in art workshops where kids can make anything from books to cool holiday-themed projects. They also host birthday parties.

Parsons The New School for Design

66 Fifth Avenue at West 13th Street

212-229-8933

www.parsons.edu

Kids in grades four and up can sign up for the Parsons School of Design pre-college academy where they can take Saturday morning art classes from 10 a.m. until 12:50 p.m. during the school year. They also have summer classes available.

Pratt Institute

200 Willoughby Avenue at Grand Avenue

Brooklyn

718-636-3600

www.pratt.edu

The Saturday Art School at Pratt lets kids study art at this world-renowned art college in Clinton Hill, Brooklyn. The program is for kids ages three and up, and classes are arranged by age. Older kids can take classes in sculpture, drawing, painting, and ceramic construction.

School of Visual Arts

209 East 23rd Street at Third Avenue

212-592-2000

www.schoolofvisualarts.edu

The continuing education department at this Manhattan art college offers kids the chance to study a variety of visual arts at the school. They also offer weeklong classes in the summer. Classes are for kids in kindergarten through ninth grade, and range from learning about mixed media to using watercolors.

Fiber Arts

Have your child learn how to sew an outfit or knit a scarf or sweater for his or her dolls. It will give your child an amazing sense of accomplishment.

Brooklyn Mercantile

335 Fifth Avenue at 4th Street

Brooklyn

718-788-1223

www.brooklynmercantile.com

This Brooklyn workshop offers Simple Sew classes for kids ages eight and up, in which they learn the basics of using a sewing machine. Kids and parents are invited to bring their own machine or use one of the machines provided. Participants learn how to make a drawstring tote bag.

Knitty City

208 West 79th Street at Amsterdam Avenue

212-787-5896

www.knittycity.com

Knitty City has an after-school kids' club for children ages seven through eleven, for all levels of experience. Kids get to knit purses, sweaters for stuffed animals, and more. They also have a parent-child knitting workshop on Sunday afternoons, where kids and their parents can choose a project and knit together while improving their skills. They invite all levels to these classes and workshops.

Lion Brand Yarn Studio

34 West 15th Street bet. Fifth and Sixth avenues

212-243-9070

www.lionbrandyarnstudio.com

Kids ages seven and up can learn how to knit and crochet at this Chelsea yarn studio that offers fun, educational classes where parents and children can learn a lifelong hobby and skill.

Pottery

Wouldn't it be cool to eat off the dish or drink from the cup that your child made? Pottery classes are a great way to have your kids strengthen motor skills while creating tons of pieces that make great gifts for Grandma and Grandpa.

Greenwich House Pottery

16 Jones Street bet. Bleecker and West 4th streets

212-242-4106

www.greenwichhouse.org

This West Village pottery studio has been around since 1909 and is a great place to introduce your kids to the beauty of clay and ceramics. On Tuesday afternoons from 3:45 p.m. until 5:15 p.m., they host a class called Creative Critters, for kids ages four through seven, in which kids can learn about shaping clay. They also have a parent and child class for kids ages six through thirteen, in which parents and their children can work on collaborative projects. The Greenwich House also offers dance, jazz, voice, and other music classes for kids.

Mugi Pottery Studio

993 Amsterdam Avenue at West 109th Street

212-866-6202

www.mugipottery.com

This Upper West Side pottery studio has hand-building and wheel-throwing classes for kids ages five and up. Mugi offers classes on Tuesdays, Thursdays, and Saturdays. Mugi also hosts birthday parties.

The Painted Pot

339 Smith Street at Carroll Street

Brooklyn

718-222-0334

8009 Third Avenue at 80th Street

Brooklyn

718-491-6411

www.paintedpot.com

With two locations in Brooklyn, in Carroll Gardens and Bay Ridge, this pottery studio offers both hand-building and wheel-throwing classes for kids ages five and up. They also have a pottery wheel summer camp for kids ages eight through fifteen. Additionally, this pottery studio welcomes drop-ins of kids and their parents.

An After-School Class at the Museum

Here are some area museums that offer after-school and/or weekend classes:

American Museum of Natural History

Central Park West at 79th Street

212-769-5100

www.amnh.org

Brooklyn Museum of Art

200 Eastern Parkway at Washington Avenue

Brooklyn

718-638-5000

www.brooklynmuseum.org

Children's Museum of the Arts

182 Lafayette Street at Broome Street

212-274-0986

www.cmany.org

New York Hall of Science

47-01 111th Street at 47th Avenue

Queens

718-699-0005

www.nyhallsci.org

Whitney Museum of American Art

945 Madison Avenue at 75th Street

212-570-3600

www.whitney.org

See also p. 47

Cooking

City kids are exposed to some of the finest restaurants in the world, so it's no wonder they crave the opportunity to become savvy chefs. Sign your child up for a cooking class and embrace the joys of cooking together.

Creative Cooks

298 Atlantic Avenue at Smith Street

Brooklyn

718-237-2218

www.creativecooks.us

Grade school kids can take the Junior Tastemakers class, which runs for twelve weeks and focuses on proper food handling and kitchen basics. Creative Cooks also offers Mommy and Me classes for the younger set as well as classes for middle school kids. They also host parties and field trips.

Institute of Culinary Education

50 West 23rd Street at 6th Avenue

212-847-0700

www.iceculinary.com

The Institute of Culinary Education offers a wide variety of classes in the recreational division, including family cooking classes where parents and their kids can make everything from sushi to pizza. They also host kids' parties.

Dance

There are local dance studios all over the city, and due to space limitations I can't list them all. I can rave about our local ballet school, Cobble Hill Ballet, and I'm sure every neighborhood has its personal favorite. Here are a few dance programs that are affiliated with some of the city's most notable dance companies, if you are looking to expand your child's dance career or if you want him or her to have the unique opportunity of getting to dance at a respected dance company. Your child must audition for many of these programs; they take dance quite seriously.

The Alvin Ailey School

The Joan Weill Center for Dance

405 West 55th Street at 9th Avenue

212-405-9000

www.theaileyschool.edu

City kids have the opportunity to study dance at the legendary Alvin Ailey School, in their spacious midtown studios. The school offers dance classes for kids ages three and up, as well as two programs in the Junior Division. One program, called First Steps, is for kids ages three to six and the other is a pre-professional program for kids and teens ages seven through seventeen. They also have separate classes for boys.

Brighton Ballet Theater at the School of Russian Ballet

2001 Oriental Boulevard at Quentin Street

Brooklyn

718-769-9161

www.brightonballet.com

Children ages two and up can take classes at this ballet school that is the home to the Brighton Ballet Company, a Russian ballet and folk dance group. Classes are held on the Kingsborough Community College campus.

Mark Morris Dance Group

3 Lafayette Avenue at Flatbush Avenue

Brooklyn

718-624-8400

www.markmorrisdancegroup.org

Children ages four and up can take dance classes at the Mark Morris Dance Center in Brooklyn, home to the renowned Mark Morris Dance Group, which performs around the world. They offer classes throughout the year.

New York Theatre Ballet

30 East 31st Street bet. Madison and Park avenues

212-679-0401

www.nytb.org

Enrollment in the New York Theatre Ballet School is by audition only, and classes are offered for children ages four and up. The official school of the New York Theatre Ballet was founded in 1978 and uses the Cecchetti method. The New York Theatre Ballet Company has a great program of family-friendly performances, like their yearly production of *The Nutcracker*. Check their Web site for show info.

Peridance Center

890 Broadway at West 19th Street

212-505-0886

www.peridance.com

Home to the contemporary dance company the Peridance Ensemble, this school offers the PeriChild program, where kids can study ballet, jazz, tap, modern, and hip-hop. Classes for children start at eighteen months (those are Mommy and Me), and they have adult classes as well.

School of American Ballet

70 Lincoln Center Plaza at Columbus and Amsterdam avenues

212-769-6600

www.sab.org

You must audition to enroll in the classes at the School of American Ballet at Lincoln Center, where classes are for children ages six and up. The school is affiliated with the renowned New York City Ballet.

Filmmaking

New York City is the setting for so many films that kids can't help but see production crews filming around the city. If you have a budding filmmaker on your hands, sign them up for one of these classes.

826 nyc

372 5th Avenue bet. 5th and 6th streets
Brooklyn

718-499-9884

www.826nyc.org

This Brooklyn nonprofit writing center hosts a series of free filmmaking workshops for kids ages ten and up. Class enrollment is determined by a lottery.

Kids Make Movies

42 West 29th Street at Sixth Avenue

917-650-2131

www.kids-make-movies.com

Kids Make Movies offers private lessons and workshops for kids ages eight through twelve. Private classes can be held at your home or in their studio, where kids receive lessons on film-shooting techniques and editing. Students learn all aspects of video production, from start to finish. Kids learn how to write scripts and storyboards as well as how to create props and costumes; they are involved with every part of the filmmaking process. They even teach iMovie for beginners and Final Cut Pro for more advanced students. In the summer they have weeklong intensive Make a Movie camp for kids ages eight through twelve.

New York Film Academy

100 East 17th Street at Park Avenue South

212-477-1414

www.nyfa.com

The New York Film Academy in Union Square offers weekend digital filmmaking camps for kids ages ten and up. They also offer a camp for acting for film at a variety of skill levels.

Language

Learn Mandarin and Spanish, along with many other languages in our multicultural city.

Language and Laughter Studio

139 Nevins Street at Bergen Street
Brooklyn
718-852-2965 or 718-802-1756
www.thelanguageandlaughterstudio.com

This Brooklyn language school offers after-school classes in French, Spanish, and Mandarin. The school integrates art, dance, and other creative arts into their language classes. The studio also has a summer camp and hosts birthday parties. Adults can take classes at the studio as well.

Language Lunch

356 Broadway bet. Leonard and Franklin streets
212-226-9926
www.languagelunch.com

Kids can study French, Spanish, Mandarin, Italian, and Russian at this TriBeCa language school, where classes are offered for kids ages two through eleven. The classes involve creative play, song, and other ways to introduce the languages in a fun atmosphere. They also have adult classes.

The Language Workshop for Children

888 Lexington Avenue at East 66th Street
212-396-0830
www.thibauttechnique.com

Your kids have the choice of learning French, Italian, Spanish, or Mandarin at this Upper East Side language school. Classes start for children as young as six months.

Manners

Do your kids need to brush up on their etiquette?

The Development and Finishing Institute

2130 First Avenue at 110 Street, Suite 2207
212-828-4530
www.thedfinstitute.com

Both boys and girls ages five through eighteen can sign up for a ten- or twenty-week course offered at the Development and Finishing Institute, which will teach your child proper table manners, voice projection, posture, money management, and other life skills. The class culminates with a graduation, and graduates receive membership to the alumni club. All classes are held at Columbia University, Zankel Hall, 120th Street between Broadway and Amsterdam Avenue

The Etiquette School of New York

212-288-5413
www.etiquette-ny.com

This etiquette school founded by Patricia Napier-Fitzpatrick offers a four-session program called Elementary Etiquette for kids ages five through eleven. The class teaches kids how to make good first impressions, as well as basic manners, conversational skills, how to dine, among other topics. Classes are one hour long, and they offer private lessons.

Music

Introduce your child to the joys of playing an instrument in this musical town with the following schools:

Bloomingdale School of Music

323 West 108th Street bet. Riverside Drive and Broadway
212-663-6021
www.bsmny.org

This Upper West Side school of music offers both private and group lessons as well as the option of joining an ensemble. They use the Suzuki method to teach the basics of violin, cello, flute, and piano. They also offer classes for adults.

Brooklyn Guitar School

44 Fourth Avenue bet. Dean and Pacific streets
Brooklyn
718-855-5400
www.brooklynguitarschool.com

This Park Slope guitar school offers classes for kids of all levels. The best part is that they have guitars at the school so you don't have the burden of carrying one to class. They also offer classes for adults.

Brooklyn Queens Conservatory of Music

58 Seventh Avenue at Lincoln Place
Brooklyn
718-622-3300

13532 38th Avenue at Main Street
Queens

718-461-8910
www.bqcm.org

At locations in Brooklyn and Queens this music conservatory offers private lessons, ensembles, and group classes.

Church Street School for Music and Art

74 Warren Street bet. Greenwich Street and West Broadway
212-571-7290
www.churchstreetschool.org

This TriBeCa school offers music and art classes for kids. Children can take a wide range of music classes, from rock or folk guitar classes to enrolling in their string ensemble. Classes are for children ages sixteen months and up and are arranged by age group. Check their Web site for their extensive list of music classes. Classes for adults are also available.

Diller-Quaile School of Music

24 East 95th Street at Madison Avenue
212-369-1484
www.diller-quaile.org

The Diller-Quaile School of Music was founded in 1920, and has a notable early childhood program. The school offers instruction in both music and voice, with classes running for the entire school year. The School of Music offers individual instruction and also has ensembles, orchestras, and a chorus for more advanced students.

Lucy Moses School

129 West 67th Street bet. Broadway and Amsterdam Avenue
212-501-3303
www.kaufman-center.org/lucy-moses-school

The Lucy Moses School has both private and group classes for a wide variety of instruments. They offer many teaching methods from Dalcroze to Suzuki. The school has ensembles, a choir, and many other music programs for children, along with dance and theater workshops. Adults interested in dance can also take classes.

Third Street Music School Settlement

235 East 11th Street bet. Second and Third avenues

212-777-3240

www.thirdstreetmusicschool.org

The Third Street Music School Settlement has been educating New Yorkers since 1894. They offer both individual and group lessons for kids in a variety of instruments, from strings to piano. They also teach classes with the Suzuki method for piano, violin, viola, cello, bass, guitar, and flute. They have performance ensembles and chamber music programs and also offer dance (hip-hop, ballet, and tap) as well as art classes and an arts summer camp.

Turtle Bay Music School

244 East 52nd Street bet. Second and Third avenues

212-753-8811

www.tbms.org

This music school has been teaching New Yorkers how to play musical instruments since 1920. The school offers children and adults instruction in a wide variety of instruments. Students have the option of performing at the school's Em Lee Concert Hall at the end of the class.

Performing Arts

From drama and stand-up comedy to circus arts to musical theater, you can learn it all in this city that serves as the mecca for so many in the performing arts community.

Comedy

Is your child the class clown? Well get them up on stage and have them show off their funny side while performing at a comedy club.

Improv 4 Kids

669 Eighth Avenue at West 43rd Street

212-568-6560

www.improv4kids.com

This improv group offers Comedy 101 classes for kids ages ten to seventeen. The classes focus on a study of performance techniques for both improv and theater, after which children learn to develop a short stand-up comedy routine. These hands-on classes are held at a Times Square off-Broadway theater and culminate in a comedy showcase for family and friends. Students also get a season pass to the improv group to sit in on their shows.

Kids 'N Comedy at Gotham Comedy Club

208 West 23rd Street bet. Seventh and Eighth avenues

212-877-6115

www.kidsncomedy.com

Your child can learn how to be the next Jerry Seinfeld at these stand-up comedy workshops and classes at the Gotham Comedy Club. The comedy club offers a monthly workshop for kids eight and up to learn about stand-up. Kids are chosen from the workshop to perform in the Kids 'N Comedy Show. They offer two-hour-long weekly classes for kids ten and up on Saturdays, which runs for nine weeks. They also offer a summer camp for kids ages ten and up. If your child is interested in comedy, but is not ready for a class, get them tickets for a Kids 'N Comedy show.

Circus Arts

If you catch your child juggling apples in the kitchen, maybe you should advance their education in the circus arts at the following schools.

Circus Minimus

215 West 88th Street at Broadway
212-874-3976
www.circusminimus.com

Kids ages six and up can sign on for the Circus Minimus after-school classes, which include programs like Circus Kids Create, where kids learn how to juggle as well as other circus arts. There are also a host of other classes including Circus Yoga for kids, Wizardy 101, comedy, tumbling, and other creative arts classes.

España Streb Trapeze Academy

51 North 1st Street bet. Wythe and Kent streets
Brooklyn
718-384-6491
www.streb.org

If your child dreams of joining the circus, you should sign them up for a class at this trapeze school in Brooklyn. Kids ages five through twelve can learn the basics of the art of trapeze in their Kid Fly classes. The one-hour class allows children of all levels to work with trained professionals and learn at their own pace. España Streb Trapeze Academy also hosts birthday parties and a summer camp.

Drama and Musical Theater

If living in a theatrical town like NYC inspires your child to pursue acting, encourage them to take the stage at these acting schools.

Acting Creatively

122 West 26th Street bet. Sixth and Seventh avenues, 11th floor
646-336-7985
www.actingcreatively.com

Acting Creatively offers acting classes for kids ages seven through seventeen, where they get to explore all aspects of acting, from improvisation to character development. In addition to acting classes, kids can also study juggling. Acting Creatively holds one-day workshops in auditioning, circus skills, and also a special class for parents who are trying to navigate their way through the world of show business.

Applause New York City

St. Jeans Community Center
184 East 76th Street bet. Lexington and Third avenues
212-717-0703
www.applauseny.com

Applause offers a wide variety of classes in the performing arts for kids of all ages. Children in kindergarten through sixth grade have their choice of classes in hip-hop, acting, musical theater, and auditioning techniques, among many others.

Atlantic Theater Company

76 Ninth Avenue at West 16th Street
212-691-5919
www.atlanticactingschool.org

Children ages four and up can study in the after-school program at this acclaimed acting school run by the Atlantic Theater Company, which was founded by David Mamet and William H. Macy. Classes vary but the focus is on performing, creating, and playwriting. Classes are available for kids of all levels. The theater also runs a summer program and have theatrical performances for kids on their main stage.

Brooklyn Children's Theatre

St. Saviour's Church
135 Prospect Park SW at Terrace Place
Brooklyn
718-369-6388
www.brooklynchildrenstheatre.net
Musical theater classes are available for kids in first grade on up at this Park Slope musical theater program. All classes stage and perform a musical at the end of the session. Performances are held at the church.

Galli Children's Theater

38 West 38th Street bet. Fifth and Sixth avenues, 3rd floor
212-810-6485
www.gallitheaterny.com
Your child can take Spanish and German acting classes through the Galli Children's Theater. If you'd like to stick to English, you can opt for a creative drama class and a kids' acting class.

H B Studios

120 Bank Street bet. Washington and Greenwich streets
212-675-2370
www.hbstudio.org

This famous West Village acting school has been around since 1945. Young people's classes are offered for children ages nine and up throughout the year and range from an introduction to make-believe to classes that focus on various acting techniques.

The Lee Strasberg Theatre and Film Institute

115 East 15th Street at Irving Place
212-533-5500
www.strasberg.com
The world-renowned Lee Strasburg Theatre and Film Institute offers all-day Saturday classes for kids ages seven and up. The classes run from 10:30 a.m. until 4 p.m. and focus on acting, movement, dance, and acting for film and TV. The school also offers summer classes.

Manhattan Children's Theatre

52 White Street bet. Broadway and Church Street
212-226-4085
www.mctny.org
Classes at this TriBeCa children's theater are for kids in pre-K and up. Classes provide a gentle introduction to the world of theater and include creative drama for children in first through third grades, where children use their imagination in a fun environment. Kids in third through fifth grades can take beginner acting classes. The theater hosts shows and birthday parties as well.

Manhattan Movement and Art Center

248 West 60th Street bet. Amsterdam and West End avenues
212-787-1178
www.manhattanmovement.com

The Manhattan Movement and Art Center offers a host of classes, including acting and musical theater for kids and a bunch of dance classes in ballet, jazz, hip-hop, and tap. The center also offers an Afro-Brazilian capoeira martial arts and an aerial circus class that combines ballet with the trapeze. They also have a circus arts class where kids can learn how to juggle and other circus skills.

The New Acting Company

219 Sullivan Street at West 3rd Street
212-254-3074
www.childrensaidsociety.org/pcc/nac
Children ages three and up can register for a variety of acting classes at this West Village acting school at the Children's Aid Society. Classes range from theater games to play labs where kids learn about acting through studying and performing a play at the end of the semester.

TADA! Children's Theater

15 West 28th Street bet. Broadway and Fifth Avenue
212-252-1619
www.tadatheater.com
Children will enjoy taking an acting class at this theater, which hosts performances by their children's ensemble. The acting school at TADA! offers musical theater and acting skill-building classes broken up into three semesters (fall, winter, and spring). Classes are divided by age group and serve school-age children. During the summer and standard school breaks throughout the year, TADA! also offers weeklong camps for various age groups. Kids get to work with artists to create their own mini musical that is performed for their families.

Science/Nature

Is your child interested in making a robot or conducting science experiments in your dining room? He or she can learn about the joys of science at these classes:

Brooklyn Art and Technology at Streb Lab

51 North 1st Street bet. Wythe and Kent avenues
Brooklyn
718-395-3742
www.brooklynartandtech.com
Brooklyn Art and Technology classes combine art and science to make an ideal program for kids that will introduce them to math and science. The group hosts various events in Brooklyn, from constructing robots with parents at a picnic in Brooklyn to weeklong robot-building workshops. Check the Web site for a list of workshops and events.

Carmello the Science Fellow

300 Atlantic Avenue at Smith Street
718-722-0000
www.carmelothesciencefellow.com
After-school classes at the Cosmic Cove, Carmello the Science Fellow's Brooklyn storefront classroom, fill up quickly and it's not surprising. Carmello explores the wonders of science with fun classes that involve extremely inventive science projects that are both educational and entertaining. Classes are for kids in pre-K through fifth grade.

Mad Science at the Scholastic Store

130 Mercer Street at Prince Street
954-344-4403
www.madscience.org

In workshops around the city, including at the Scholastic Store, Mad Science offers science workshops for kids ages three and up. The themed programs involve age-appropriate activities to engage kids and expose them to the world of science.

Mohr's Explorers
212-568-2820
www.mohrs-explorers.com
This after-school program offers kids the chance to explore New York City and engage in outdoor activities like fort building, bird watching, and hiking. Mohr's Explorer's program is run through participating Manhattan schools, but can you can sign your kids up for their Open Group that meets on the southeast corner of 81st Street and Central Park West at 3:45 p.m. until and 5:15 p.m. Check the Web site for enrollment and dates. They also offer birthday parties, camping trips, and summer programs.

Science Teacher Sarah
1182 Broadway at West 28th Street, Suite 1004
212-683-2010
www.scienceteachersarah.com
Kids in pre-K and above can sign up for one of Science Teacher Sarah's after-school programs at her classroom. The programs focus on everything from weather to biochemistry in a fun environment. Science Teacher Sarah also hosts birthday parties and a summer camp.

Sports
From horseback riding to golf, your city kid can participate in a wide variety of sports in the city.

Horseback Riding
You can take lessons or guided rides at these riding academies:

Jamaica Bay Riding Academy
7000 Shore Parkway
Queens
718-531-8949
www.horsebackride.com

Kensington Stables
51 Caton Place at Coney Island Avenue
Brooklyn
718-972-4588
www.kensingtonstables.com

Riverdale Equestrian Center at Van Cortlandt Park
West 254th Street at Broadway
Riverdale, NY
718-548-4848
www.riverdaleriding.com
For more riding academies located in city parks, check out www.nycgovparks.org.

Fencing
If a trip to the Renaissance Festival has gotten your child in the mood to joust, check out these fencing schools:

Empire United Fencing
145 West 30th Street bet. Sixth and Seventh avenues
212-594-2118
www.empireunited.net
Empire United has a starter package for kids, which

includes three private lessons and four group lessons. They recommend that your child take the private lessons before attending the group classes. This package is the only opportunity for nonmembers to take private lessons from a coach. Beginner's foil for kids ages seven and up is offered, among other classes. Empire also hosts birthday parties.

Manhattan Fencing Center

225 West 39th Street bet. Seventh and Eighth avenues
212-382-2255
www.manhattanfencing.com
Kids ages six and up can take all levels of fencing lessons at Manhattan Fencing. They also offer a weeklong summer camp session as well as host birthday parties. The site has an informative Kids & Parents page that discusses the benefits of fencing.

Sheridan Fencing Academy

2035 Second Avenue at East 104th Street
212-831-0764
www.sheridanfencing.com
Sheridan Fencing Academy offers a wide variety of fencing classes for kids ages seven and up.

Golf

Golf isn't just for parents. If your child learns to master the game, you can take them on your next golf trip.

City Parks Foundation

www.cityparksfoundation.org
The City Parks Foundation offers free golf lessons throughout the city for kids and teens ages six through seventeen. The group also runs the **Junior Golf Center** (8850 14th Avenue, 718-259-2999) in

Dyker Heights, Brooklyn, which has a 6-hole golf course, practice putting, chipping greens, a covered driving range, and clubhouse with classroom space.

The Golf Club at Chelsea Piers

Pier 59 at 23rd Street
212-336-6400
www.chelseapiers.com
The Golf Club has an after-school program for junior golfers. The one-hour sessions run for seven weeks.

Gymnastics

Most of the one-stop shopping centers I mentioned on pages 20–22 offer gymnastics.

Asphalt Green

555 East 90th Street bet. York and East End avenues
212-369-8890
www.asphaltgreen.org

Chelsea Piers Sports and Entertainment Complex

Pier 62 at 17th through 23rd streets
212-366-6500
www.chelseapiers.com

Little Gym

Check the Web site for locations throughout New York City.
www.littlegym.com
The Little Gym is an international chain that offers gymnastics classes in a noncompetitive environment for infants as well as grade school aged children. Little Gyms are also popular places for birthday parties.

Powerplay Kids

432 Third Avenue at 7th Street
Brooklyn
718-369-9880
www.powerplaykids.com
Kids can take gymnastics, rock climbing, and dance classes at this popular Park Slope gym. Younger kids will enjoy a romp around the indoor play space after class. Powerplay also hosts a summer camp.

Baseball

If your child is interested in getting instruction off the Little League field, sign up for a baseball class.

The Baseball Center NYC

202 West 74th Street at Amsterdam Avenue
212-362-0344
www.thebaseballcenternyc.com
The Baseball Center NYC is centrally located on the Upper West Side in an old bank and offers kids private baseball lessons, an after-school program, a summer camp, and birthday parties.

Little League Baseball Teams

There are tons of Little League teams in the city; here are just a few:

Downtown Little League

www.downtownlittleleague.org

Little League Online

www.littleleague.org
This Web site has a handy search feature that will help you find New York City–area Little League teams.

Manhattan Babe Ruth Little League

www.nycbaberuth.org

Prospect Park Baseball Association

www.ppba.info

West Side Little League

www.westsidebaseball.org

Skateboarding

Your child can learn some cool new moves at these skateboarding schools:

Everyday Athlete Studio

136 Union Street bet. Columbia and Hicks streets
Brooklyn
347-529-6377
www.everydayathletekids.com

Uptown Skate School

420 East 76th Street bet. York and First avenues
646-852-6397
www.uptownskateschool.com

Soccer

Does your child want to be the next David Beckham? Kids can enjoy soccer all around the city at these soccer classes and leagues.

American Youth Soccer Organization

800-872-2976
www.soccer.org

Cosmopolitan Junior Soccer League

850 62nd Street bet. Eighth and Ninth avenues
Brooklyn

718-491-4009

www.cjsl.org

Kidsmove for Soccer

Nethermead in Prospect Park

212-253-9383

www.kidsmoveforsoccer.com

Manhattan Soccer Club

www.manhattansc.org

Modern School of Soccer

718-204-8534

www.themodernschoolofsoccer.com

Super Soccer Stars

606 Columbus Avenue at 89th Street

212-877-7171

www.supersoccerstars.com

Swimming

Just because we live in a city that is surrounded by water that you aren't allowed to swim in, doesn't mean your child shouldn't pick up this important life skill.

Asphalt Green

555 East 90th Street bet. York and East End avenues

212-369-8890

www.asphaltgreen.com

Aqua Skills Swim School

212-206-6979

www.aquaskills.com

Classes take place throughout the city; check the Web site for more information.

The Berkeley Carroll School

718-534-6624

www.berkeleycarroll.org

This pool is a popular place to take swim classes in Park Slope, Brooklyn.

Imagine Swimming

41 Union Square West at East 17th Street

212-253-9650

www.imagineswimming.com

Classes take place throughout the city; check the Web site for more information.

Physique Swim School

512 East 11th Street bet. avenues A and B

212-725-0939

www.physiqueswimming.com

Classes take place throughout the city; check the Web site for more information.

SwimJim

3 West 102nd Street at Central Park West

212-749-7335

www.swimjim.com

Classes take place throughout the city; check the Web site for more information.

Take Me To the Water

888-794-6692

www.takemetothewater.com

Classes take place throughout the city; check the Web site for more information.

Tennis

If your child learns how to play tennis, you'll have someone to volley with on your next vacation.

BumbleBee Tennis

Check Web site for locations throughout Manhattan.
347-284-6061
www.bumblebeetennis.com

Champion Tennis Club

1918 1st Avenue at East 100th Street
212-876-7766
www.championtennisclub.com

City Parks Foundation

Check Web site for locations throughout New
York City.
www.cityparksfoundation.org
The City Parks Foundation offers free tennis lessons
at thirty-six city parks for kids ages five through
seventeen.

Prospect Park Tennis Center

50 Parkside Avenue
Brooklyn
718-436-2500
www.prospectpark.org

Riverside Clay Tennis Association

Riverside Park at 97th Street
212-870-3078
www.rcta.info

Writing Workshops and Book Clubs

New York City is the publishing capital of the country
and home to many writers. Children shouldn't be left
out of this literary scene. Children have amazing imaginations and it's always great to hear the tales they tell,
so sign them up for a writing class and see what creative stories your children write. The New York Public
Library, the Brooklyn Public Library, and the Queens
Public Library host writing workshops as well; check
the Web site of the library nearest you for schedules.

Creative Arts Studio

310 Atlantic Avenue bet. Smith and Hoyt streets
Brooklyn
718-797-5600

119 Union Street at Columbia Street
Brooklyn
718-243-0658
www.creativeartsstudio.com
The Creative Arts Studio offers a writing class for kids
ages nine and up. The Writer's Collective is a class
that introduces kids to the world of writing short
stories, novels, and plays. At the end of the class
children get to participate in a professional reading.

826 NYC

372 Fifth Avenue at 5th Street
Brooklyn
718-499-9884
www.826nyc.org
This nonprofit center in Brooklyn offers both drop-in
tutoring for kids as well as a diverse selection of writing workshops for free. The classes are quite popular, so enrollment is determined by lottery. Volunteer
writers, artists, educators, and publishing professionals teach classes at the center. Classes range
from writing about heroes and villains to learning
about epic novels. The course list is diverse; there
are even classes on creating board games.

Yoga

The stress of the city can impact even our kids, so it's great to get them started on yoga so they know how to keep calm in our hectic city and can also reap the health benefits from this practice.

Karma Kids Yoga

104 West 14th Street at Sixth Avenue
646-638-1444
www.karmakidsyoga.com

Next Generation Yoga

Check Web site for locations throughout New York City.
212-595-9306
www.nextgenerationyoga.com

SonicYoga Center

754 Ninth Avenue at West 51st Street
212-397-634
www.sonicyoga.com

Volunteering

Here are a list of programs that will encourage parents and children to volunteer together. There are many ways that you can get your child involved in giving back.

❋ Build a lemonade stand to sell cookies and sugary summertime drinks to passersby with all profits benefiting a charity of your choice.

❋ Go through old toys and clothes and donate them to a homeless shelter.

❋ Answer a child's letter to Santa and buy a child a present through Operation Santa. You can pick up letters sent to Santa written by children in need at the James A. Farley Post Office (the main branch) at 421 Eighth Avenue, during the holiday season. Once you pick a letter, it's up to you to follow through and send the present the child requested.

❋ Knit baby blankets for a hospital nursery.

❋ Help out at a local animal shelter or foster a cat or dog for a local animal group.

❋ Donate old coats to a coat drive.

❋ Collect food for the hungry.

Children for Children

6 East 43rd Street at Fifth Avenue, 25th floor
212-850-4170
www.childrenforchildren.org

This nonprofit organization teaches children the value of volunteering and hosts events around the city. If you have a child age six through thirteen, sign up for the Children's Action Board, which will send you updates on ongoing projects and the service project of the month. You will receive a CAN card to keep track of the events that your child participates in (they put a sticker on the card). The more your child participates, the more gifts she or he will receive, like T-shirts and service pins.

Dorot USA

171 West 85th Street at Amsterdam Avenue
212-769-2850
www.dorotusa.org
This Jewish nonprofit works to enhance the lives of the elderly through intergenerational programs. Kids ages five through twelve can sign up for their after-school programs to volunteer for activities like visiting seniors and making birthday cards.

New York Cares

214 West 29th Street bet. Seventh and Eighth avenues, 5th floor
212-228-5000
www.nycares.org
New York Cares has an extensive database of family-friendly volunteer activities, from delivering food for Meals on Wheels to planting city gardens. Look through their Web site for listings of volunteer activities that will inspire your family to pitch in together.

Chapter Three

Take Me Out on the Town:

Art Museums, Theater, Music, and Other Fun Activities

Even if your kids have an 8 p.m. bedtime, they can reap the benefits of living in a city that never sleeps. From jazz brunches with live music to kid-focused museum tours, one of the greatest joys of raising kids in the city is that they are exposed to a variety of cultural experiences. After checking out these interesting and educational activities for your kids, you'll understand again why, in deciding to stay with your kids in a city of millions, you sacrificed space for city living. Take advantage of residing just blocks from world-class paintings by Monet and mere minutes from some of the best dance performances in the world. Turn off the TV and explore the wonders of this great city.

Museums

Museums are a great place to introduce your kids to everything from history to the practices of other cultures. You may enjoy a leisurely stroll through a museum, but even the best behaved eight-year-old might find the museum overwhelming and announce their boredom. Most of the museums that I've chosen to include below have family programs tailored to specific age groups, so that kids can learn to appreciate museums on their own level. From guided tours to art workshops, there are great ways to introduce your children to the beauty of our city's museums.

Some tips when visiting museums: Don't try and cover the entire museum, but instead, focus on specific rooms or works of art. After taking countless museum tours with my kids while researching the book, I've noticed that most kid-focused museum tours only study one or two pieces of art on a tour. This way the kids get a real understanding of one work and aren't bombarded with too much information. After going on all of the tours, I found that quick visits to the museum are more enjoyable with my kids. We tend to spend an hour or less at a museum and we really get a lot out of the visit. If you make a short trip, your kids will want to return, which I believe will encourage a love for museums.

American Museum of Natural History and The Rose Center for Earth and Space

Central Park West at 79th Street
212-769-5100
www.amnh.org

The American Museum of Natural History is like a second home to most New York City kids. Who doesn't enjoy a visit to see the famous blue whale hanging in the Milstein Hall of Ocean Life and the dinosaur skeletons? This treasured museum offers kids a room of their own at the Discovery Room where kids can put fossils together to make a dinosaur skeleton or dig for dinosaur bones. If your child wants to get even more out of a visit to the museum, you should consider signing up for a weekend workshop or class that is available at the museum—and is often free with admission. Classes fill up fast, so I'd suggest signing up before you visit. They also offer a popular summer camp. Check the Web site for information on all family programs and Imax movies that are perfect for grade-school children who can appreciate stunningly visual educational films on science. When my family visited, the museum was offering a great Imax film about dinosaurs.

Just walking through the museum and exploring the various exhibits can take all day. If you need to grab a bite to eat during your visit, you can dine at the café in the museum, but note that the lines are often quite long and finding a seat can be a challenge. Before your visit, peruse the museum's Web site and discuss what your kids would like to see. This will make your trip more relaxed. If you are a frequent visitor to the museum you might want to sign up for a family membership, which entitles your family to free admission to the museum and members-only events as well as discounts on movies.

Does your child want to grow up to be an astronaut? Even if they aren't hopeful space explorers, kids of all ages will love seeing a space show at the Hayden Planetarium. In 2009 they added a wonderful new space show, *Journey to the Stars*, narrated by Whoopi Goldberg. To avoid long lines, you can buy advance tickets for the space show on the museum's Web site. The show runs every half hour from 10:30 a.m. through 4:30 p.m. except Wednesdays, when the first show is at 11 a.m.

A Unique Sleepover: Night at the Museum

Kids ages eight through twelve and an accompanying parent can spend the night at the Museum of Natural History. The sleepover starts at 5:45 p.m. and ends at 9 a.m. This unique experience allows kids to sleep on a cot at the museum, but before you call it a night, kids see an Imax film, explore fossils by flashlight, see a live animal presentation, and get some activities to take home. You are treated to an evening snack and breakfast the next day. Call to book a night at the museum and see if the artifacts really come to life after hours. Check the Museum of Natural History's Web site for dates or give them a call (212-769-5200). Just to note, this is quite popular and fills up quickly, so make your reservation early.

Brooklyn Museum of Art

200 Eastern Parkway at Washington Avenue
Brooklyn
718-638-5000
www.brooklynmuseum.org

The fountains outside of this Brooklyn museum will excite your kids, with its streams of water shooting up high into the air. The Brooklyn Museum of Art is a great place to introduce kids to the world of art as well as other cultures (they have an amazing exhibit about ancient Egypt). On weekends you can partake of their popular Arty Facts program for children ages four through seven (they discourage bringing younger children, so leave the younger siblings with your partner while you enjoy this activity with your older child). Arty Facts takes place from October through June at 11 a.m. and 2 p.m. The ninety-minute program is free with admission and includes a mini tour of the museum galleries and an art project that relates to exhibits that the children view. When we were there, my daughter and I were invited back to the studio to paint a picture using the colors we had seen in a bright painting. It was great to see the kids dressed in smocks, armed with paintbrushes and working really hard to create a piece of art. The leader was encouraging and enthusiastic and helped the kids understand basic concepts in art. If your child is a fan of Arty Facts, you might consider signing for the Gallery/Studio program where kids ages six and up can take art classes at the museum.

If you want help figuring out what exhibits appeal to kids, the museum has a family guide, so that you can explore the museum together. The guide is designed for young people to tour the museum on their own or with a parent.

On the first Saturday of every month, the Brooklyn Museum of Art hosts Target First Saturdays, a program of free music and entertainment from 5 p.m. to 11 p.m. At this event, the quiet museum transforms to a vibrant and festive atmosphere and there are many kid-focused activities, from art projects to music. Get there early as it gets crowded.

Science Stores

You can't believe the stuff for sale at these unique NYC shops that will appeal to city kids (and their parents):

Evolution Nature Store
120 Spring Street at Greene Street
800-952-3195
www.evolutionnyc.com
This Soho shop sells natural history collectibles. If you have a child that thinks getting a replica of a human skull is better than getting a Wii gaming system, then you should head to this shop. Evolution is stocked with a variety of interesting items from butterflies encased in glass to other insects. A visit to the shop is like a trip to a small museum, except you can actually buy everything in the shop.

Maxilla and Mandible
451 Columbus Avenue at West 82nd Street
212-724-6173
www.maxillaandmandible.com
This Upper West Side shop sits just blocks from the American Museum of Natural History (see p. 41) and is the perfect place to search through a vast selection of natural history items if a visit to the museum has inspired your child to collect fossils. From a fossilized shark tooth to seashells, this is a must visit.

Solomon R. Guggenheim Museum

1071 Fifth Avenue at 89th Street

212-423-3500

www.guggenheim.org

This museum designed by Frank Lloyd Wright will appeal to kids, who enjoy forgoing the stairs for a ramp that leads visitors through the various floors and museums exhibits. My daughter loved figuring out what level we were on and also enjoyed stopping on the ramp to look at the art.

If you are looking for a structured family visit, you should consider participating in one of their family workshops. The popular family workshops are for parents and their kids ages five through ten and range from printmaking workshops to painting and sculpture workshops. The Guggenheim also has a Second Sunday Program, on the second Sunday of every month, when there are guided tours for families, which are thematically based and vary each month. The Second Sundays allow kids and their family to tour the museum with fun activities like scavenger hunts. The workshops and Second Sundays are an additional charge to admission. On Wednesdays from 1 p.m. until 4 p.m., the museum offers a Just Drop In program, where an art educator sets up a table on one of the galleries, and offers kids guided art projects based on the art in the gallery. Just Drop In is also offered during school vacation weeks, and is free with museum admission. Also, for kids ages eight through eleven, the Guggenheim offers after-school classes as well as camps for spring break and summer.

If you don't want to commit to a family workshop or tour, you can pick up a Family Activity Pack at the Aye Simon Reading Room, which is offered free during your stay, until 4 p.m. You need to leave an ID like a driver's license to borrow the pack, which includes a binder with tons of kid-friendly activities that correspond with the artwork on display and correspond to changing exhibits. When we went, the pack included a great book related to one the paintings at the museum as well as a sketchpad, colored pencils, and an eraser, so young artists can simply sit and sketch while surrounded by priceless inspirational works of art. There were also art projects, like making a postcard inspired by one of the works at the museum, which we were able to take home. My daughter and I had such a good time following their tour on our own and I felt as if I were seeing the art all over again through a child's eyes; it gave me a better appreciation of the works at the Guggenheim.

If you are in need of libations, there is a cafeteria on the ground level with everything from salad to sandwiches. The gift shop is located near the entrance and has a nice section of art books and toys for kids, as well as books about New York City.

Metropolitan Museum of Art

1000 Fifth Avenue at 82nd Street

212-535-7710

www.metmuseum.org

Every city kid has to visit the Met because it's an NYC classic. My childhood dream was to be locked up in the Met overnight like the fictional characters Claudia and Jamie in the children's classic *The Mixed-Up Files of Mrs. Basil E. Frankweiler*. Besides the amazing exhibit about ancient Egypt on the first floor, with a wall of windows exposing the stunning views of Central Park, there are tons of kid-friendly aspects of this amazing museum. The Met's family program hosts kid-focused film screenings and tours divided by age as well as a kid-friendly tour, Start for Art, that is great for kids ages three to seven. Tours focus on various exhibits around the museum and they usually have the kids draw pictures based on the art they viewed. We've taken the tours and were quite impressed with the educators, who do an amazing job teaching the kids about art and how to appreciate the works at the museum. For kids ages six through twelve, the museum offers more detailed tours and classes. If you'd like to view the museum on your own without a tour, they offer audio tours for families. These tours are suggested for kids ages six through twelve.

If you are heading to the museum for a family program, you can enter from the street-level entrance at the Education Center, which is great since you can skip being immersed in the crowds that often gather in the lobby. Pay your entrance fees and make sure to pick up a free children's map of the museum (my daughter loves carrying this colorful map around the museum). If you'd like to take a more substantial memento home besides a museum map, there are many opportunities to purchase souvenirs at the Met gift shops as well as a kids' shop, where you can pick up educational toys and art books.

There is also a great cafeteria at the museum, which serves kids' meals in a cardboard taxicab. Although the meals here are on the pricey side.

Before you head to the museum, check out the kids' section on the Met museum's Web site. This will help you and your child prepare for your visit. The kids' section has the latest info on all the family-friendly activities as well as interactive educational games and activities.

If you head uptown, you can visit **The Cloisters** in Fort Tyron Park (212-923-3700), which is another historic museum run by the Met. The Cloisters has family programs for children from ages four through twelve. The program is an hour long and allows families to explore this medieval museum and garden. The family programs take place on the first and third Saturdays and the first Sunday of each month at 1 p.m. Other family events occur throughout the year.

Museum of Arts and Design
2 Columbus Circle at West 58th Street
212-299-7777
www.madmuseum.org

Families can enjoy programs such as Studio Sundays, a hands-on art workshop that focuses on touch and its relation to art. Museum staff introduces children to various materials like clay, metal, and fiber to create art that is inspired from exhibits at the museum. The program takes place every Sunday from 2 p.m. until 4 p.m. unless otherwise noted, and it costs $10 per person, with the price of materials included. The museum also has houses a working artist's space, so kids can see artists at work in their studios.

Museum of Modern Art
11 West 53rd Street bet. Fifth and Sixth avenues
212-397-6980
www.moma.org

The Museum of Modern Art is a kid's paradise with lots of colors and lights. The MoMA also has many family programs including the popular Tours for Fours, where kids who are four years old can take a tour geared toward their age group. For kids ages five through ten, there are family programs, thematically organized with a new theme each month, where you can tour the museum. These tours fill up fast (when we arrived twenty minutes before the museum was to open, we were already closed out of a tour). If you take a child-friendly tour, you and your child also get free admission to the museum.

The New Museum

235 Bowery at Prince Street
212-219-1222
www.newmuseum.org

This hip museum on the Bowery contains the latest in modern art and hosts New Museum First Saturdays for Families program on the first Saturday of each month, where kids can screen films sponsored by Brooklyn International Film Festival's KidsFilmFest, complete with hands-on art activities, and enjoy family tours. The program is designed for kids ages five through fifteen and is free of charge.

Noguchi Museum

9-01 33rd Road at Vernon Boulevard
Queens
718-721-2308
www.noguchi.org

This serene museum in the heart of industrial Long Island City is a place most city folks go to get some peace and quiet. Ironically enough, kids are also drawn to this museum (in fact my daughter always asks to go). Yes, parents hush their kids a lot, but families can enjoy viewing the collection of Noguchi's sculptures. The museum also has a popular family art workshop that fills up quite quickly. A tip: Get on their mailing list and sign up for the workshop as soon as you get the brochure.

Queens Museum of Art

Flushing Meadows Corona Park
NYC Building, Avenue of the States
Queens
718-592-9700
www.queensmuseum.org

When I was a city kid, one of my favorite places in NYC was the Panorama of the city at the Queens Museum of Art. The Panorama is a 9,335-square-foot architectural model that was built by Robert Moses for the 1964 World's Fair. The model includes every single building constructed before 1992 in all five boroughs, totaling 895,000 individual structures. It's amazing to see the enormity of this large city in this model.

In addition to the Panorama, the museum hosts free drop-in art workshops on Sundays from 1:30 p.m. until 4:30 p.m. for children ages five and up. There are other family programs too, as well as revolving exhibits and a permanent collection.

Rubin Museum of Art

150 West 17th Street at Seventh Avenue
212-620-5000
www.rmanyc.org

You'll learn a lot about Himalayan art and culture at this museum. On Saturdays kids ages five and up can participate in family workshops from 2 p.m. until 3:30 p.m., when families get to explore exhibits and afterward, make their own works of art. If you have younger kids, the museum offers separate family programs for two- to five-year-olds. Twice a year in the spring and fall, the museum hosts family festivals, so check its calendar for dates.

Museum Mile Festival

www.museummilefestival.org

For over thirty years during this educational block party, the museums of the noted Museum Mile have opened their doors to the public at no charge. The festival spans from 82nd to 105th streets along Fifth Avenue and usually runs on the evening of the second Tuesday in June. There are musical performances in the streets, art workshops, and tons of kid-friendly activities. It's also exciting to walk down a car-free Fifth Avenue and pop into all of these museums for a flavor of this historic block in New York. The nine museums that participate in the festival are: El Museum del Barrio, the Museum of New York City, the Jewish Museum, the Cooper-Hewitt National Design Museum, the National Academy Museum of Fine Arts, the Solomon R. Guggenheim Museum, the Neue Gallerie New York, the Goethe Institute-German Cultural Center, and the Metropolitan Museum of Art.

The Skyscraper Museum

39 Battery Place at Little West Street

212-968-1961

www.skyscraper.org

Learn all about how buildings are constructed at the family programs on Saturday mornings at the Skyscraper Museum. With workshops where you make a skyline with your body to programs that focus on going green, kids ages five and up will learn about their urban environment and the enormous buildings that surround them. Check the Web site for their calendar of upcoming family programs. Registration for these programs is required by 5 p.m. on the Friday before the event. The program asks a suggested donation of $5 per child. Older kids will appreciate the museum's exhibits on skyscrapers and architecture.

Whitney Museum of American Art

945 Madison Avenue at 75th Street

212-570-3600

www.whitney.org

The Whitney Museum has a host of family programs for kids ages six through twelve. They also offer Saturday family workshops, where every month they explore different themes inspired by different pieces from the Whitney collection. There is a $10 fee for the two-hour family fun workshop. These programs fill up quickly, so sign up in advance on the Web site. The Whitney also offers after-school classes.

American History

If you want to bring American history to life, check out these historic sites around the city:

Ellis Island and the Statue of Liberty

www.statueofliberty.org; www.ellisisland.org

You don't have to be a tourist to take the ferry to Ellis Island and the Statue of Liberty—both are a huge part of our great city's history. The Immigration Museum on Ellis Island is for older-grade school-aged children while the Statue of Liberty can be enjoyed by kids of all ages. The crown on the Statue of Liberty was closed after 9/11 but reopened on July 4, 2009. You can book tickets through Statue Cruises (877-LADY-TIX, www.statuecruises.com).

Historic Richmond Town

441 Clark Avenue
Staten Island
718-351-1611
www.historicrichmondtown.org

You don't have to be a history buff to enjoy a day visiting the twenty-seven buildings at this museum village from the 1600s. The restored village includes old homes, outhouses, a courthouse, and many other buildings. It's a great place to stroll around and the staff is extremely friendly and eager to discuss the history of the town. There are many family events year-round including fairs, festivals, and concerts. Children in grades three through six can enjoy a sleepover at this historic town as well; inquire about dates and rates by phone.

Historic House Trust of New York City

212-360-8282
www.historichousetrust.org

The Historic House Trust represents over twenty-three historic homes in New York City, from farms to mansions. Pick up their passport of homes, and travel around the city visiting these historic landmarks. Many of the homes have kid-friendly activities and offer stamps for the passport for each one you visit. Homes with kid-friendly activities include the Morris Jumel Mansion in Manhattan and the Lefferts House in Brooklyn, among many others.

Teddy Roosevelt Birthplace

28 East 20th Street at Broadway
212-260-1616
www.nps.gov

Older children who are learning about the presidents will enjoy seeing the place where Teddy Roosevelt was born. This isn't the original brownstone, but it has been rebuilt to look like the original and is in the same location. City kids will also be happy to know that Teddy was a city kid too, and can tour the rooms or look through a display of his personal belongings on the ground level.

Lower East Side Tenement Museum

91 Orchard Street at Broome Street
212-431-0233
www.tenement.org

If your child is reading the All-of-a-Kind Family books or has Rebecca, the American Girl doll from the Lower East Side, then she will enjoy a visit to this tenement turned museum. Families should sign up for the forty-five minute tour of the Confino apartment, the home of Sephardic Jewish immigrants led by a teenage guide dressed as Victoria Confino, a member of the family. Tickets sell out quickly, so buy them on the Web site before you go. They recommend the tour for kids ages five and up. Don't forget to take the kids to Guss's Pickles (www.gusspickle.com), which is down the block at 89 Orchard Street, so they can taste some fresh Lower East Side pickles.

Children's Museums/ Science Museums

You can touch everything you'd like at these interactive museums designed specifically for kids. Tour these NYC museums or make a fun day trip out of a visit to museums that are within ninety minutes or less from the city:

Brooklyn Children's Museum

145 Brooklyn Avenue at St. Mark's Avenue
Brooklyn
718-735-4400
www.brooklynkids.org

The Brooklyn Children's Museum was renovated and expanded into a "green" museum in 2008. All the favorites are still there, like the room filled with drums from around the world, as well as the toddler area. Exhibits like the World Brooklyn exhibit featuring re-creations of local Brooklyn shops like L & B Spumoni Garden, where kids can pretend to bake pizza and serve spumoni, or the Mexican Bakery where kids can bake bread with pretend dough, are sure hits with the younger set. My kids love driving the stationary bus and making up scenarios about traveling around the city. The museum now offers folks the opportunity to dine at their café on the second floor, which also showcases revolving exhibits. The museum hosts tons of family programs and events on a daily basis, so be sure to check its calendar before you visit. Announcements over the PA system indicate when different programs are starting, so you don't have to look at the schedule while you're visiting the museum.

Children's Museum of Manhattan

212 West 83rd Street bet. Broadway and
Amsterdam Avenue
212-721-1223
www.cmom.org

This Manhattan children's museum is known for its interactive exhibits geared toward the under-five set, with a Dora and Diego exhibit and the popular Playworks; however, older children will enjoy exhibits like Gods, Myths, and Mortals, and the out-

door water area. The museum also has family programs each weekend for kids ages five and older. The museum hosts birthday parties (even sleepover parties for kids ages six through eight) and is a great place to stop by if you are on the Upper West Side.

Intrepid Sea-Air-Space Museum

Pier 86 at 46th Street
877-957-7447; 212-245-0072
www.intrepidmuseum.org

Although not a kids' museum, the USS *Intrepid* belongs here because I think that its museum teaches kids about science and space. In 2009, the *Intrepid* reopened after an extensive five-year renovation and so you can once again spend your day on an aircraft carrier while you explore the exhibits of old planes like the B-52 bomber and the Concorde—the luxury airliner that used to speed across the ocean from France and London to New York. There are numerous interactive exhibits where kids can learn about the science behind the aircrafts and ships. Kids of all ages will enjoy the Intrepid Exploreum, which includes a flight simulator and other cool features for kids. It's great fun to visit for Fleet Week, which takes place each May with tons of festivities and so kids can see the sailors while they are on leave.

New York Hall of Science

47-01 111th Street at 47th Avenue
Queens
718-699-0005
www.nyhallsci.org

There is much to see at this kid-focused science museum where you can shoot baskets and learn about the science behind sports. Each exhibit has numerous interactive stations where children can learn about basic concepts in science and, weather permitting, kids can play in the outdoor Science Playground. The New York Hall of Science always has drop-in workshops that usually charge a small materials fee. When my family went, my daughter made a butterfly stick puppet. There is a host of family programs through this museum, including an after-school science club and birthday parties are available (see p. 109). This museum really makes science fun and don't forget to pick up some space ice cream at the gift shop. If you also find this ice cream tasteless, walk down the block to our favorite: **Lemon Ice King of Corona** (5202 108th Street, Queens; 718-699-5133; www.theicekingofcorona.com) for a proper scoop.

Staten Island Children's Museum

1000 Richmond Terrace
Staten Island
718-273-2060
www.statenislandkids.org

Play chess with extra-large chess pieces at this children's museum located at Snug Harbor. The museum has exhibits on bugs as well as a huge fire truck where kids can dress up and pretend to be firefighters. There is a wonderful library with reading areas for the kids, and the museum offers a bunch of family programs on a daily basis—from story times to craft projects—so just check the schedule for dates. When we visited, my kids got to design their own family coat of arms made out of oak tag.

Children's Museums Around the City

One of the perks of becoming a member of a children's museum like the Brooklyn Children's Museum (see p. 49) and the Children's Museum of Manhattan (see p. 49) is certain memberships include free access to all of the accredited children's museums and science museums throughout the United States. All you have to do is show them your membership card to enter. For a nice day trip outside of town, consider taking a trip to these children's museums, which are within ninety minutes or less of New York City.

Liberty Science Center

251 Phillip Street
Jersey City, New Jersey
201-200-1000
www.lsc.org

Head across the water to New Jersey to visit the newly renovated Liberty Science Center, where your family can be schooled on the interesting world of science. Rated one of the top ten science centers by *Parents* magazine, exhibits focus on the world of medicine, the environment, and many other science topics. They also have an Imax dome theater and 3-D digital theater. Additionally, they offer an area called IExplore for younger kids, ages two through five, if you have a younger sibling in tow.

Long Island Children's Museum

11 Davis Avenue
Garden City, New York
516-224-5800
www.licm.org

Your child can literally stand inside a bubble at this Long Island children's museum. Other exhibits include exploring what it's like to be disabled by visiting a wheelchair-accessible house and getting to sit behind the wheel of a handicap-accessible van. There are many interactive exhibits, such as a woodshop, where kids can build and construct. The museum has a theater and hosts many performances. There are art activities and other drop-in workshops at the museum. Kids enjoy climbing through the enclosed rope ladder that take you to the second floor of the museum. Pack a lunch because they don't have a café but a cafeteria where families are invited to eat; however they don't serve food and just have a few vending machines.

Children's Museum of the East End

376 Bridgehampton at Sag Harbor Turnpike
Bridgehampton, New York
631-537-8250
www.cmee.org

This children's museum located in the posh Hamptons has interactive exhibits, including a fantasy tree-house bedroom and an East End farm, where kids can pretend to buy local veggies. They also have an outdoor amphitheater with tons of theatrical events ranging from puppet shows to musical performances. There is also drop-in art studio where kids can participate in free art projects.

Hudson Valley Children's Museum

75 North Water Street
Poughkeepsie, New York
845-471-0589
www.mhcm.org

For over twenty years this Hudson Valley children's museum has offered kids fun and educational enjoyment. They have daily art activities and exhibits on the region like the River Town exhibit, which explores the cultural diversity of the area. They also have historically focused exhibits in which you can see what the Hudson Valley was like during the Revolutionary War.

New Jersey Children's Museum

599 Valley Health Plaza
Paramus, New Jersey
201-262-5151
www.njcm.com

With pirate adventure weekends and a play area where kids get to dress up like doctors and pretend to drive an ambulance, this museum is well worth the trip to New Jersey. The museum is a great place for kids of all ages, and even adults will enjoy watching the model trains on the giant train set. Eat before you go because they don't have food at the museum, although the museum's Web site lists some family-friendly area restaurants.

Stepping Stones Museums at Mathews Park

303 West Avenue
Norwalk, Connecticut
203-899-0606
www.steppingstonesmuseum.org

This Norwalk Children's Museum has interactive exhibits for the five-and-over set, ranging from health to inventions. The museum's Build It exhibit goes over the concepts of building and addresses the topic of the museum's own "green" construction project. If you are up for another adventure, consider taking a ride over to the **Maritime Aquarium** (10 North Water Street; 203-852-0700; www.maritime-aquarium.org), where you can feed the seals, see an Imax film, or see other marine life.

Cultural

Even though New York City is a melting pot, it's never too early to expose your children to the beauty of other cultures. There are many cultural institutions in the city, but I've listed the ones with great kids' programs.

Asia Society
725 Park Avenue at 70th Street
212-288-6400
www.asiasociety.org
The Asia Society hosts various family programs like the Coca-Cola Family Day Program Series, a series of family days where kids can tour galleries, do hands-on activities, and see live performances. Check the Web site for additional family programs. They also offer a shuttle bus to the Noguchi Museum (see p. 46).

Japan Society
333 East 47th Street bet. First and Second avenues
212-832-1155
www.japansociety.org
The Japan Society has many family festivals and events including a New Year's Day celebration, a doll's festival, a children's day, and many others. Check the schedule for upcoming events. The Japan Society is an interesting place to explore with your children. They also offer workshops in subjects like anime and classes for students.

Jewish Children's Museum
792 Eastern Parkway at Kingston Avenue
Brooklyn
718-467-0600
www.jcmonline.org
This museum, suitable for children of all ages and faiths, opened in the winter of 2005. The museum has a series of engaging and educational exhibits on the food, culture, and history of Judaism as well as family workshops like making latkes for Chanukah. From shopping in a kid-size kosher supermarket to pretending to cook in a kosher kitchen, the museum has many Jewish themed exhibits including the Six Holes of Life mini golf! In observance of Shabbat, the museum isn't open on Fridays or Saturdays during the day, but it opens after sundown on Saturday nights. Check the Web site or call for specific hours since they change seasonally.

The Jewish Museum
1109 Fifth Avenue at 92nd Street
212-423-3200
www.thejewishmuseum.org
On the second Sunday of the month, at 11:15 a.m., the Jewish Museum hosts family tours. They also have family programs, like their popular weekend concert series. On holidays and school breaks, they have drop-in activities ranging from arts and crafts to story times. Every Sunday from 1 p.m. until 4 p.m., they also have a drop-in arts and crafts program at the activity center for families on the fourth floor. Check the schedule for holiday programming and other special events.

National Museum of the Native American

Alexander Hamilton U.S. Custom House
1 Bowling Green at Broadway
212-514-3700
www.nmai.si.edu

The National Museum of the Native American hosts annual family festivals as well as provides a handy guide to direct your family through seven highlights of the museum that would interest families. The museum also has family days four times a year and offers family tours. Kids will enjoy exploring the interesting exhibits at this free museum.

The New York Chinese Cultural Center

390 Broadway bet. White and Walker streets
212-334-3764
www.chinesedance.org

Located in Soho, the New York Chinese Cultural Center is a performing arts and educational organization designed to foster the appreciation of Chinese culture. Although it's not a museum, the organization runs a festival for the lunar New Year as well as Chinese dance performances. They also have a summer camp and dance classes, so check the schedule for events. I am on the mailing list and receive e-mails about many upcoming performances and art workshops.

Scandinavia House

58 Park Avenue at 38th Street
212-879-9779
www.scandinaviahouse.org

Although the playroom at the Scandinavia House is better for the tot crowd, there is much to occupy an older child. One rainy day, my daughter and I had a great time visiting the museum. She built Lego structures, and we read Scandinavian classics like *Heidi* and *Pippi Longstocking* from the amazing library. There were revolving kid-centric exhibits next to the kids' room, and while we were there, an igloo occupied my five-year-old while I sat and read. If you live on the East Side, you might consider buying a pass to their kids' room. It's a great back-up plan for bad weather and a gentle way to introduce your child to other cultures.

United Nations

First Avenue and 46th Street
212-963-TOUR
www.un.org

There's no better way to teach your children about international relations than a trip to the United Nations. Upon entering the U.N., you are officially leaving New York City and America and crossing into international territory. Kids will get a kick out of the airport-like atmosphere of getting to watch your bag go on a conveyor belt through security and also trying to recognize the flags from all the countries that line the entrance to the U.N. The United Nations offers tours on weekdays from 9:45 a.m. until 4:45 p.m. The tours are forty-five minutes long and are only for children over age five (they are fairly strict about this policy). The U.N. tours are geared toward older kids, and I personally recommend only taking children who are ten years and up. But if you have younger kids in tow, you can still enjoy a trip to the U.N., as the lobby houses rotating photography and art exhibits.

If your children would like a unique souvenir, you can get their photo put onto a U.N. stamp that can only be sent from the United Nations. Just head to the lower level for a trip to the U.N. post office, and you can put it on a postcard and send it anywhere in the world. The lower level also houses a gift shop and a bookshop that carries travel-themed and internationally themed items for kids, like wooden Melissa & Doug puzzles of maps as well as children's books. In addition, there is a booth that sells kid-related items to benefit UNICEF along with a small café where you can grab lunch. While at the bookshop, we purchased a coloring book that is published by the United Nations, entitled *The United Nations in Our Daily Lives*. We sat on the bench and read the book while taking breaks to discuss the importance of the United Nations. This talk helped my daughter appreciate what the U.N. does for the world.

Just a parental warning, if you haven't broached subjects like war, famine, drugs, and refugees with your child, these are topics that may come up while on a visit to the U.N. My six-year-old daughter asked a slew of questions and many of them were difficult to answer since I didn't think a girl on the brink of six would be able to digest these concepts.

Cultural Festivals

We all know about the Chinese New Year and the many parades celebrating other cultures, but here are a few kid-friendly cultural celebrations in NYC that are off the beaten pavement:

June
Egg Rolls and Egg Cream Festival
(www.eldridgestreet.org)
July
Bastille Day at Bar Tabac
(www.bartabacnyc.com)

August
The Hong Kong Dragon Boat Festival in New York (www.hkdbf-ny.org)
October
Czech Street Festival (www.czechcenter.com)
September
Brazil Day Festival (www.brazilianday.com)
Korean Harvest and Folklore Festival in Flushing Meadows (www.nycgovparks.org)
Tibetan Festival at the Jacques Marchais Museum of Tibetan Art
(www.tibetanmuseum.org)

Performing Arts

From theater to jazz shows for kids at a popular jazz club, there are a lot of activities in the city to entertain your city kid.

Theater

Take your child on a theatrical tour of the city. There is a plethora of Broadway theater productions available to your city kid, like the Disney productions and other kid-friendly shows like *Mama Mia*. Here is a list of children's theaters in the NYC area:

Atlantic For Kids

336 West 20th Street bet. Eighth and Ninth avenues
212-691-5919
www.atlantictheater.org
The children's theater productions at this well-respected theater company range from a play based on the Frog and Toad book series to one based on the popular young adult novel *Holes*. The actors are

professionals, so adults will appreciate the performances, too. This theater company has two different productions each year, and the players perform the show on Saturday and Sunday mornings. After the performance the cast meets with the children in the lobby and will answer any questions or will sign programs. Check the Web site for their schedule. Additionally, the company runs the Atlantic Acting School, where there are acting classes for kids in Pre-k until high school.

Blue Man Group
434 Lafayette Street at Broadway
800-982-2787
www.blueman.com

Children eight and older can enjoy a performance of this long-running performance art show where men who are completely painted in blue create music and dance. The group recently founded the Blue School—an elementary school for kids (each year they add a new grade and by 2014, the school will have its first fifth grade class). There is also a popular after-school program open to all kids, offering classes in art (they have one class where you work with various working artists each week), movement, music, and science. (www.theblueschool.org).

Brooklyn Center for the Performing Arts at Brooklyn College
2900 Campus Road at East 21st Street
Brooklyn
718-951-5400
www.brooklyncenteronline.org

For over twenty years the Brooklyn Center's Family Fun series has been entertaining kids ages three and up, along with their parents. From acrobats to folk singers to productions of *The Wizard of Oz* and the *Nutcracker*, Family Fun has great programs for kids. In 2008 Target began sponsoring the program and offering discounted tickets, which start at $6.

Galli Fairytale Theater
38 West 38th Street bet. Fifth and Sixth avenues
212-810-6485
www.gallitheaterny.com

This German theater company located on the third floor of a Midtown building performs productions of classic fairy tales like *The Princess and the Pea* and *Rumpelstiltskin*. Plays run throughout the year and you can buy tickets online at the Web site. The theater also hosts birthday parties. Note that the elevator only fits a few people at a time, so get to performances early.

Gazillion Bubble Show
340 West 50th Street bet. Eighth and Ninth avenues
212-239-6200
www.gazillionbubbleshow.com

This popular and unique show has been entertaining families for over three years. The interactive show combines bubbles and laser lights, and kids are invited onstage to participate.

Kingsborough Children's Theater
Kingsborough Community College
2001 Oriental Boulevard at Quentin Street
Brooklyn
718-265-5343
www.kbcc.cuny.edu/kcc_arts/lively_arts.html

You can't go wrong at this children's theater located on the Kingsborough Community College campus, where tickets are a real bargain at $10. Each season they show a variety of kid-friendly theater, from clown acts to the more traditional puppet show. This is a nice weekend activity for families. Kingsborough also hosts the Brighton Ballet Theater and other dance and musical groups.

Literally Alive Children's Theatre at The Players Theater

115 MacDougal Street at West 3rd Street
212-866-5170
www.literallyalive.com

This theater company has been performing plays inspired by great works of literature for over ten years. The plays take place at the Players Theater and are extremely professional. We went to see a production of *Treasure Island* that appealed to kids ages three and up, which is quite tough given the material of the book. For an additional charge, your kids can participate in a preshow activity that relates to the production, so for example, we made treasure chests before seeing *Treasure Island*. They also host birthday parties (see p. 112).

Puppetworks

338 Sixth Avenue bet. 3rd and 4th streets
Brooklyn
718-965-3391
www.puppetworks.org

This marionette puppet theater in the heart of Park Slope is for kids three and up, and performs such classics as *Jack and the Bean Stalk*, *Hansel and Gretel*, and many other wonderful puppet shows. The theater is only open to the public on weekends, and the performances fill up quickly, so I'd suggest that you buy tickets early. It is also open during school breaks and hosts parties (see p. 113).

Manhattan Children's Theatre

52 White Street at Church Street
212-226-4085
www.mctny.org

For seven years this popular Tribeca children's theater has been hosting such performances as *Peter and the Wolf* and *Harry the Dirty Dog*. They also offer acting classes for kids as well as opportunities for kids to enjoy their birthday at the theater.

The New Acting Company at the Children's Aid Society

219 Sullivan Street at West 3rd Street
212-254-3074
www.childrensaidsociety.org/pcc/nac

This theater run by the Children's Aid Society has professional productions for kids at a West Village location. Plays are based on popular children's books and tales like *Wild Thing*, which was based on the book *Where the Wild Things Are*. They also have a popular acting school for kids.

The New Victory Theater

229 West 42nd Street bet. Seventh and Eighth avenues
646-223-3010
www.newvictory.org

Housed in a gorgeous restored theater on 42nd Street, the New Victory Theater hosts productions from all over the world. We've been members of this theater for years and have seen everything from a Swiss circus to a Romanian acrobatic group. The offerings are quite diverse and the theater has performances for all ages. If you buy tickets for three different performances for the season, you automatically become a member and get discounted seats. You can also sign up for the educational theatrical workshops, and often before the curtain goes up there is a craft project for kids in the lobby. The New Victory Theater hosts a summer camp as well as camps for the weeklong school breaks during the year.

Paper Bag Players

800-277-2247

Check the Web site for participating venues

www.paperbagplayers.org

Founded in 1958, the Paper Bag Players have been entertaining kids ages four through nine for over fifty years. The shows they perform have to do with the everyday experiences of a kid's life and props are simple products you'd find around the house. Kids should be inspired by their shows and realize that it doesn't take a huge fancy set to create theater.

The Circus Comes to Town

See trained animals and amazing acrobatic feats at these circuses that make annual (sometimes biannual) appearances in the city:

Big Apple Circus

June:

Cunningham Park, Fresh Meadows

December:

Lincoln Center

www.bigapplecircus.org

CIRCUSundays

Sundays in June

www.waterfrontmuseum.org

New York Circus Arts

A New York–based circus arts program

www.nycircusarts.com

Ringling Brothers Circus

March

Summer at Coney Island: Coney Island Boom A Ring

www.ringling.com

Russian American Kids Circus

A New York–based circus with an all-kid cast

www.rakidscircus.org

Slam Show at Streb Lab

March through May

This isn't a circus, but they do aerial performances and many other feats with kids who are students at Streb. Popcorn is served and kids get to see folks their own age participate in the show.

www.streb.org

UniverSoul Circus

Wollman Rink at Prospect Park

www.universoulcircus.com

Story Pirates at the Drama Book Shop

250 West 40th Street bet. Seventh and Eighth avenues

310-880-4725

www.storypirates.org

On Saturdays at 2 p.m., the Story Pirates host a weekly bookshop show where they perform plays written by kids. This inventive acting troupe lets kids create their own play that the players then perform for them. It's so exciting to see the kids so enthusiastic about creating their own play. At the end of the show, kids are treated to ice cream and cookies. Tickets cost $20 dollars and sell out quickly due to the Story Pirates increasing popularity. They also perform birthday parties (see p. 113).

Improv 4 Kids

Ha! Comedy Club
63 West 46th Street at Seventh Avenue
212-352-310
www.improv4kids.com/NYShows.html
On Saturdays at 3 p.m., kids and their families can enjoy some comedy by the folks from Improv 4 Kids. Head to this comedy club in the Times Square area and enjoy some laughs with your kids. They also teach comedy class for children.

Swedish Marionette Theater at Central Park

Central Park at 79th Street
www.cityparksfoundation.org
212-988-9093
This historic puppet theater in Central Park hosts puppet shows like *Peter Pan* and *Beauty and the Beast*. The shows are wonderful and it's quite an experience to sit in the gorgeous historic theater designed specifically for kids. Just to note, you must reserve tickets in advance as the shows fill up quickly.

TADA! Children's Theater

15 West 28th Street at Broadway
212-252-1619
www.tadatheater.com

Enjoy a musical production performed by kids in the TADA! Ensemble, which is comprised of kids age eight through eighteen. The musicals are one hour long and are performed on weekends. Productions are specifically created for kids; children will enjoy seeing their contemporaries on the stage. Children can take acting classes at TADA! or have their birthday parties at the theater.

Teatro Sea at Los Kabayitos Puppet Theatre

107 Suffolk Street at Rivington Street
212-529-1545
www.sea-ny.org
Housed in an old public school, this Lower East Side Latino children's theater company has bilingual puppet shows on Saturdays at 3 p.m. during the school year. Check the schedule on the Web site for upcoming productions.

13th Street Repertory Company

50 West 13th Street at Sixth Avenue
212-675-6677
www.13thstreetrep.org
The 13th Street Repertory Company has two shows for kids that they perform at different times on Saturdays and Sundays. The first show is the popular *WiseAcre Farm*, where kids are invited to try to help Cliffy the Pig save his cake from a mean fox. The second show includes a musical version of *Rumpelstiltskin*. They also have the Imagination Show, which can be performed for a child's birthday (see pp. 113-114). Tickets are only $10 for each performance.

Vital Theatre Company

2162 Broadway at 76th Street

212-579-0528

www.vitaltheatre.org

Vital Theater Company has been running the popular musical version of the beloved book *Pinkalicous* since 2007. Recently the Upper West Side theater has moved the production to 45 Bleecker Street, and has various other family friendly productions at their Upper West Side theater. The theater also offers a junior performance camp.

Free Theatrical Festivals and Concerts

Spend a day outdoors enjoying these theatrical festivals and concerts around the city hosted by Broadway on Broadway (www.BroadwayonBroadway.com). For over seventeen years this organization has been hosting a free concert in Times Square that takes place in September.

Broadway in Bryant Park (www.bryantpark.org) In the summer months at lunchtime, Brynat Park showcases performances from popular Broadway musicals. It also has an annual evening performance in the spring called "Broadway under the Stars."

Jazz Mobile (www.jazzmobile.org) Every Wednesday night at 7 p.m. in the summer you can see a jazz show at Grant's Tomb on 122nd Street and Riverside Drive.

River to River (www.rivertorivernyc.com) This summerlong performance series in downtown Manhattan showcases family-friendly shows all over the downtown area. Check the Web site for list of performances.

Music and Dance

Take in a musical or dance performance from great halls to a small jazz club.

American Ballet Theater

890 Broadway at West 19th Street

212-477-3030

www.abt.org

The American Ballet Theater hosts ABT Kids shows that are ideal for kids ages four through twelve. Kids are invited to participate in a pre-performance workshop.

Apollo Theater

235 West 125th Street bet. Seventh and Eight avenues

212-531-5300

www.apollotheater.org

The historic Apollo Theater has a family program, which performs about five family shows a year including a holiday show for Kwanzaa. There are educational projects and events at the shows as well as free movies for kids at the theater. Older kids may appreciate a backstage tour of the theater. The theater also has a gift shop where you can buy Apollo souvenirs.

New York City Ballet

David H. Koch Theater

70 Lincoln Center bet. Columbus and Amsterdam avenues

212-870-4071

www.nycballet.com/families/families.html

Enjoy *The Nutcracker* and other ballets at the New York City Ballet. The New York City Ballet doesn't admit children under age five (the only exception is for *The Nutcracker*). They offer a fun family subscription where kids can get discounted tickets for shows throughout the year.

Tribeca Performing Arts Center

199 Chambers Street at Greenwich Street

212-220-1459

www.tribecapac.org/children.htm

The Tribeca Performing Arts Center Family Series has shows that appeal to kids of all ages, from plays based on the works of children's book author, Mo Willems, to kid-focused mysteries. They also host concerts, dance performances, and puppet shows. Join the "10 club," for which you get ten tickets to the family series for $120.

Carnegie Hall

154 West 57th at Seventh Avenue

212-974-1150

www.carnegiehall.org

Family concerts at this historic hall only cost $9 and you can choose from a wide variety of performances throughout the season. Kids receive a copy of Kids Notes at the show, which is filled with activities concerning the concert. This incredible family program for kids ages five through twelve will take your family on a musical journey from ethnic music like the Slavic Soul Party to orchestra symphonies.

Jazz at Lincoln Center for the Performing Arts

70 Lincoln Center bet. Columbus and Amsterdam avenues

212-258-9800

www.jalc.org

This series provides kids with great introduction to jazz. The conductor not only offers a jazz band playing great tunes, but he explains the history behind the composer whose music they have just played. When my family went to a tribute to Benny Goodman show, we were walked through Benny's life, and the interactive show involved us in swing dancing in the aisles.

Jazz for Kids at Jazz Standard

116 East 27th Street at Lexington Avenue

212-576-2232

www.bluesmoke.com

On Sundays during the school year, the Jazz Standard hosts jazz shows for kids by kids in the Jazz Standard Youth Orchestra. If you're hungry you can order from the exceptional Blue Smoke brunch menu. After the concerts the kids are allowed to check out the instruments.

The Little Orchestra Society

330 West 42nd Street at Ninth Avenue, 12th Floor

212-971-9500

www.littleorchestra.org

For over sixty years the Little Orchestra Society has been introducing music to kids and fostering musical appreciation wherever they go. Their Happy Concerts for Young People is suited for kids ages six through twelve. Concerts are held at Town Hall in Midtown.

Metropolitan Opera at Lincoln Center for the Performing Arts

70 Lincoln Center bet. Columbus and Amsterdam avenues

212-362-6000

www.metoperafamily.org

In addition to seeing opera classics like *The Magic Flute* in one of the most famous theaters in New York City, you can also sign up for Opera Explorers, the Metropolitan Opera Guild's program designed to introduce children ages five through twelve and their parents to opera. Older children will also enjoy a backstage tour of this world-class opera house.

New York Theatre Ballet

30 East 31st Street at Madison Avenue, 5th Floor

212-679-0401

www.nytb.org

The New York Theatre Ballet has several ballet performances throughout the year. It hosts an extremely popular version of *The Nutcracker*. Most shows last under an hour and are performed in a smallish theater so everyone has a good seat. Outside of the show there is a table set up to sell ballet books and other merchandise that will attract prospective ballerinas.

New York Philharmonic

Avery Fisher Hall at 57th Street

10 Lincoln Center Plaza

212-875-5900

www.nyphil.org

The New York Philharmonic hosts a popular Young People's Concert series throughout the season at 2 p.m. in the afternoon for children ages six through twelve, with shows ranging from Mozart to Debussy. My cousins have been taking their kids to this series

for over six years and they rave about the concerts here. It's never too early to expose your children to the joys of classical music. Before every concert there is an interactive music fair where kids get to try playing instruments as well as musical games and more.

Symphony Space

2537 Broadway at 95th Street

212-864-5400

www.symphonyspace.org

From family concerts and book clubs to movies and author readings (Judy Blume read here in 2009)—these are just a few of the family programs that this Upper West Side performance arts venue offers for NYC kids. Check the schedule for the extensive listing of programs. You can also have your child's birthday party at Symphony Space, where kids can watch a show and then have pizza and cupcakes.

Film, TV, and More

Although the world sits right outside their windows, even city kids watch way too much TV. To add an educational element to the world of TV and film, you must take your children to one of these museums or tours. From a behind-the-scenes look at how an animated TV series is produced to workshops where kids can make their own old-time radio show, there is much to see once you turn off the TV and learn about the process and history behind this ubiquitous piece of technology.

Little Airplane Studio Tour

South Street Seaport

207 Front Street bet. Fulton and Beekman streets

212-965-8999

www.littleairplane.com

These are the studios of Little Airplane production company, which created the popular animated series *Wonder Pets*, as well as *Oobi*, *Go Baby*, and other kids' TV shows. The extremely informative forty-five-minute kid-friendly tour of their studio located in a historic South Street Seaport building includes a meeting with writers, storyboard artists, producers, and animators who explain what fun it is to create an animated series. Highlights include a visit to the recording booth where kids get to record a character's voice and hear it dubbed in a *Wonder Pets* episode. The guided tours, costing $10 per person, are given on Tuesdays and Thursdays at 11 a.m. and 4 p.m., but you must book in advance. Do not forget to stop by the gift shop, which carries a large supply of *Wonder Pets* merchandise and other toys. You do not need to take a tour to stop by the shop. In the summer of 2009 they added a concert venue, Little Airplane Café, where they have a concert series for kids at the intimate café at the studio.

Museum of the Moving Image

35 Avenue at 37th Street

Queens

718-784-4520

www.movingimage.us

This museum is a perfect place to introduce kids to the film world. Located across from a film studio, the museum has tons of interactive exhibits where kids can learn the basics of film editing, sound effects, and animation. My daughter and I had a fun time making a flipbook, which we got to take home as a memento from our visit. The museum hosts family workshops like the one in which we learned the history of early animation. The workshop culminated with my daughter learning to make a Thaumat-rope—a moving picture toy from the Victorian era. The educators at these economical workshops are fantastic, and taking these classes gives kids a better understanding of the world behind their cartoons and video games. The classes are divided by age and are recommended for kids ages six and up.

If your kid is a gamer, he or she will love the collection of retro arcade games like Ms. Pacman (a personal favorite), which is housed at the museum, as well as the cases of memorabilia like original costumes from various films, old toys, Star Wars action figures, and other film and TV-related goodies. If you are in the mood for a film, check out daily screenings of family films at the kitschy Tut Fever Film Palace, an Egyptian-themed movie theater in the museum. See the film schedule to make sure you can plan your day around the screening. We had such a great time at the museum, and I think it had to do with the fact that so many exhibits were interactive and kids feel as if they are a part of the filmmaking process. The trip will also open up discussions on how filmmaking has evolved after viewing collections of old cameras and equipment used to produce early film. It really gave my daughter a greater appreciation for the hard work behind all the movies we see and how many people are involved in the process, and the importance of working together.

When we toured the museum it was undergoing a major renovation and expansion. After construction is finished, the museum will have a three-story addition including a café. The museum hosts birthday parties for kids ages seven and up, starting at $500 for ten kids. Parties include a private tour and film screening. If your family is a bunch of film buffs, consider getting a family membership to the museum, which will entitle you to discounted educational workshops and free admission.

Paley Center for Media

25 West 52 Street bet. Fifth and Sixth avenues
212-621-6800
www.paleycenter.org

I know my kids can't believe that there was life before DVR and cable, so taking them to the Paley Center for Media gave them a chance to see how TV and radio have changed throughout the years. The museum houses an archive of over 140,000 TV shows, commercials, and radio programs in their library and you can choose which tape you'd like to see from their database. Spend a rainy afternoon exposing your kids to noneducational cartoons that you grew up on, like *Tom and Jerry*, just make a reservation at their library, or you can listen to radio shows in the radio room. The museum also has daily screenings throughout the day and you can download the schedule from their Web site. The public programs are sometimes better suited for older kids, so check the schedule for events.

If you'd like to show your child what life was like before TV, sign up for a Re-creating Radio Workshop, a two-hour workshop where kids ages nine and up get to produce a radio drama using scripts, sound effects, and music. Each week the program produces a different show based on old radio programs like *The Lone Ranger, The Shadow*, and other favorites. At the end of the class, you get to take home a copy of your radio program on a disc. Since space is limited, they ask that you call ahead to reserve a spot. They also host birthday parties at the workshop.

Sony Wonder Technology Lab

550 Madison Avenue bet. West 55th and 56th streets
212-833-8100
www.sonywondertechlab.com

Tech-savvy city kids will love checking out all the exhibits at Sony Wonder Lab, but especially the "sensi-tile" wall, which creates images when you touch it. Kids get to create their own digital profile before they explore the other exhibits, which include a look at how electronic devices work and the world behind technology. Some parents (like me) will actually learn something on a trip to the lab. Sony Wonder Technology Lab has a seventy-three-seat high-definition theater to screen children's films like *Elmo's World* and *Dora the Explorer*. You should book tickets a week in advance, as there are a limited number of tickets and they fill up quite quickly. Admission is free to the screenings.

Kids Film Fest

www.kidsfilmfest.org

The Brooklyn International Film Festival runs the KidsFilmFest, an annual June event dedicated to kids. Kids have the opportunity to meet filmmakers at the festival with its many programs, workshops, and Q&As after the screenings. The film fest also screens films that have been shown in previous festivals on the first Saturday of every month at the New Museum First Saturday series at the New Museum (see p. 46).

Zoos and Aquariums

You don't have to travel around the world to see exotic animals; you can see them at your local zoos. If you become a member of the Wildlife Conservation Society (www.wcs.org), you can get unlimited free admission to all NYC zoos and the New York Aquarium, excluding the Staten Island Zoo.

Bronx Zoo

2300 Southern Boulevard in Bronx Park
Bronx
718-220-5100
www.bronxzoo.com

What can I say about the Bronx Zoo? This city zoo is awesome and is filled with a large assortment of animals from around the world. The zoo is quite large, so plan on spending an entire day there. They also have restaurants at the zoo, like the spacious Flying Crane Café, but consider packing a lunch since the food can be quite pricey. The Children's Zoo has interactive exhibits and kids will love riding the bug carousel. The Bronx Zoo has many family education programs and you can even spend the night camping at the zoo with the popular overnight program.

New York Aquarium

Surf Avenue at West 8th Street
Brooklyn
718-265-FISH
www.nyaquarium.com

Located in Coney Island, this aquarium has a cool cave-like shark room and an amazing sea lion show in an outdoor theater, among other interactive exhibits. The relatively small size of this aquarium makes it extremely kid-friendly, since it's not too large or overwhelming. On Fridays after 3 p.m., the aquarium offers "pay as you wish," which makes for an interesting and economical way to end the school or work week.

Prospect Zoo at Prospect Park

450 Flatbush Avenue
Brooklyn
718-399-7321
www.prospectparkzoo.com

Kids are transfixed by the sea lions located in the center of this zoo, and you can see them being fed at various times throughout the day. The Prospect Park Zoo is divided into three sections in which you can see animals from around the world. The zoo is quite small and is a great activity for a short day trip. Remember to pack some food as there is no cafeteria and it's a bit removed from food options since it's located in Prospect Park. In the warmer months the zoo also hosts puppet shows (my kids love these). You can also pretend to milk a wooden cow, which sounds silly but is actually quite fun. After a visit to the zoo, take a walk in the park and ride the carousel located outside the zoo's entrance.

Queens Zoo Wildlife Center

53-51 111th Street bet. 53rd and 54th avenues
Queens
www.queenszoo.com

The Queens Zoo Wildlife Center has a fun petting zoo where kids can feed and pet the farm animals. The highlight of this zoo is the amazing aviary where you can see gorgeous birds fly around. They also have great family programs like getting up close with an animal in the discovery room or other animal-themed craft projects. The zoo isn't too large and can be easily combined with a visit to the New York Hall of Science (see pp. 49–50), which is right down the block.

Staten Island Zoo
614 Broadway at Colonial Court
Staten Island
718-442-3100
www.statenislandzoo.org

This zoo is not apart of the Wildlife Conservation Society, but offers great family programs like the Breakfast with the Beasts program, where kids ages five and up get a tour of the kitchen used to prepare food for the animals, as well as help make breakfast for their furry friends. You also get to see the animals eat the food they've prepared and even meet a few up close. Check the calendar on the Web site for program dates. Admission costs $10 for members and $13 for nonmembers of the zoo. You can also enjoy a stroll around the zoo, checking out their wide variety of animals.

Cool animal-focused road trips:

If your child loves animals, consider a trip to these animal-themed excursions that range from spending a night at a working farm to a day trip to a Long Island game farm, there are many reasons to spend the weekend exploring the region.

Hull-O-Farms
10 Cochrane Road
Durham, New York
518- 239-6950
www.hull-o.com

Have a farm vacation at this family-friendly Catskill farm that will put your kids to work doing an assortment of fun and interesting farm chores, from gathering freshly laid eggs to milking cows. You can also spend quality time with the animals on the farm and engage in fun family activities like bonfires and making s'mores. The farm offers guests a choice of three private guesthouses if you'd like to spend the night.

Long Island Game Farm Wildlife Park and Children's Zoo
638 Chapman Boulevard
Manorville, New York
631-878-6670
www.longislandgamefarm.com

Head for a fun day trip (en route to the Hamptons/North Fork if you are heading east) to the Long Island Game Farm, which is also a wildlife park and zoo. Kids can see donkeys, tigers, alligators, and many other animals with animal shows and rides.

Woodstock Farm Animal Sanctuary
35 Van Wagner Road
Woodstock, New York
www.woodstockfas.org

If you are in the Woodstock area, head to this animal sanctuary where families can tour the farm and meet the animals. Tours take place from April through October from 11 a.m. until 4 p.m.

Take a Trip Back to the Middle Ages

Enjoy a trip back in time with these fun, kitschy, and family-friendly day trips.

Medieval Times

149 Polito Avenue
Lyndhurst, New Jersey
888-WE-JOUST
www.medievaltimes.com

You are never too young or old to eat with your bare hands and watch a jousting match. I actually had my twenty-ninth birthday party here among many ten-year-olds and their birthday parties. Kids will enjoy the show and the festive atmosphere at this New Jersey Medieval Times, located just fifteen minutes from Midtown Manhattan. Buses are available from Port Authority to the show.

New York Renaissance Faire

600 Route 17A
Tuxedo, New York
845-351-5171
www.renfair.com

Kids will appreciate the theatrics at the annual New York Renaissance Faire in Tuxedo, New York, that runs in August through mid-September. Located a little over an hour from the city, the Faire grounds are made to look like a medieval village with jousting matches and tons of interactive shows. You can actually rent costumes to wear at the festival. You won't go hungry at the Faire either—my family and gorged ourselves on treats like pickles and apple dumplings. There is a Shortline bus from Port Authority that goes to the Faire.

Chapter Four

Dining Out:

Kid-friendly Restaurants

Now that you're no longer weighed down by a stroller and diaper bag, and fueled by a desperate search for a restroom with a changing table, you're open to a whole new world of New York City restaurants. Of course that doesn't mean that fussy eaters won't limit your dining choices, but the whole experience of eating out with the kids gets a lot easier once they've outgrown their booster seats. However, I would suggest holding off on making reservations at the city's finest restaurants, because even the most best-behaved child is not always keen on the meaning of "volume control" and you don't need the stress of getting through a meal while other diners glare at your family (believe me, I've been there).

Eating in the city as a kid can feel a bit like taking a culinary trip around the world. City kids are exposed to a variety of cuisines—from eating with their hands at an Ethiopian restaurant to chowing down a bowl of chili underneath pictures of famous cowgirls at the kitschy Cowgirl restaurant. The truth is that kids will have fun at any one of New York City's eateries. Unlike most of America, where kids have limited dining options—the local diner or a large chain restaurant—NYC kids can dine on dim sum in Chinatown or eat dosas from a food cart at Washington Square Park. City parents know that half the reason they live in the New York is for the good grub that's widely available, and your kids should reap the benefit of the city's eclectic restaurants.

I've tested all the following restaurants with my kids and all of them come recommended by NYC parents. Obviously for a city as large as New York City, I could have written an entire book on dining out with your kids, so I've limited the list to some exceptional finds around Manhattan and the boroughs.

Chinatown

Golden Unicorn

18 East Broadway bet. Catherine and Market streets

212-941-0911

www.goldenunicornrestaurant.com

Dim sum is a parent's dream. You can order many rounds of food served in small kid-friendly portions while your children occupy themselves as they try to master the art of eating with chopsticks and sample various forms of dumplings. This Chinatown favorite is a fun and friendly place to introduce your kids to the joy of dim sum, served on large tables in the atmospheric dining room. Kids will love the fact that you take an elevator to the restaurant and that waiters walk around the dining room floor with carts filled with dumplings, stopping at each table to offer up their selections. If you want another dim dum option, check out **Dim Sum Go Go**, just down the block (5 East Broadway; 212-732-0796), which serves up over twenty types of dumplings. If you'd like to extend your day, consider taking the kids for a scenic walk across the Brooklyn Bridge after the meal. It's the perfect NYC ending to a warm afternoon or evening.

TriBeCa

Bubby's Pie Co.

120 Hudson Street at N. Moore Street
212-219-0666

1 Main Street at Plymouth Street
Brooklyn
718-222-0666
www.bubbys.com

New Yorkers have been lining up to indulge in a hearty brunch and a slice of one of Bubby's famous pies since 1990. Bubby's American-eclectic menu has everything from matzoh balls to bacon-wrapped meatloaf. The kid's menu is filled with favorites like the sautéed wild Coho salmon or build-your-own chicken soup. There's an outpost in DUMBO, so Brooklynites won't have to travel across the bridge. Call the Brooklyn location before visiting since it can be closed for private events.

Landmarc

179 West Broadway bet. Leonard and Worth streets
212-343-3883

10 Columbus Circle at Eighth Avenue
212-823-6123
www.landmarc-restaurant.com

A favorite among NYC parents, the kid's meal at this notable TriBeCa restaurant will please any picky eater. Who could resist an order of green eggs with ham or a slice of cheesy spaghetti pie? The regular menu at this upscale bistro, where your kids are certainly welcome, will not disappoint discerning adults in need of proper food.

Moomah

161 Hudson Street bet. Hubert and Laight streets
212-226-0345
www.moomah.com

This family-friendly café serving organic food offers kids the chance to engage in art projects while they eat. This place is an amazing find because although it's a kid-centric café, they don't settle on a menu of simple diner fare. The tasty menu is filled with healthy food like Yummus, which consists of homemade hummus and a basket of blue corn chips. Other favorites include an assortment of homemade soups, spinach and caramelized onion flatbread quesadillas, and many more. If you have a picky eater with you, Moomah offers a Super Tryer Menu, where kids get a chance to taste any six items off a list that includes dates, green peas, Greek yogurt, and more. Once your child has tasted all of the foods from their Super Tryer platter, they receive a stamp on their Super Tryer card. An accumulation of three stamps is awarded with a free T-shirt.

The Odeon

145 West Broadway bet. Duane and Thomas streets

212-233-0507

www.theodeonrestaurant.com

This popular TriBeCa restaurant has a menu of comfort food and amazing fries. A major part of 1980s culture in New York City, the restaurant is still a celebrity magnet. Have a wholesome family meal at this New York institution that's also a good choice for a downtown brunch.

The Soda Shop

125 Chambers Street at West Broadway

212-571-1100

www.sodashopnewyork.com

Step back in time at the Soda Shop in TriBeCa, where you can order such NYC classics as an old-fashioned egg cream or a lime rickey. The old-school atmosphere of tin ceilings, a working soda fountain, and old advertisements and soda bottles will appeal to kids and adults alike. The menu is filled with New York–style comfort foods, so you can indulge in a Stuyvesant High grilled cheese or a Lower East Side liverwurst sandwich. There is no escaping this soda parlor without picking up some retro candy for your kids (and yourself) from their awesome candy collection, which is stocked with candy buttons, Charleston Chews, and other fun goodies.

Soho

Kelly and Ping

127 Greene Street bet. West Houston and Prince streets

212-228-1212

www.eatrice.com

This Soho Thai restaurant has a children's menu filled with creatively named dishes like the Bowl of Sunshine, which consists of a broth with noodles and roast chicken or Naughty Noodles, Pad Thai topped with chicken skewers much like lollies. At lunch you may order from the counter and relax with your kids while drinking a sugary Thai iced tea.

Rice to Riches

37 Spring Street bet. Mott and Mulberry streets

212-274-0008

www.ricetoriches.com

After a lunch in Soho, you might want some dessert. In a city filled with ice cream shops, it's nice to find a place that pays homage to the often forgotten delights of rice pudding. Kids can choose from a variety of rice puddings with a number of flavors and ingredients. The folks at Rice to Riches are extremely friendly and offer samples of the rice pudding to taste—making it easier for you to decide between "the corners of cookies and cream" and "coconut coma."

Soho Park

62 Prince Street at Lafayette Street

212-219-2129

www.sohoparknyc.com

Not your typical hot dog joint, this casual Soho restaurant invites diners to indulge on an assortment of grilled lunchtime favorites like hot dogs, burgers, grilled cheese sandwiches with two types of cheese, fries, and other American fare inside the large, immaculate restaurant or the "airy garage-garden," which is always the popular choice. Once you place your order, you are given an old license plate to hold as your order number. Kids will get a kick out of sampling the different homemade dipping sauces for the fries, like the roasted red pepper aioli and spicy sambal ketchup.

Spring Street Natural
62 Spring Street at Lafayette Street
212-966-0290
www.springstreetnatural.com
A personal favorite of mine, Spring Street Natural has been serving up organic cuisine since 1973. Families can choose from an array of healthy eats, and the staff is extremely friendly and accommodating. Open for breakfast, lunch, dinner, and brunch, this is an ideal stop for folks looking for tasty healthful food like free-range chicken and vegetable-tofu-and-cashew croquettes.

The Villages (East, West, and Greenwich)

Cowgirl
519 Hudson Street at West 10th Street
212-633-1133
www.cowgirlnyc.com
How can you go wrong bringing your kids to a place that serves ice cream in the shape of a baked potato? It will be hard to save room for dessert at this kitschy West Village staple that has been our family favorite for years. The hearty menu gives city kids the chance to dine on western classics like fried catfish and fried chicken. Beyond the crayons and activity sheet, the large complimentary bowl of nachos and black-eyed-pea salsa, there is even more to occupy kids.

While you wait for food, head over to their general store, set near the entrance, which sells everything from sheriff's pins to candy lipsticks.

Ditch Plains
29 Bedford Street at Downing Street
212-633-0202
www.ditch-plains.com
If you're in the mood for some beach grub but can't make it to the ocean, head to Ditch Plains, where you can watch surf movies on their flat-screen TV, and dine on fish tacos or fish and chips. If you have kids that aren't big fans of fish, they also have hot dogs, which can be topped with mac 'n' cheese and accompanied by a side of fries. When the check arrives it is placed in a cup filled with salt water taffy.

Favela Cubana
543 LaGuardia Place at Bleecker Street
212-777-6500
The festive atmosphere at this West Village Cuban restaurant is perfect for short attention spans. There is much to distract an active child here—from the live band to the wall of magazines. The food is tasty and the brunch is quite reasonably priced. Kids will love having a meal at the counter, where the bar stools are actual bongo drums. Favela also has a nice outdoor deck overlooking LaGuardia Place, which is perfect for people watching or a game of I Spy.

Max Brenner
841 Broadway bet. 13th and 14th streets
212-388-0030
www.maxbrenner.com
Calling all chocolate lovers! Max Brenner's chocolate

treats will make you fall in love with the place. The children's menu, entitled Max and the Secret Chocolate Menu reads more like a kid's picture book than a menu. The diverse menu options include a crispy mac 'n' cheese as well as peanut butter and banana sandwiches. My kids were so excited to sit indoors to roast s'mores, since we usually only get to make them on our camping trips and at beach bonfires. One word of advice, save room for goodies like the melting marshmallow crepe or the "Ivory Heart," a chocolate cake layered with melting white chocolate and chocolate cream.

Peanut Butter & Co

240 Sullivan Street at West 3rd Street

212-677-3995

www.ilovepeanutbutter.com

Any restaurant that offers the option of drinking from a "crazy" straw and has a menu filled with a variety of peanut butter and jelly sandwiches is perfect for kids. This kitschy West Village restaurant redefines the art of the peanut butter and jelly; families can dine on everything from a peanut butter B.L.T. to the Elvis—a grilled peanut butter sandwich that is stuffed with bananas and honey. If you're not a fan of peanut butter, there are many peanut-free options on the menu, like turkey or grilled cheese sandwiches.

Stand Burger

24 East 12th Street bet. University Place and Fifth Avenue

212-488-5900

www.standburger.com

Washing a burger down with a pumpkin shake or a honey-lavender chocolate shake is something both kids and their parents can appreciate. This casual Village burger joint serves up burgers with an assortment of toppings like bacon and egg, or sliced Portobello mushrooms. They have a unique twist on the usual side of fries, offering mashed sweet potatoes and Parmesan. If you aren't a beef eater, you may also choose a salmon or a veggie burger instead.

Sweetie Pie

19 Greenwich Avenue at Christopher Street

212-337-3333

www.sweetiepierestaurant.com

How can you go wrong at an atmospheric West Village restaurant that has Tater Tots on the menu? Other kid- and parent-friendly eats at Sweetie Pie include Tunamato, a bowl of tomato soup with a scoop of tuna and silver dollar pancakes. Don't eat too much since their tempting dessert menu offers such classics as ice cream sundaes and a trio of mini ice cream cones.

Think Coffee

248 Mercer Street bet. 3rd and 4th streets

212-228-6226

1 Bleecker Street at Bowery

212-533-3366

www.thinkcoffeenyc.com

Think Coffee is the ideal place to stop and have a casual lunch with the family. Overtired parents will perk up when they peruse its extensive coffee selection and kids can choose from sandwiches and salads. When you are downtown and need a quick meal or break, this cafe is a nice alternative to Starbucks.

After-school Snacks

Obviously you can line up for a cone from the ubiquitous Mr. Softee truck, or you can head to one of these local ice cream shops, bakeries, or candy stores and indulge in some real treats.

Ice Cream

Here's a scoop, enjoy some homemade ice cream after school at these area shops:

Alphabet Scoop

543 East 11th Street between avenues A and B
212-982-1422
www.alphabetscoopicecream.com
You not only get a scoop of artisanal ice cream at this East Village ice cream shop, but you also help NYC kids since this ice cream shop is part of a mentoring program for teaching job skills to city kids. The ice cream is made on the premises and your own kids will love having a scoop and then taking a walk around the vibrant East Village.

Brooklyn Ice Cream Factory

1 Water Street
Brooklyn
718-246-3963

97 Commercial Street
Brooklyn
718-349-2506
The DUMBO location is housed in an old fire-boat house on the pier, so you can have a scoop of creamy ice cream and watch the boats go by. This is one of my family's favorite ice cream shops, and I am hopelessly addicted to the vanilla with chocolate chips. The old firehouse has almost a New England appeal to it, and unless you look back at the NYC sky-line, you might think you're in a small-town parlor. The Brooklyn Ice Cream Factory also has a location on Commercial Street in Green-point, Brooklyn. You can choose from any one of their tasty eight flavors.

Blue Marble Ice Cream

420 Atlantic Avenue at Bond Street
718-858-1100

186 Underhill Avenue at Sterling Place
718-399-6926
www.bluemarbleicecream.com
Made with all-organic dairy products from Natural by Nature, an organic milk from grass-fed cows, you won't feel guilty when you finish a scoop of Blue Marble's excep-tionally delectable ice cream. The ice cream shop on Atlantic Avenue has a play area for kids as well as a back patio where you can eat your ice cream. They have a large ice cream menu with the traditional chocolate and vanilla, as well as more inventive flavors like butter pecan and pumpkin. They also have frozen yogurt and sorbet.

Chinatown Ice Cream Factory

65 Bayard Street at Mott Street
212-608-4170
www.chinatownicecreamfactory.com
After dim sum, head to the Chinatown Ice Cream Factory for a cone of almond cookie,

black sesame, or green tea ice cream. Stroll through Chinatown as you finish your cone.

Eddie's Sweet Shop

105-29 Metropolitan Avenue at 72nd Avenue
718-520-8514

Order a cone or sundae at this retro ice cream parlor complete with tin ceilings and other original details, like an old-fashioned cash register. Enjoy the atmosphere while you have this timeless treat in a wide variety of flavors. We stuck with chocolate as we sat at the counter. I felt like our family was in the 1950s, at a local soda shop for an after-school snack. After your cone has disappeared, walk off the ice cream with a casual stroll through Forest Hill Gardens, a gorgeous neighborhood filled with old Tudor-style homes located just blocks from the parlor.

Eggers Ice Cream Parlor

1194 Forest Avenue at University Place
Staten Island
718-981-2110

In the charming town of Tottenville, just a short walk from the beautiful historic Conference House and its surrounding park, sits the timeless Eggers Ice Cream Parlor. People travel from all over to eat their delicious homemade ice cream. The Parlor has been there since the 1930s and has a small-town feel to it. Neighborhood kids sit outside with their bikes, and you'll feel as if you're in the middle of America and not in New York City.

Jacques Torres Ice Cream

62 Water Street

Brooklyn
www.mrchocolate.com

When I heard that one of our favorite chocolate shops was opening an ice cream parlor, I had to check it out. For years Jacques Torres carried an extremely popular ice cream sandwich that would sell out quickly. Now folks can get their ice cream fix next door to the chocolate factory at the new ice cream shop.

Il Laboratorio Del Gelato

95 Orchard Street at Broome Street
212-343-9922
www.laboratoriodelgelato.com

Okay, it's not ice cream, but the gelato at Laboratorio Del Gelato appeals to both kids and adults. With a large variety of flavors including nutmeg, vanilla saffron, ginger, kiwi, and a long list of many interesting flavors, there is much to love about this Lower East Side gelato shop.

Max and Mina's

71-26 Main Street at 71st Road
Queens
718-793-8629
www.maxandminasicecream.com

If you have ever wanted to try lox ice cream, you should head to this Queens ice cream parlor for some of the tastiest homemade ice cream in the city. Max and Mina's has a diverse selection of ice cream from Mounds-flavored to horseradish-flavored ice cream. We like to stop here on the way home from the New York Hall of Science (see pp. 49-50), the Queens Zoo Wildlife Center (see pp. 64-65), or the Queens Botanical Gardens (see pp. 133-134).

Ronnybrook Farm Dairy

75 9th Avenue bet. 15th and 16th streets

212-741-6455

www.ronnybrook.com

Whenever we are in the Chelsea Market, we stop by Ronnybrook Ice Cream for a scoop of their creamy and unbelievably tasty ice cream. The shop also carries Ronnybrook's other dairy products, like yogurt drinks and milk.

Sundaes & Cones Inc.

95 East 10th Street at Third Avenue

212-979-9398

www.sundaescones.com

From tiramasu to vanilla, you'll find your favorite flavor at this popular East Village ice cream shop. They also make incredible birthday cakes.

Traveling Desserts

We all know about ice cream trucks, but in recent years there has been a new trend in dessert trucks. You can follow these trucks on Twitter, for up-to-the-minute updates on where the trucks are parked:

CupcakeStop Truck

718-490-5155

www.cupcakestop.com

twitter.com/CupcakeStop

Track down this truck if you have a cupcake-addicted child, and what child isn't? At CupcakeStop, they serve freshly made cupcakes from a truck. From red velvet to chocolate swirl, the cupcakes appeal to both sophisticated palates and little eaters.

Street Sweets

www.streetsweetsny.com

twitter.com/streetsweets

Croissants, cookies, muffins, and other sweets are stocked on this truck. If you are in search of a good afternoon treat, you'll find it here. They also cater birthday parties.

Treats Truck

212-691-5226

www.treatstruck.com

twitter.com/thetreatstruck

From bite-size cookies that are perfect for little kids to over-size Rice Krispie treats, you can't go wrong when you order a treat from the Treats Truck, affectionately named "Sugar." The truck is usually stopped on Broadway on the lower eighties on Saturdays, so stop by after hanging out with the dinosaurs in the American Museum of Natural History (see pp. 41-42).

Van Leeuwen Artisan Ice Cream Truck

www.vanleeuwenicecream.com

twitter.com/Vlaic

This ice cream truck travels around the city from Park Slope, Brooklyn, to Soho and Midtown in Mahattan. We always get it in the afternoons on 7th Avenue and Carroll Street in Park Slope. Not your average Mr. Softee truck, Van Leeuwan carries high-end homemade ice cream. The server was extremely friendly when we approached the truck and gave us samples before we settled on their extremely creamy and decadent strawberry ice cream.

Wafels and Dinges Truck
646-257-2592
www.wafelsanddinges.com
twitter.com/waffletruck
My kids are waffle-obsessed, so we love to head to this Belgian waffle truck for their Liege waffle on a stick. You can order a waffle with dinges (toppings) like strawberries, cream, and other sweets.

Chelsea

Chelsea Market

75 Ninth Avenue bet. 15th and 16th streets
www.chelseamarket.com
The old National Biscuit Company warehouse is now a marketplace filled with good eats. If your family is in search of a sugar high, you'll be sure to find it at the Chelsea Market. Renowned shops like the **Fat Witch Bakery** (www.fatwitch.com), **Sarabeth's Kitchen** (www.sarabeth.com), **Amy's Breads** (www.amysbread.com), and **Eleni's Cookies** (www.elenis.com) make the market a perfect place to stop for an after-school snack. Stroll through this old factory as you browse through the many shops. Young chefs and their parents should check out the cooking supplies at **Bowery Kitchen Supply** (www.bowerykitchens.com) to make sure you have the right tools to make a delicious meal at home. In addition to amazing dessert venues, there are restaurants for grabbing a bite, including **Friedman's Lunch** (www.friedmanslunch.com), where comfort is definitely on the menu.

Cookshop Restaurant & Bar

156 Tenth Avenue at 20th Street
212-924-4440
www.cookshopny.com
Friends of ours make this café a regular locale for Saturday morning brunch before they take their kids to tour the **Chelsea art galleries** (www.chelseaart-galleries.com). They say it's the perfect way to spend a cold or rainy afternoon since the restaurant is near all the galleries, including some within the same building. Dine on a frittata or some huevos rancheros at this notable Chelsea restaurant.

Rocking Horse Cafe

182 Eighth Avenue at 19th Street
212-463-9511
www.rockinghorsecafe.com
This Chelsea Mexican restaurant has a menu filled with delicious Mexican soups, burritos, and free-range chicken dishes. The brunch menu has classic brunch items like eggs and pancakes. This is a good stop with kids if you're en route to the **Atlantic Theater** (www.atlantictheater.org) or heading the **Chelsea Piers** (www.chelseapiers.com). The staff is very accommodating to kids, making this cafe a relaxing find on lively Restaurant Row.

Union Square and the Flat Iron

Big Daddy's Restaurant

See Web site for locations throughout Manhattan.
www.bigdaddysnyc.com

Go retro in this atmospheric diner. Younger kids can occupy themselves coloring and doing the activities on the kid's place mat while older ones can pass the time asking each other questions from the Trivial Pursuit cards provided on each table. With televised sporting events, retro tunes, and a 1980s pop culture mural including Spiderman and the Atari logo, there is a lot going on in this brightly lit diner. Portions tend to be quite large, but don't forget to make room for their famous Tater Tots. The tasty comfort food will satisfy everyone at the table. Big Daddy's also does catering for kids' parties.

Blue Smoke

116 East 27th Street bet. Park and Lexington avenues
212-447-7733
www.bluesmoke.com

The popular East Side restaurant also houses the music venue, the Jazz Standard. On Sunday afternoons during the school year the Jazz Standard runs a Jazz concert series for kids where kids can order from the Blue Smoke menu while listening to great jazz from a rotating list of players. Blue Smoke is family-friendly and the food is phenomenal. They have a kid's menu with kid favorites like mac 'n' cheese and healthy options like grilled salmon. A very charitable restaurant, Blue Smoke will donate one dollar from any kid's meal ordered to Spoons Across America, a nonprofit organization dedicated to educating children, teachers, and families about healthy eating habits.

Chat 'n Chew

10 East 16th Street bet. Union Square West and Fifth Avenue
212-243-1616
www.chatnchewny.com

One of my family's favorite restaurants in the city, Chat 'n Chew has a menu filled with hearty comfort food. There is much on the menu to please any child, such as the creamy skin on smashies (mashed potatoes) or the nacho appetizer. The restaurant is lively, making it ideal for loud children. If you'd like to keep them quiet, bribe them with one of Chat 'n Chew's decadent desserts.

The Coffee Shop

29 Union Square West at 16th Street
212-243-7969

For years the Coffee Shop was the "it" place to grab a drink or a bite and is now a serious part of Manhattan's history. I feel as if I've spent a large portion of my adult life dining at the Coffee Shop and spotting celebrities at the booths (I've seen a ton here). So take your kids people watching and expose them to some American diner fare with flair at this NYC staple.

Republic

37 Union Square West bet. 16th and 17th streets
212-627-7172
www.thinknoodles.com

If your child is a noodle lover, head to Republic for a culinary journey beyond spaghetti and marinara sauce. At Republic kids can dine on a variety of noodles with chicken dunked in superb broths with tons of veggie options. The sleek design and the casual atmosphere of the place will add an extra element of sophistication to the noodle dining experience.

The Shake Shack at Madison Square Park

Madison Avenue and East 23rd Street, southeast corner
212-889-6600

366 Columbus Avenue at 77th Street
646-747-8770
www.shakeshacknyc.com

Folks brave the long lines at both locations of the Shake Shack for the tasty burgers, hot dogs, frozen custard, and the decadent shakes. Convince yourself that you are in fact ordering something healthy for the kids with the Vitamin Creamsicle Shake made with juice or just indulge in a chocolate hand-spun shake.

Midtown East and West

Ben's Kosher Deli and Restaurant

209 West 38th Street bet. Seventh and Eighth avenues
212-398-2367
www.bensdeli.net

Sometimes you get a craving for an overstuffed sandwich and a knish followed by half of a sour pickle and coleslaw (well, at least I do). New York City delis are a dying breed, and this kosher classic will satisfy any carnivore's craving (except if you're in search of pork). A nice place to grab a meal before you head to the theater district or if you need a break from shopping at Macy's and 34th Street, Ben's also caters.

Prime Burger

5 East 51st Street bet. Madison and Fifth avenues
212-759-4729
www.primeburger.com

Aside from Prime Burger's long history of serving up tasty burgers since 1938, the allure of this burger joint is the kistchy décor like the wooden chairs attached to trays in lieu of a proper table, which makes dining easy. Kids will love dining on these old-school seats and chowing down some of the options from their delicious classic diner menu. This is a great place to stop if you're headed to the MoMA since it's just two blocks away. With its time-less appeal, you might feel as if you are dining in a midtown luncheonette in the 1940s rather than at Prime Burger in the present day. A tip from the wise, don't forget to order the seasoned curly fries.

Serendipity 3

225 East 60th Street bet. Second and Third avenues
212-838-3531
www.serendipity3.com

You aren't a city kid until you've had your first frozen hot chocolate. A staple in my own city kid history, this restaurant is a fun place to splurge for a birthday meal. The food is yummy, but people really come here for the decadent desserts. If you have younger ones in tow, it's important to note that the restaurant does not allow strollers. If you'd like to have a birth-day celebration, you can reserve a table with a max-imum of eight people.

Smörgås Chef
58 Park Avenue at 38th Street
212-847-9745
www.smorgaschef.com

Check Web site for locations throughout Manhattan

The café at the Scandinavia House serves up authentic Scandinavian cuisine in a bright atmosphere with modern furniture that is reminiscent of Ikea, but a bit higher end. Devour some Swedish meatballs, lingonberries, and other regional favorites. If you have a Pippi Longstocking fan with you (like my daughter), head to the gift shop across from the café. They have many other locations throughout the city.

The Burger Joint at the Parker Meridien
118 West 57th Street bet. Sixth and Seventh avenues
212-708-7414
www.parkermeridien.com

A friend of mine describes this place as a scene "straight out of *Happy Days*." Located behind a large curtain in the glamorous Parker Meridien Hotel, the wood-paneled walls will remind you of Arnolds' living room, where the Fonz and the gang once hung out. The prices are surprisingly reasonable, so order a hamburger, fries, or grilled cheese followed by a thick milk shake.

Theater District

Carmine's
200 West 44th Street at Seventh Avenue
212-221-3800

2450 Broadway at West 91st Street
212-362-2200
www.carminesnyc.com

If you are pulling together a large group or planning a family reunion, this spacious family-style restaurant is an excellent choice. With a convenient location, it's the ideal place to meet up before a matinee or for a nice dinner. Enjoy their generous portions of hearty Italian fare.

Five Napkin Burger
630 Ninth Avenue at 45th Street
212-757-2277
www.fivenapkinburger.com

We happened upon this restaurant before seeing a Broadway matinee and were quite impressed with the menu and the quality of food. If you are in search of a tasty burger, you are sure to find it here. They have a diverse brunch menu and many vegetarian options despite being billed as a burger joint. It's also quite spacious and the staff is very accommodating.

Hourglass Tavern
373 West 46th Street at Ninth Avenue
212-265-2060

Expect speedy service at this tavern in the heart of the theater district, where you can enjoy a pre-theater meal. With a menu of American fare, there is something for all members of the family. If you want your kids to hurry along, just remind them that time is running out before the start of the show or show them the time left on the hourglass that they leave on the table!

Ollie's Noodle Shop
411 West 42nd Street at Ninth Avenue
212-921-5988

This Times Square Chinese restaurant is extremely kid-friendly and serves large portions of Sichuan-style food. On a street filled with many national chain restaurants like Chevy's, this is another option when trying to avoid the ordinary. The menu at this well-known restaurant includes soups, noodles, and other delicacies. There are other locations throughout the city.

Upper East Side

Barking Dog Luncheonette
1453 York Avenue between 77th and 78th streets
212-861-3600

1678 3rd Avenue between 94th and 95th streets
212-831-1800

With walls plastered with pictures of dogs and a kid-friendly menu, this is a great find for families. A neighborhood favorite with outdoor seating in front of the restaurant in the warmer weather, the Barking Dog also offers tons of comfort food. It tends to get very busy on weekends, so get there early if you don't want to wait for a table.

E.A.T.
1062 Madison Avenue at 80th Street
212-772-0022
www.elizabar.com

Fans of Zabar's, will love E.A.T., a casual café located right near Museum Mile. Grab lunch here instead of the museum café—their selection of salads, sandwiches, and soups is top-notch and never disappoints.

Lexington Candy Shop
1226 Lexington Avenue at 83rd Street
212-228-0057
www.lexingtoncandyshop.net

New Yorkers have been dining at the Lexington Candy Shop since 1925, and the retro décor will make you feel as if you've gone back to a simpler time. Before you embark on a day on Museum Mile, introduce your kids to the real NYC dining history of the once-popular luncheonettes and soda shops. Sip Lime Rickeys, egg creams, and fountain soda in a restaurant that looks straight from a set of the *Patty Duke Show* or the movie *Pleasantville*. Kids will love the menu filled with pancakes, French toast, grilled cheese, and many other kid-friendly favorites. The restaurant is quite small and tends to get a bit crowded for breakfast, so get there early. The Lexington Candy Shop can be rented out for parties. It's also been featured in many movies including *The Nanny Diaries*, in which the nanny played by Scarlett Johansen takes her charge to this renowned diner.

Upper West Side

Artie's Delicatessen
2290 Broadway at 83rd Street
212-579-5959
www.arties.com

This Jewish deli on the Upper West Side seems as if it's been here for decades but it actually only opened in 1999. The menu is filled with deli favorites including pastrami on rye, chopped liver with onions on toast, and hot brisket of beef. Wash it all down with a Dr. Brown's soda and your family has had a true New York Jewish deli experience. Just be sure to save room for some ruggelach.

Boat Basin Café
390 West 79th Street at Riverside Drive
212-496-5542
www.boatbasincafe.com

Dine outdoors and waterside at this seasonal café that offers families stunning views of the water as they dine on hummus, burgers, and other casual fare. This is a nice way to spend an early spring or summer evening, watching boats dock at the pier and New Yorkers slow down as they relax by the water.

Good Enough to Eat

483 Amsterdam Avenue at 83rd Street
212-496-0163
www.goodenoughtoeat.com

This well-regarded Upper West Side restaurant has a diverse menu and a separate kids menu with mac 'n' cheese and burger bites. If your kid shows in an interest in cooking up grub at home, Good Enough To Eat offers cooking classes for kids ages eight and up, where they get to try their hand at recipes from the restaurant's own menu, Check the Web site for a class schedule. They also sell the cutest T-shirts for kids and adults. My daughter loves the fact that there is a white picket fence out front, so it feels more as if we are eating in someone's front yard rather than just a roped-off section of Amsterdam Avenue.

Josie's NYC

300 Amsterdam Avenue at 74th Street
212-769-1212

565 Third Avenue at 37th Street
212-490-1558
www.josiesnyc.com

We love this organic restaurant that offers kids meals like turkey meatballs and pasta. The menu is diverse and you can choose from various healthy dishes like the butternut squash soup, salads, and many veggie-friendly entrees. The folks there are so kid-friendly

that when our friend's toddler covered the floor around her with food, they never even batted an eye.

Mama Mexico

2672 Broadway bet. 102nd and 103rd streets
212-864-2323

214 East 49th Street bet. Second and Third avenues
212-935-1316
www.mamamexico.com

This Upper West Side Mexican staple has a menu filled with all the classics from burritos to bowls of guacamole. They also serve breakfast so you can order a hearty brunch of Mama pancakes—fresh flapjacks topped with banana and strawberry slices and drizzled with maple syrup. Vegetarians will be satisfied their extensive veggie menu. The restaurant gets quite loud, making it the perfect place to dine with kids who can't keep their voices down. They have another location on East 49th Street and another in Englewood Cliffs, New Jersey.

Pinch and S'mac

474 Columbus Avenue at West 83rd Street
646-438-9494

S'mac

345 East 12th Street at 1st Avenue
212-358-7912
www.pinchandsmac.com

Located just a block from the Museum of Natural History, this Upper West Side restaurant that specializes in gourmet pizza and mac 'n' cheese is the right stop for carb-addicted kids. They also do a fine job of adding veggies to their food—my daughter finished an entire pizza covered in spinach and goat cheese. Parents can enjoy chatting among themselves, as kids will be drawn to the kids' programming on an enormous flat-screen TV. If you're downtown, stop by S'mac, a restaurant that solely specializes in gourmet mac 'n' cheese—something which appeals to foodie parents and their mac 'n' cheese–loving kids.

Tapas Floridita Bar & Restaurant
3219 Broadway at West 129th Street
212-662-0225

My daughter Lucy and I had the nicest meal here after our visit to the Madame Alexander Doll Factory tour (see p. 194). Located at the foot of the entrance for the 125th Street subway, this tapas restaurant doesn't disappoint while being extremely reasonably priced. Although we didn't save room for dessert, I've been told the flan is exceptional.

Themed Restaurants in Manhattan

Have a fun dinner at one of these themed restaurants. You don't have to be a tourist to enjoy these kid-centric haunts.

American Girl Café
609 Fifth Avenue at 49th Street
877-247-5223
www.americangirl.com

Kids and their American Girl dolls are welcome at this café, which offers brunch, lunch, dinner, and afternoon tea. If your child doesn't have a doll, they will lend you one for the meal or you can pick one up in their shop (see p. 186). The meals at the café are prix fixe and tend to be on the pricey side, so this is a great place for a special event. Menu items include Tic-tac-toe Pizza, turkey potpie, and other entrees.

Brooklyn Diner
155 West 43rd Street bet. Broadway and Sixth Avenue
212-265-5400

212 West 57th Street bet. Broadway and Seventh Avenue
212-977-1957
www.brooklyndiner.com

This spacious Brooklyn Diner offers an array of ethnic eats like hummus, Cuban chicken, and lasagna, which pay tribute to Brooklyn's cultural melting pot. The staff is extremely friendly and the portions are incredibly enormous.

Ellen's Stardust Diner
1650 Broadway at West 51st Street
212-956-5151
www.ellensstardustdiner.com

This retro fifties-themed diner is owned by a former Miss Subway. Have your kids dine on meatloaf and other comfort food at this Midtown diner. It's a great place to grab a bite if you're going to the theater since the service is fast and the menu has many options, like hot dogs and grilled cheese, that will please even picky eaters.

ESPN Zone
4 Times Square Plaza at Broadway
212-921-3776
www.espnzone.com

This sports-themed restaurant boasts a menu of pub grub and as many televised sports events that you can watch at once. Kids will eat all their veggies for a chance to play video games and other sports-related games at the restaurant. I'll admit I didn't even want to leave their floor of games—it really sparked the inner kid in me. ESPN Zone also hosts birthday parties.

Hard Rock Café
1501 Broadway at West 44th Street
212-343-3355
www.hardrock.com
Located in the heart of Times Square, this chain restaurant has a concert venue and a shop. Surrounded by walls of rock memorabilia, the menu is filled with kid favorites like twisted mac 'n' cheese, hickory-smoked chicken wings, steak, and much more. You'll have a fun time at this atmospheric restaurant.

Jekyll & Hyde Pub and Club
91 7th Avenue bet. West 4th and Barrow streets
212-989-7701

1409 Avenue of the Americas bet. West 57th and 58th streets
212-541-9505
www.jekyllandhydeclub.com
For a spooky time, have a meal at either the Jekyll & Hyde Pub and Club. Both locations will entertain kids with floorshows and spooky mechanical creatures coming out from the walls. Themed restaurants are fun and kitschy—kids love them—but please be aware that the restaurant is quite dark and can get a bit scary and overwhelming for little ones. However, for older children this is a good spot for birthday parties, so check the Web site for the list of birthday party themes and packages. The same owners also run the Slaughtered Lamb Pub in the West Village.

Mars 2112
1633 Broadway at 51st Street
212-582-2112
www.mars2112.com
Take a visit to the red planet via a NYC elevator in midtown. Kids will get a kick out of the Martian that visits your table and happily take pictures with you. Dine on cuisine that is out of this world—like Orbital BBQ Ribs and Cosmos Cobb Salad. The design is unique and families will get a kick out of the ride down to Mars.

Manhattan chains

Blockheads
Check Web site for locations throughout Manhattan.
www.blockheads.com
In need of a quick burrito fix? Head to one of the six Blockheads located in Manhattan, where the menu has all of the Mexican classics, from quesadillas to burritos. If your kids can't eat an entire burrito, the restaurant offers mini burritos that are perfect for kids. Blockheads is also great for catering parties.

Burger Heaven
Check Web site for locations throughout Manhattan.
www.burgerheaven.com
This reliable NYC diner chain has six locations throughout Manhattan and has been serving up tasty burgers since 1943. There are a bunch of Midtown locations, which comes in handy if you are in search of food while on a visit to the MoMA or the

Paley Center for Media. The diner menu is filled with hamburgers (of course) and other diner staples like eggs and salads.

E.J.'s Luncheonette

1271 3rd Avenue bet. East 73rd and 74th streets
212-472-0600

432 Sixth Avenue bet. West 9th and 10th streets
212-473-5555

447 Amsterdam Avenue bet. West 81st and 82nd streets
212-873-3444

Get there early if you are in search of breakfast or brunch, because this popular chain gets quite busy with the morning crowd on the weekends. Its diner fare in a homey atmosphere attracts families, so you won't be the only people in the restaurant with meal companions that sometimes forget to use their indoor voice.

Jackson Hole Burgers

Check Web site for locations throughout New York City.
www.jacksonholeburgers.com
If your child's diet is low in iron, head to this famous burger joint for a quick dose of a good burger. With five locations in Manhattan and two in Queens, this is a New York City staple. Although mostly a restaurant for those with an affinity for meat, they also have vegetarian options on the menu.

John's Pizzeria

260 West 44th Street at Eighth Avenue
212-391-7560
408 East 64th Street at First Avenue

212-935-2895
www.johnspizzerianyc.com
This is one of our favorite places to grab a pie with the family. The pizza parlor chain is consistently good and serves other classics like spaghetti and meatballs if you aren't in the mood for pizza.

Le Pain Quotidien

Check Web site for locations throughout Manhattan.
www.lepainquotidien.com
Indulge in a French-inspired treat or sandwich at one of the long wooden table's at this popular chain, but save room for one of their rich desserts. I commend them for the attention to detail in the presentation of their dishes, which can make an ordinary sandwich look like a feast.

Patsy's Pizzeria

Check Web site for locations throughout Manhattan.
www.patsyspizzeriany.com
Since 1933 Patsy's has been serving pizza to New Yorkers. In addition to pizza this family-friendly New York chain has a wide variety of pastas, salads, and classic Italian desserts like tiramisu.

Sarabeth's Kitchen

Check Web site for locations throughout Manhattan.
www.sarabeth.com
If you're in need of some homemade breakfast goodies to get you through the day, head to Sarabeth's Kitchen. With locations in Lord & Taylor and the Chelsea Market, Sarabeth's is quite popular for brunch, so bring something to distract the kids while you wait or just get there early. It's the ideal place to fill up on some comfort food before a day exploring the Museum of Natural History.

Vynl

754 Ninth Avenue at 51st Street
212-974-2003

1492 Second Avenue at East 78th Street
212-249-6080

102 Eighth Avenue bet. West 15th and 16th
streets
212-400-2118
www.vynl-nyc.com

This funky music- and pop-culture-themed restaurant has three Manhattan locations that dish up fun comfort food like mac 'n' cheese or a meatloaf sandwich—you can even order breakfast all day. The décor pays tribute to pop stars with bathrooms dedicated to Britney Spears amongst other celebrities. If you have kids that sleep in, you might like the fact that they serve breakfast all day.

Whole Foods

Check Web site for locations throughout Manhattan.
www.wholefoodsmarket.com

The dining area at the popular organic market is the perfect place to get a quick fix of wholesome eats. If you'd like to prepare a picnic but don't want to be bothered with food preparation, pick up already prepared food and libations at the buffet. Note that the capacity of the café varies from location to location; the Union Square outpost has a large seating area upstairs while other Whole Foods stores have more modest seating arrangements.

Downtown Brooklyn

Junior's Cheesecake

386 Flatbush Avenue Extension at Dekalb Avenue
718-852-5257

West 45th Street bet. Broadway and Eighth
Avenue
212-302-2000
www.juniorscheesecake.com

This famous Brooklyn restaurant is known for its exceptional cheesecake. An old favorite of mine, the menu is filled with Reuben sandwiches, Hungarian beef goulash, salmon cakes, and many other dishes. But whatever your family orders, you must save room for cheesecake. The restaurant is a part of Brooklyn history as it has been in the same location since 1950, and especially with the promise of their fantastic cheesecake, children will adore it. There is also another location on West 45th Street and one in the Grand Central Terminal.

Brooklyn Heights and Dumbo

Grimaldi's Pizza

19 Old Fulton Street at Elizabeth Place
Brooklyn
718-858-4300

242-02 61st Avenue at Douglaston Parkway
Queens
718-819-2133
www.grimaldis.com

Rain, snow, or sleet there is always a line for this

popular Brooklyn pizzeria. If you have kids that can patiently wait in line for exceptional pizza, you should definitely pay a visit to Grimaldi's. If you visit the Brooklyn location, you must also take a walk down the block for some frozen dessert at the Brooklyn Ice Cream Factory or for chocolate at Jacques Torres (www.mrchocolate.com) after your meal. They also have a location in Queens.

Heights Café

84 Montague Street at Hicks Street
718-625-5555
www.heightscafeny.com

Right by the scenic Brooklyn Heights Promenade sits a restaurant that offers families a chance to dine on pizza, sandwiches, wraps, and other food. The brunch menu is filled with goodies like the Brioche French Toast and the Spinach and Feta Cheese Tart. Enjoy a stroll on the promenade after your meal or have your child burn off their meal at the playground next to the promenade.

The Moxie Spot

81-83 Atlantic Avenue at Hicks Street
718-923-9710
www.themoxiespot.com

It will be hard to pry your kids away from the play space on the second floor of this kid-friendly restaurant in Brooklyn Heights. (I know I had a tough time.) The Moxie Spot offers a Friday night film series that features popular kid flicks, which they also repeat on Saturday mornings. With a menu filled with kid-friendly eats and a playful Wonka-like vibe, this restaurant will satisfy the whole family. Don't miss the weekly family dance party on Saturday evenings, or simply visit any day of the week to use the play space filled with everything from computers to dollhouses.

Noodle Pudding

38 Henry Street bet. Market and Catherine streets
718-625-3737

This beloved Brooklyn Height's Italian restaurant has extremely tasty food, which makes it a popular spot for Brooklynites. Dine on gnocchi, among other Italian dishes, at this local Brooklyn gem, but get there early, as there is often a wait before seating.

Theresa's

80 Montague Street at Hicks Street
718-797-3996

Fans of Polish food will love the perogies at this Brooklyn Heights restaurant. If boiled perogies or an amazing potato pancake doesn't appeal, the menu has soups and a menu of diner fare. Located a block from the Brooklyn Heights Promenade on the Height's main drag, this is a family favorite of ours, especially for a relaxing weekend brunch. In the summer they have a large outdoor eating area on Montague Street.

Cobble Hill and Carroll Gardens

Bocca Lupo

391 Henry Street at Verandah Place
718-243-2522

If you arrive at Bocca Lupo at 5 p.m., you'll see the tons of Brooklyn families having dinner. The kid's meal comes with hazelnut pudding, which we use as a bribe to get our kids to finish one of the many dishes, like pasta and meatballs (my son's favorite), offered at this restaurant. Most parents will delight in a glass of wine from Bocca Lupe's well-respected wine list. Owned by a local parent, this restaurant is a staple in the area.

Buttermilk Channel

524 Court Street at Huntington Street
718-852-8490
www.buttermilkchannelnyc.com

Dine early at Buttermilk Channel with a menu filled with local specialty foods like Caputo's pasta. The kid's menu offers crowd pleasers like buttermilk-fried chicken and an organic beef hot dog. Kids will also love the clown sundae that comes with the kid's meal. This restaurant is quite popular and gets lots of press, so a word of advice is to get to there early.

Eton

205 Sackett Street at Henry Street
718-222-2999

Our week isn't complete without a meal from Eton. This Brooklyn dumpling shop makes your dumplings fresh, so after placing your order, it takes around twenty minutes until you get your food. My kids don't mind waiting while they watch the dumplings being made. If your kids aren't in the mood to wait, call ahead and they'll start on your order—there are also some comic books and magazines to keep them occupied. The menu is fairly simple: all kinds of dumplings. Choose from a variety of three, including pork, chicken, and tofu mixed with shredded vegetables. In the winter they expand the menu to serve noodle soups and in the summer they serve shaved ice. Eton is available to cater parties as well.

Frankies Spuntino

457 Court Street bet. Luquer and 4th Streets
718-403-0033

A neighborhood favorite, parents and their kids will feast on Frankies Spuntino's classic Italian food, ranging from crostinis and antipastos to plentiful Italian entrees. The meatballs are a hit with kids, and the atmosphere and wine list are for the adults. However, the word is out about Frankies and it is often pretty crowded. This is one of the few restaurants where neighborhood folks always spot celebrities. In the summer they open up their spacious outdoor garden for dining.

Layla Jones

214 Court Street at Warren Street
718-624-2361
www.laylajones.com

Owned by local parents who named the restaurant after their two kids, the pizza at this low-key restaurant is extremely tasty. In the summer, the backyard is packed with local families taking in the nice weather and the good eats. The staff is very accommodating to children (as I found out when my son broke a saltshaker). This is a good choice for a caterer if you are hosting a birthday party at the **Little Gym** (www.thelittlegym.com) or at **Carmello the Science Fellow's Cosmic Cove** (www.carmelothesciencefellow.com), both located on Atlantic Avenue. They also host make-your-own-pizza parties at the restaurant and in their spacious yard.

Lucali

575 Henry Street at First Place
718-858-4086

Folks start lining up at the door to get a table when Lucali opens at 6 p.m. Owned by a neighborhood family, this Carroll Gardens pizzeria, tucked away on residential Henry Street, is a real crowd pleaser. They have a short menu of pizza or calzone, but these Italian specialties are baked in a brick oven, which render them exceptional. You'll never again question the lines outside Lucali.

Pacifico

269 Pacific Street at Smith Street
718-935-9090

This atmospheric Mexican restaurant owned by well-known Brooklyn restaurateur Alan Harding has been serving Mexican food to families in an oversize outdoor area for years. The restaurant is quite spacious and attracts a fun crowd, so kids can make some noise without being shushed. Dine on some grilled corn topped with cheese or order a taco for the kids.

Pit Stop

127 Columbia Street at Kane Street
718-875-4664

www.pitstopny.com

This car-themed and French-influenced restaurant serves up food with a French flare like seared tuna steak Niçoise and poached tilapia Antiboise. They also have burgers, salads, and a menu for little eaters that includes chicken fingers. Located in Carroll Gardens West, the Pit Stop has been serving up food to Brooklyn families for years and is an extremely well regarded. With a Web site that says, "kids welcome," you'll feel right at home. Although the famed play area has decreased in size, it's still a fun place to eat.

Ted and Honey

264 Clinton Street at Verandah Street
212-842-2212

www.tedandhoney.com

Located across from Cobble Hill Park, this casual neighborhood café is the perfect place to start out the day or to stop for lunch. Order a Nutella-and-banana panini from the kid's menu with a Mexican hot chocolate and let your little ones devour their food as you relax at the table with an iced coffee and a sandwich. Don't forget to pick through the selection of books by local authors (lots of choices in this literary neighborhood) and recharge with the family at this nice addition to a residential street. Ted and Honey also offers catering.

Union Smith Cafe

305 Smith Street at Union Street
718-643-3293

Located just a block from the Carroll Street subway station, this spacious restaurant caters to families with kids of all ages. Older children will be awestruck by their cool rocket-ship high chairs. (My kids wanted to sit in them even though they've already outgrown them.) The menu offers standard American café fare including salads, homemade pastas, and the world's creamiest mashed potatoes. The kid's menu offers the usual suspects like grilled cheese, chicken breast, and meatballs.

Red Hook

Hope and Anchor

347 Van Brunt Street at Wolcott Street
718-237-0276

This Red Hook restaurant has amazing eats, and parents and kids will appreciate the friendly service as they dine on such goodies as tofu potpie, grilled cheese, and very tasty fries. The vibe here is almost like a restaurant in a small town, although it's in Brooklyn. After a meal here, head a few doors down to the decadent **Baked** (359 Van Brunt Street; 718-222-0345; www.bakednyc.com) for a slice of cake.

Ikea Café

One Beard Street at Otsego Street

718-246-4532

www.ikea.com/us/en/store/brooklyn

Okay, Ikea is mostly a furniture store, but it's also a great place to grab a meal with the kids. First of all, the store has a playroom where you can drop off your kids while you shop, and the dining area offers kid's meals for under $3. Kids can gorge themselves on Swedish meatballs and then head downstairs for a $1 frozen yogurt. Show the folks at the water taxi your receipt and you'll get a free ride across to Manhattan; it makes a fun afternoon.

Red Hook Vendors

www.myspace.com/redhookfoodvendors

From May through October, you can dine on a range of Latino cuisine from the vendors at the Red Hook ball fields—a culinary tradition that has been going on for over thirty years. This is a great place to grab a bite after a swim at the neighboring Red Hook pool or you can just sit at a picnic table and dine while your kids run around the field.

Park Slope and Prospect Heights

Applewood

501 11th Street at Seventh Avenue

718-788-1810

www.applewoodny.com

Owned by a local family, Applewood is a Park Slope neighborhood favorite. The owners take food seriously, as you can plainly see on their American fare menu. This restaurant only prepares wild fish and hormone- and antibiotic-free meat and poultry, and only uses organic products and produce from local farms. Bring the kids for a nice brunch where a kid-appropriate portion of eggs or French toast is only $3.

Brooklyn Fish Camp

162 Fifth Avenue bet. Lincoln Street and St. John's Place

718-783-3264

www.brooklynfishcamp.com

This Park Slope outpost of the famed Fish Camp in the West Village is extremely kid-friendly. Have your child grab a meal from the Little Salty Dog menu, which includes maritime favorites like fish-and-chips and fried baby shrimp, as well as hot dogs or grilled cheese for land-loving children. Adults can dine on tasty entrees like one half of a Maine lobster.

The Chip Shop

383 Fifth Avenue at 6th Street

718-832-7701

www.chipshopnyc.com

If you can't find the time to escape to London, but you want your kids to experience some English-style cooking, head to the Chip Shop where your kids can indulge in some tasty fried fish served with French fries. Our family makes an annual trip to get our fill of fish-and-chips. If you are in the Brooklyn Heights area, check out their other location at **The Atlantic Chip Shop** (129 Atlantic Avenue; 888-FRYCHIP).

Dizzy's

511 9th Street bet. Eighth and Ninth avenues
718-499-1966
www.dizzys.com

This Park Slope diner has been dishing out comfort food for years and is a popular brunch spot with the locals. Just a block from Prospect Park and one block from the F train subway stop, this is a convenient place to take the kids before heading to the park. They offer plastic cups with straws for kids to minimize spillage during the meal. My kids especially love that they serve chocolate milk.

Perch Café

365 Fifth Avenue bet. 5th and 6th streets
718-788-2830
www.theperchcafe.com

This café on Park Slope's Fifth Avenue appeals to parents and kids alike. Colorful and well designed, the cafe has couches in the back so you can sit and relax with your little one, as well as a small open area for the tots to move about. Open at 7:30 a.m. for early risers, Perch also serves up breakfast until 4 p.m. for those parents who find it hard to get out early. Perch's menu of light fare includes delicous sandwiches and salads, as well as a large selection of kid's meals. Aside from good food, Perch also hosts free kid-centric activities. They have sing-alongs for tots on Mondays and Thursdays at 10 a.m. with Courtney, and sing-alongs on Tuesdays at

10:30 a.m. and Wednesdays at 3:30 p.m. with Randy. Story time takes place every Wednesday and Friday at 10 a.m., so grab some morning Joe and sit back while your little one listens along and sings some fun children's tunes. Oh, and did I mention the spotless bathroom with a changing table? Perch is Park Slope's welcome addition to Fifth Avenue.

Tom's Restaurant

782 Washington Avenue at Sterling Place

You'll think you went back to 1950s-era Brooklyn when you enter this extremely beloved classic Brooklyn restaurant. Order a Lime Rickey, egg cream, or a fountain soda, and dine on some diner food from their menu. The staff is very friendly and it's perfect for families. The restaurant is a bit small and quite popular so arrive early to avoid crowds. Tom's is definitely worth a detour on your way to visit the **Brooklyn Museum of Art** (www.brooklynmuseum.org), the **Brooklyn Botanical Garden** (www.bbg.org) or the Central Branch of the **Brooklyn Public Library** (www.brooklynpubliclibrary.org).

Two Boots Brooklyn

514 2nd Street bet. Seventh and Eighth avenues
718-499-3253
www.twobootsbrooklyn.com

Two Boots is one of the most kid-friendly pizza parlors around, aside from the Chuck E. Cheese franchise. Kids are able to watch their pizzas being made while their parents drink microbrews; there is also ample outdoor space. Two Boots attracts a very hip night crowd when it doubles as a music venue—a very unique combination of family friendliness and nightlife. Although quite popular, Two Boots in Brooklyn has plenty of room, so you don't have to wait all that long for a table. They have a bunch of locations throughout the city; check their Web site to find a Two Boots near you.

'sNice

315 5th Avenue at 3rd Street
718-788-2121

This vegetarian restaurant in Park Slope has tasty food and is very kid-friendly. If you want your kids to eat their veggies this is the ideal place to expose them to the world of vegetarian food, and all kid's meals come with a cookie (we use this to bribe our kids to finish their food). It's a perfect place to grab lunch and is located down the block from J. J. Byrne Park playground where kids will happily burn off their post-meal energy. They have a large outdoor area on Fifth Avenue, so you can people watch while you're minding your young'uns.

Willie's Dawgs

351 Fifth Avenue bet. 4th and 5th streets
718-832-2941
www.williesdawgs.com

Not your typical hot dog restaurant, Willie's Dawgs serves up hot dogs with a variety of toppings making it a great place to score a funky foot-long. Do you serve your kids hot dogs on challah, rye, or whole grain buns? Doubt it, so that is reason enough to make the trip to this popular Park Slope hot dog restaurant. Vegetarians aren't left out since they have a Phoney Baloney Dawg, which is really a grilled marinated carrot. In warm weather, opt for a space outside in their outdoor dining area. They also do catering.

Tea Time: Unique NYC places to have an afternoon tea with your kids

Alice's Tea Cup
102 West 73rd Street at Columbus Avenue
212-799-3006

156 East 64th Street at Lexington Avenue
212-486-9200

220 East 81st Street bet. Second and Third avenues
212-734-4832
www.alicesteacup.com
Relax at an afternoon tea at this *Alice in Wonderland*–themed tea lounge. It has three locations in Manhattan where kids can sip tea or dine on treats like a yummy breakfast or lunch.

Madeline Tea at the Carlyle Hotel
35 East 76th Street bet. Fifth and Madison avenues
212-744-1600
www.thecarlyle.com
Fans of the classic *Madeline* books will like afternoon tea at this posh East Side hotel. Take your afternoon tea surrounded by murals by the famed Ludwig Bemelmans (he illustrated the *Madeline* books) in the aptly named Bemelmans bar, as your kids sip tea and dine from a buffet of eats. The tea luncheon costs $40 per person for kids ages three and up. Kids under three have a discounted admission price of $20.

appeal and allure of 67 Burger. The menu is simple—burgers and incredibly delicious fries—but what makes 67 Burger unique are the creative toppings for the burgers. An interesting combination of cheeses, various sauces, and added vegetables will make any veggie burger stand out. The kids' meals are extremely economical, with the standard fare of grilled cheese and chicken for kids who shy away from burgers. Conveniently located a block from the Brooklyn Academy of Music, this Fort Greene burger joint is the perfect place to take the kids and eat some gourmet burgers with sweet potato fries.

Clinton Hill and Fort Greene

Choice Market

318 Lafayette Avenue at Grand Street

718-230-5234

www.choicemarketbrooklyn.com

Located down the block from the kids' clothing store Still Hip Brooklyn (see pp. 157-158), Choice Market's café attracts a family-friendly crowd. Order a panini or a salad with your child as you dine at the long dining room table. It's also a convenient place to pick up some food if you're en route to visit the **Pratt Sculpture Garden** (www.sculpture.org/pratt) or if your child is taking an art class at Pratt. It's a great restaurant in this increasingly kid-friendly 'hood.

67 Burger

67 Lafayette Avenue at South Elliott Place

718-797-7150

www.67burger.com

Despite being a vegetarian, I can still appreciate the

Williamsburg and Greenpoint

Bliss Café

191 Bedford Avenue at North 7th Street

718-599-2547

Located on bustling Bedford Avenue, this Williamsburg vegan café will make health-conscious parents extremely happy with its selection of organic entrees. I've been taking my kids here since they were born and the staff has always been very accommodating to us. If your family likes tofu, this is the place to go, since you can order it alongside scrambled eggs or with rice.

Peter Pan Donut and Pastry

727 Manhattan Avenue at Norman Avenue

718-389-3676

Doughnut fans will love the fresh doughnuts made daily at this Greenpoint café. In addition to some of the most amazing doughnuts you'll ever taste, and that rival any Dunkin Donut—Peter Pan Donut also serves bagels with eggs. Indulge on other pastries (my son ate a large muffin that was filled with jam) and wash it down with a hot cup of coffee (or milk for the kids).

Farm at Adderley

1108 Cortelyou Road at East 11th Street

718-287-3101

www.thefarmonadderley.com

My kids fell in love with this place the minute they saw the small bucket of plastic farm animals at the entrance. I fell in love with it when I tasted their amazing grilled trout. The Farm at Adderley also has a separate children's menu. If you are heading to the Farm on a weekend, reservations are a must for parties of five or more.

Picket Fences

1310 Cortelyou Road at Argyle Road

718-282-6661

www.picketfencebrooklyn.com

This Ditmas Park Restaurant was one of the first to open on Cortelyou Road, and it has been a neighborhood favorite ever since. In the warmer weather, sit outside in their nice garden. Picket Fence has a kids' menu with turkey meatloaf and grilled chicken among other kid-friendly favorites. The restaurant bathroom also has a changing table if you have younger kids in tow.

Roberta's Pizza

261 Moore Street bet. White and Bogart streets

718-417-1118

www.robertaspizza.com

Have your pick of pizza, or entrees of roasted chicken, duck, and other favorites at this East Williamsburg/Bushwick restaurant. Kids will love choosing toppings for their pizza and parents will like their extensive wine list. This restaurant is cash only.

Midwood

Anopoli Ice Cream Parlor and Family Restaurant

6920 3rd Avenue at Bay Ridge Avenue

718-748-3863

This Bay Ridge diner offers folks some casual dining in a retro atmosphere. Don't fill up on omelets, burgers, and grilled cheese, because you'll want to save room for their excellent ice cream. If your family is looking for an old-school Brooklyn dining experience, this is the place.

Arirang Hibachi Steakhouse

8812-14 4th Avenue at 88th Street

718-238-9880

www.partyonthegrill.com

Kids will love watching their food being made by chefs at their table. The chefs really put on a show, and you'll be guaranteed to have a good time at this hibachi steak house and "samurai lounge." They also have a location in Staten Island, one in New Jersey, and another in Pennsylvania.

Di Fara Pizzeria

1424 Avenue J at East 15th Street

718-258-1367

www.difara.com

Expect a wait at this famed pizza parlor in the heart of Orthodox Midwood. Always highly rated in the press as one of the city's best pizza places, the slices are thin and extremely delicious. This is really worth the visit and is only a block from the F train subway stop. If you are there on a Sunday, check out vibrant Avenue J, filled with kosher marts and bakeries.

Hinsch's Confectionary

8518 5th Avenue at 85th Street
718-748-2854

This classic and quaint Brooklyn diner is right down the block from Century 21 (see p. 188) so you can have lunch here after a day sifting through the children's section at the famed discount department store. The food at Hinsch's is excellent and their homemade chocolate is certainly worth the calories. The staff is very friendly; when my son had a runny nose, they basically told me I had to give him their chicken soup—now, that's caring!

L & B Spumoni Gardens

2725 86th Street at West 10th Street
718-449-1230

www.spumonigardens.com

This Dyker Heights pizzeria has some of the best pizza you'll find in Brooklyn. In the warmer months, you can sit outside and dine on pizza and spumoni. During the Christmas season, take an after-dinner stroll to see the Christmas lights that light up the houses in the neighborhood. It's worth the trek out to Dyker Heights.

Randazzo's Clam Bar

2017 Emmons Avenue at East 21st Street
718-615-0010

www.randazzosclambar.com

The last remaining clam bar in Sheepshead Bay, Randazzo's is a fun place to grab some seafood or Italian food. Afterward you can take a walk along the water or take the kids fishing on one of the many

commercial fishing boats that dock across the street. This is also a good stop if you're heading to Kingsborough Community College to see a children's theater show, just a short drive from the clam bar.

Roll-n-Roaster

2901 Emmons Avenue at East 25th Street
718-769-6000

www.rollnroaster.com

Since I grew up going to Roll-n-Roaster in Queens, I had to include this in *City Kid New York*. For over thirty-six years, this restaurant has been serving slow-cooked fast food with a menu of roast beef sandwiches, chicken breast heroes, and hamburgers.

Queens

Buddha Bodai

4296 Main Street at Cherry Avenue
718-939-1188

www.chinatownvegetarian.com

If you want to show your kids that eating their veggies is fun and that tofu is yummy, head to this kosher vegetarian restaurant in Flushing's Chinatown. The food at Buddha Bodai is served family style, so don't order too much. This is also a nice place to grab some food if you are visiting the nearby Queens Botanical Gardens (see p. 133) or the New York Hall of Science (see p. 49). If you are driving, they have a convenient parking lot. Buddha Bodai has another location in Manhattan's Chinatown. If you are in search of some grilled meat, head down Main Street towards 39th Avenue for a slew of restaurants and carts selling barbecue skewers and dumplings, or you can eat at one of the vendors at the Flushing Mall. Walking through Flushing is a fun and educational day trip of sampling foods from the many culinary regions of China.

Carosello Restaurant

162-54 Cross Bay Boulevard bet. 162nd and 163rd avenues
718-322-7600
www.carosellorestaurant.com

Our family discovered this Howard Beach Italian restaurant en route to the Jamaica Bay Wildlife Preservation (literally just a few miles down the road; see p. 131) and my kids quickly decided it was their favorite NYC restaurant and now beg to come here all the time. Maybe it's because the restaurant is designed to look like a circus with a big-top ceiling and clown decorations, or maybe it's because they have an arcade for after-meal playtime. Nevertheless, the tasty Italian food on offer is truly authentic. How many places in New York City can you play skee ball after you eat? The portions are extremely large, so have the kids spilt an entree or you'll be bringing food home.

Jackson Diner

37-47 74th Street at 37th Road
212-672-1232
www.jacksondiner.com

This popular Indian Restaurant in the heart of Jackson Height's Little India is a gem for folks who enjoy tasty ethnic eats. Kids will love drinking a mango lassi while feasting on North Indian cuisine, and on Sundays the whole family can partake in their lunch buffet. Jackson Diner also has an upstairs room available for parties. Note that some of the dishes can be quite spicy, so if your kids aren't fans of hot food, make sure to ask for mild versions of dishes on the menu.

Jahn's

81-04 37th Avenue at 81st Street
Jackson Heights
718-651-0700

Sadly, this location's décor isn't straight out of the 1940s, like its sister parlor's recently closed Richmond Hill location, but Jahn's is part of NYC history as one of the last remaining ice cream parlors from a famed area chain. Although the décor is much like a typical East Coast diner, you can still order their famous Kitchen Sink ice cream sundae alongside the obligatory diner fare. The ice cream is superb—definitely worth the visit.

Nick's Pizza

108-26 Ascan Avenue at Austin Street
718-263-1126

This Forest Hill favorite serves light and tasty pizza and the atmosphere is relaxing for parents—the place is filled with children so you don't have to shush your child every time they get a bit loud. A tip: This place is popular and gets crowded quickly, so get there early.

Pinang Malaysian and Thai Cuisine

111-10 Queens Boulevard at 75th Avenue
Forest Hills
718-268-9135

This Forest Hills Malaysian restaurant, located just a few blocks from bustling Austin Street, serves up authentic cuisine in a kid-friendly atmosphere. The spacious restaurant has large round tables to accommodate large families. When we dined here with our kids, they loved chowing down on chicken, dumplings, and an assortment of noodle dishes while washing it down with a mango drink. The staff was extremely friendly and helpful in suggesting dishes.

Bronx

Dominick's Restaurant

2335 Arthur Avenue at Crescent Avenue
718-733-2807

When I asked a bunch of NYC parents where to get authentic Italian eats on famous Arthur Avenue, several people raved about Dominick's. A family-style Italian restaurant that serves up Italian delicacies in a vibrant atmosphere, Dominick's is the perfect place to take the kids. Don't expect a menu at this family-run restaurant, you just order what you want at this uniquely New York City restaurant. To help plan your trip to the Bronx's Little Italy and to discover more Arthur Avenue restaurants and shops, check out www.arthuravenuebronx.com.

JP's Waterside Restaurant

703 Minneford Avenue
718-885-3364

It might have been years since you wore a bib, but your family will be wearing these at JP's as they dine on lobsters. Ask for a seat outside where you can dine by the water and watch the fishing boats pass. JP's doesn't kid around with their portions. Dine off huge plates of tasty seafood classics. If you aren't a fan of fish, they have a large selection of other Italian specialties. They also have a kids menu with many options for both land and sea lovers. After dinner take a walk down City Island's main drag to **Lickety Split Ice Cream** (295 City Island Avenue; 718-885-9195), a place reminiscent of a New England ice cream parlor. Next to Lickety Splits is a park where you can sit and kids can crawl on the statues of maritime life.

Staten Island

Bay Street Luncheonette

1189 Bay Street near Hylan Boulevard
718-720-0922

Sip a real fountain soda from this Staten Island luncheonette where your family can dine on scrumptious breakfast and lunch meals accompanied by an egg cream or other old-school favorites. After lunch take a walk down the block to the historic Alice Austen House (www.aliceaustin.org) and soak in the stunning views.

The Burrito Bar

585 Forest Avenue at Regan Avenue
718-815-9200
www.theburritobar.com

Kids can order from the Little Amigos menu at this kid-friendly Staten Island Mexican place. Menu items include a Tyrannosaurus Mex burger or a Mexican pizza among other goodies. The vibe is laid-back and friendly.

Denino's Pizzeria Tavern

524 Port Richmond Avenue at Hooker Street
718-442-9401

This atmospheric Staten Island pizzeria has been dishing out delicious pies for years. Read about the history of the restaurant while you wait for your table at this festive pizza parlor that packs in a crowd every night.

Dining Tips

• Even though you are an experienced parent now, it's always good to try and eat out early to avoid a wait from the brunch/lunch/dinner rush.

• Depending on your child's age, bring something to keep him busy at the table. We always have our kids bring books. Another idea is to carry a small sketchpad and some colored pencils, so your children can draw while they waits for the food to be brought out. Yes, ideally this should be a time to engage in family conversation, but sometimes it's nice to have a backup plan.

• Even if a restaurant offers a kid's meal, they are often filled with mac 'n' cheese platters or a variety of breaded chicken dishes. Instead of ordering off the kid's menu, consider ordering your child an appetizer, or if you have two kids, order them an entree to split; this way you aren't limited and your kids can try a range of different foods.

Chapter Five

97

Chapter Five. Time to Party: How to Throw an Unforgettable Bash for Your Kids

Time to Party:

How to Throw an Unforgettable Bash for Your Kids

Throwing a birthday party in New York City doesn't need to be a chore. I know that between your job and helping your kids with their homework and escorting them to weekend soccer games or music lessons, it's hard to find the time to clean your apartment, let alone plan a birthday party. Once your city kid turns five, most parties tend to be "drop-off parties," and many parents go wild with the range of birthday party venues. However you don't have to feel pressured to throw a big bash. Some of my daughter's favorite parties that she has attended have been small ones with just a few girls at someone's apartment, where they decorated cookies or had pillow fights. My son likes any party that has a cake and a loot bag filled with candy.

I love finding interesting and unique venues like museums, historic houses, and theaters for my children's parties, and I've never spent a million dollars or had to do much planning. Obviously there are tons of places where you can throw a fun bash, but here is my list of top picks for birthday party venues in New York City that are sure to please (and are hassle-free).

From birthday party venues to cakes, I've arranged the basics for planning an amazing party for your child based on theme. For those of you on a budget, I've highlighted birthday parties that are under $300 with a star. So put on some party clothes and start stuffing those goody bags, we have some celebrating to do!

Art

From painting pottery to creating an art project, these venues will offer kids group-led craft projects that you won't have to clean up afterward. Many of the craft stores and studios on page 98 also host parties. Here is a list of some popular art party venues:

*The Artful Place

171 Fifth Avenue at Lincoln Place
Brooklyn
718-399-8199
www.theartfulplace.com
Decorate a T-shirt, make jewelry, or paint a treasure chest at this Park Slope art studio and shop. Artful Place parties are for kids ages five through twelve. Party packages include supplies, juice boxes, paper products, and goody bags for ten kids, but you can invite up to fifteen (there is an additional

charge for each child). Parties start at $250. You also have the option of having an Artful Place party in your own home.

Children's Museum of the Arts
182 Lafayette Street at Broome Street
212-274-0986
www.cmany.org
The amazing Children's Museum of the Arts offers parties throughout the day, from a Birthday Breakfast Party to an Art in the Evening Party. All parties offer partygoers a private party room, and art projects led by two instructors. Some parties offer free play in the museum. You can choose from a variety of art projects like the Pablo Picasso, for which guests make a mask using Picasso's cubist style, or the Georgia O'Keeffe, for which guests can make a garden of paper flowers. Parties start at $475.

The Craft Studio
1657 Third Avenue at East 93rd Street
212-831-6626
www.craftstudionyc.com
You decorate anything from a lamp to a skateboard at this popular Upper East Side craft and toy store. Parties include an activity of your choice, a Häagen-Dazs ice cream cake, juice boxes, face painting, balloons, and much more. Prices for parties vary by activity but average between $700 and $900 for ten kids.

Hi Art!
212-757-7565
www.hiartkids.com
This notable art program for kids runs a sophisticated art party for ages two through twelve. Choose from various art projects including drawing manga

(like Japanese anime), photo projects, and learning the basics of design while creating a candy sculpture. Parties start at $700 for ten kids, and prices vary by party. Although parents must supply food, Hi Art! provides all of the art supplies as well as someone to help set up, serve, and clean.

Little Shop of Crafts
431 East 73rd Street bet. York and First avenues
212-717-6636

711 Amsterdam Avenue at West 95th Street
212-531-2723
www.littleshopny.com
Choose an activity for your party from a menu of crafts featuring painting, plaster crafts, pottery, mosaics, beading, or creating a cuddly stuffed animal. Party packages include use of a private party room, a custom T-shirt for the birthday boy or girl signed by all the guests, craft materials, invitations, party supplies, food, and other fun treats like karaoke and face or hand painting. All you have to do is invite guests and bring your child to the party and they will take care of the rest, including the cleanup. Packages start at $530 for ten kids.

*The Painted Pot
339 Smith Street at Carroll Street
Brooklyn
718-222-0334

8009 Third Avenue at 80th Street
Brooklyn
718-491-6411
www.paintedpot.com
With two Brooklyn locations, in Carroll Gardens and

Bay Ridge, the Painted Pot offers fun, economical birthday parties. You can choose from an array of artistic activities like painting pottery, clay building (actually making your own pottery), beading, making mosaics, and building a plush animal. The parties include everything except for food (they do however provide juice boxes and all paper supplies). Prices are $28 per child.

*Textile Arts Center

320 2nd Street bet. Fourth and Fifth avenues
718-369-0222
www.textileartscenter.com
This Park Slope weaving studio offers kids ages six and up the chance to celebrate their birthday while picking up a unique skill. Children will learn basic weaving techniques and take home their woven designs. You supply the food and other party-related materials and Textile Arts supplies an instructor and all crafting supplies. Parties start at $200 with a $50 materials fee for eight kids (maximum ten kids) and an additional charge of $25 for each child over the maximum. The crafting sessions are usually two and half hours long.

Beauty

If your little girl loves playing dress up and being fancy, she'll love a party at the following salons and spas in New York City:

Cozy's Cuts for Kids

1416 2nd Avenue at 74th Street
212-585-2699

448 Amsterdam Avenue at 81st Street
212-579-2600

1125 Madison Avenue at 84th Street
212-744-1716
www.cozyscutsforkids.com
Girls (and boys) can have fun getting their hair styled at this beloved NYC salon for kids. Parties are private, meaning that your kids have the run of the entire salon during the party. Guests can have their hair styled in any look they'd like, from braids to Mohawks. In addition to hair styling, they offer art projects as well as a runway show, where kids can get dressed up in sunglasses, tiaras, and boas to strut their stuff for their friends. Parties can also include mini manicures, temporary tattoos, makeup application, and face painting. Cozy will also customize parties to suit your child if she'd like to bring her favorite doll in for a new hairstyle as well. Party packages start at $695 for a basic party for ten kids, without food. Parties with food start at $795 for ten kids with a $30 charge for each additional child (maximum of thirty kids). You may also opt for party favors, which can be provided at an additional cost.

Dashing Diva

Check Web site for locations throughout New York City.
www.dashingdiva.com
This adult nail salon offers kids the chance to glam it up with their signature mani/pedi at one of their Dashing Diva birthday parties. Parties and prices vary by location, so call your local Dashing Diva to make an appointment and to get their pricing. Some locations, like the one on Madison and 93rd Street (212-348-8890; www.dashingdivamadison.com), provide cupcakes for up to twenty guests, while other locations only accommodate eight guests without the option of party snacks.

Dimples Spa

91 Montague Street at Hicks Street
Brooklyn
718-330-0000
www.dimpleskidspa.com

Kids ages five and up can get dolled up at this kid spa, where your child can choose from an extensive menu of spa treatments like facials (they have chocolate facials), manicures, pedicures, and hair styling as well as fun activities like face painting and temporary tattoos. Parties are private (so the kids get the run of the spa) and last about two and a half hours. Prices start at $300 for five kids and $50 for each additional child for a maximum of eight kids in total. They can also provide goody bags filled with hairbrushes, bath balms, and candy for an additional fee. Parents must provide cake and balloons. Since there isn't much room to eat a proper meal, Dimples suggests that you only bring a cake. If you'd like to have a party with more than eight guests, Dimples Spa can host a party in your home.

Doodle Doo's

542 Hudson Street bet. Perry and Charles streets
212-627-3667
www.doodledoos.com

Have a private party at this hip kids' salon in the West Village. Glam parties are held on Sunday mornings, when they close the salon down for birthday guests to have their hair styled, fingernails and toes painted, among other beauty-related fun. Parties also include art projects with princess themes like decorating crowns and mirrors. Parties start at $800 for twelve kids.

Cooking

It's never too early to expose children to the joys of cooking, and what better way to get them started in the kitchen but at a birthday party. Throw on some fancy aprons and cook up some fun at these food-themed party venues.

Creative Cooks

298 Atlantic Avenue at Smith Street
Brooklyn
718-237-2218
www.creativecooks.us

Creative Cooks will host your child's birthday party at their Atlantic Avenue location in Brooklyn (near most major subway lines). The ninety-minute parties include the preparation of a meal, followed by a creative dessert option like a chocolate fountain, popcorn sculptures, cake decorating, cookie decorating, and a sundae bar, among many other choices. The parties are $425 for fifteen children, with a $25 charge for each additional guest with a maximum of eighteen kids. If you have an older child (ages ten through thirteen), you might arrange a Dinner-and-a-Movie Birthday Bash for Tweens, where kids get to prepare munchies to chow down on while watching their favorite film on a big-screen projector (available indoors or outdoors). The cost per party is $625. They also host a Tween Iron Chef party.

Cupcake Kids

Check Web site for participating restaurants throughout New York City.
646-789-5554
www.cupcakekids.com

Kids get to decorate aprons and don a chef's cap as

they roll out the dough for whole wheat pizzas or other age-appropriate dishes like lasagna or soft pretzels at these popular ninety-minute parties that were rated "The Best of New York" in *New York* magazine. After the savory dish has been gobbled up, kids get to decorate their own cupcakes or cakes. Parties are hosted at various restaurants and venues in the city, or you can arrange to have a Cupcake Kids party in your own home. Party packages include everything from ingredients to party favors, and cost $1,000 for ten kids with a charge of $50 for each additional child.

The International Culinary Institute Center

50 West 23rd Street at Sixth Avenue
212-847-0700 ext 83
www.iceculinary.com

Why not throw a party at this respected culinary institute? Parties for kids include a two-hour class where your child and their guests will learn how to cook a meal of the birthday child's choosing—from Asian offerings to All-American fare. Kids receive menu packets and chef hats to decorate and bring home. The Institute will provide juice, chips with dip, and aprons for the kids. Parties start at $2,700 for twenty kids, with a charge of $60 for each additional child. Note that there is a maximum of thirty guests.

Kids Cook!

170 Hicks Street at Love Lane
Brooklyn
718-797-0029
www.kidscookbrooklyn.com

Best suited for children ages five and up, Kids Cook! works with parents to choose an ideal menu to teach the guests to prepare for their child's party. Popular party menus include Chinese dumplings, Mexican tortillas, or Italian pasta, and the kids get to make dishes by hand. There is even an option available to allow the kids to decorate the birthday cake. A basic party for eight children runs around $550; it can be held at their Brooklyn Heights location or in your own home.

Milk and Cookies Bakery

19 Commerce Street at Bedford Street
212-243-1640
www.milkandcookiesbakery.com

Kids can bake and design their own cookies or hold an ice cream social at this popular West Village bakery. Spend a fun afternoon with party guests picking out mix-in items to spice up cookies or decorate six cupcakes with an assortment of toppings. If you have four or fewer partygoers, you can have the party while the bakery is still open. Groups of five or more will have to rent the bakery for $200 an hour, with prices starting at $18 to $24 per guest, depending on the party you plan on booking. Milk and Cookies Bakery suggest a maximum of eighteen kids for optimal fun.

Mini Chef

Check Web site for participating restaurants throughout New York City.
212-727-2703
www.minichefnyc.com

Kids get to act like real chefs at cooking parties hosted by Mini Chef at some of the city's hottest restaurants. In addition to cooking and baking up a bunch of delectable delights, kids also get to watch a magic show while their food simmers away. The

101

Chapter Five. Time to Party: How to Throw an Unforgettable Bash for Your Kids birthday kid gets to choose from a variety of party themes like Create-A-Cupcake, Pizza Party, La Fiesta, Pretzel Factory, and Dim Sum Fun. Party packages begin at $1,380 and can also be hosted at home.

Tribeca Treats

94 Reade Street bet. West Broadway and Church Street
212-571-0500
www.tribecatreats.com

Kids can pretend they're pastry chefs at this Tribeca bakery's parties, where kids get to bake and decorate cupcakes and cookies. If your child is eight and older, they offer an All About Chocolate party where children learn how to work with chocolate ganache. Party packages include aprons for the children to take home, thematic activities, games, and stories, bagel brunch or pizza, juice boxes and a fruit platter for kids, coffee for the adults, paper products, and a standard eight-inch round birthday cake with polka dots. Parties are ninety minutes long and cost $750 for twelve kids. Tribeca Treats can also prepare a fabulous and scrumptious custom cake to take home with you.

Dance Parties

My memories of childhood birthday parties always involve dancing to songs from Michael Jackson's *Thriller* in someone's living room or basement in Queens. Of course, times have changed and now kids can have sophisticated types of dance parties given in a real dance studio. Below I have listed a number of the best dance party companies that will make sure the floor is packed with twirling little children. Just to note, many local dancing schools (for example, Park Slope Dance Studio in Brooklyn) offer

parties where you can rent out the studio for the afternoon and have an instructor-led dance class for the kids; so inquire at your local dance school about the possibility of having a party. Now put on your dancing shoes and get ready to party!

Deb's Family Disco

Check Web site for a complete list of venues throughout New York City.
212-586-7425
www.familydisco.com

Held in the off-hours at various clubs throughout the city, Deb's Family Disco brings in the music and dancers for a very lively party. Kids choose the music, and the MC and dancers choreograph dance routines to the songs. They also play games on the dance floor like the chicken dance (sometimes they even have someone dressed as a chicken to lead the dance) and freeze dance, among others. The birthday child gets VIP treatment to make sure they have a good time, and to encourage them to try out new dance moves. If your child is a fan of *High School Musical*, you're in luck as they offer a party to the music of that movie. Parties are an hour and a half in length and include food, decorations, a temporary tattoo artist, glitter stickers, and disco ball necklaces. Parties start at $950 for twelve kids, with a cost of $20 for additional child.

New York Kid's Club

Check Web site for locations throughout Manhattan.
212-721-4100
www.nykidsclub.com

Music and dance lovers will want either a dance- or karaoke-themed party at this popular kid's club for children ages seven and up. Learn some cool hip-hop moves at their street dance party or belt out a tune at their karaoke-themed party. Basic hip-hop parties start at $625 for ten kids with a cost of $18 for each additional child, and the all-inclusive party (food and party supplies) runs about $895, with a cost of $25 per additional child. Karaoke parties start at $725, with a cost of $23 for each additional child. The all-inclusive package costs $995, with a cost of $30 for each additional child. All parties run an hour and a half in length.

Make-Your-Own Toys, Dolls, and Books

From stuffing your own bear or designing a robot to creating a book or having a sleepover in a luxury NYC hotel, you can take your pick of personalized DIY fun at the following party locations.

American Girl

609 Fifth Avenue at 49th Street

877-247-5223

www.americangirl.com

From a tea party in the American Girl Café to a salon party where a stylist comes in and does the hair of the guests' dolls, fans of the beloved American Girl dolls will love a party at the American Girl store in Midtown (see p. 186). Café parties start at $33 per guest (plus tax and gratuity) and include invitations with matching thank-you notes, a meal of sandwiches and other food for all of the guests followed by a pink peppermint ice cream cake, as well as a surprise keepsake for the birthday girl, and a goody bag for each party guest.

*Build-A-Bear Workshop

565 Fifth Avenue at 46th Street

877-789-2327

www.buildabear.com

At Build-a-Bear, you can customize your child's birthday party just as your child can customize the plush teddy bears, which means Build-a-Bear Parties work within everyone's budget. Basic parties start at $10 per person and if you book a party with six or more kids, you get some free "pawsome" party stuff. If you decide to book the private party room, you can have it for two and a half hours for an additional $400, plus the price of each child's animal.

"Live Like Eloise" Slumber Party at the Plaza Hotel

Fifth Avenue at Central Park South

212-759-3000

www.fairmont.com/thePlaza

For a unique sleepover that the kids will remember forever, the Plaza Hotel offers a package for up to six guests to spend the night like Eloise, the cheeky little girl who lived with her nanny and turtle in the master suite of the Plaza Hotel in the popular children's books. Guests receive a copy of the book *Eloise*, snacks, and superduper sundaes from room service and DVDs of the *Eloise* movies. The package costs $3,595.

FAO Schwarz

767 Fifth Avenue at West 59th Street

212-644-9400

www.fao.com

FAO Schwarz is every child's dream toy store, so why not throw your child's next blow-out bash at this historic NYC landmark? Have an ice cream or pizza party on a weekday, hosted by a world-famous toy soldier inside a party room decorated with balloons and your child's favorite toys from the FAO Schwarz collection. Another party option is to host a private party with toy demonstrations on the second floor of the store. FAO Schwarz will even host an after-hours party for your special birthday child where you can have the whole place to yourself. Parties range from $750 to $25,000.

Madame Alexander

615 West 131st Street at Broadway
212-283-5900
www.madamealexander.com
Book a party at this historic doll factory and your kids will get a behind-the-scenes tour of the factory (see p. 194) and the chance to design their own nine-inch play doll in their Create-a-Doll workshop. They have a gorgeous party room with many customizable party options, including a lovely tea party where the kids can dine with their favorite dollies. Parties range from $38 to $99 per guest.

The Scholastic Store

557 Broadway at Prince Street
212-343-6166
www.scholastic.com/birthday
Kids (ages five and up) can become pint-sized publishers at the book factory party offered at the Scholastic Store. Each child gets to design, write, and publish his or her own wire-o-bound book. If you don't want a literary bash, you can also have a choice of the young wizards party (kids get to make a wizard's wand), a super science party, a pajama party, among many others. Parties are ninety minutes long and include a party host, cupcakes, juice boxes, and paper goods, and start at $550 for ten kids with a cost of $30 for each additional child.

Toys "R" Us

1514 Broadway
646-366-8800
www.toysrus.com
The Toys "R" Us in Times Square hosts robot galaxy birthday parties (www.robotgalaxy.com) where kids get to design and take home their own robots. Parties start at $34.95 for each of the first ten kids, and then $29.95 for each additional child. Parties are held in a private room that overlooks Times Square and the Toys "R" Us ferris wheel, and are complete with pizza, chicken fingers, and robot stickers. Parties typically run about ninety minutes.

Museums

From fire department museums to the Museum of Natural History, throw a party with an educational twist.

Linda Kaye's Partymakers

195 East 76th Street bet. Lexington and Third avenues
888-321-PARTY
www.partymakers.com
If you want to plan a party at the American Museum of Natural History or the Central Park Zoo, contact extremely popular Partymakers, who will put together a wonderful bash for you. You can choose from a variety of age-appropriate themes for each of these locales. Packages for ten children start at $710 for a party at the American Museum of History and $660 for the Central Park Zoo, although you must be a contributor-level member of the museum to throw a party there. If you want to have a party at another venue or in your home, Linda Kaye's Partymakers

have an extensive menu of thematic parties that are perfect for savvy city kids, from bake-a-cake parties to fairy-tale adventure parties. Linda Kaye has been planning parties for over twenty-five years and is just the person to help you plan the perfect party for your child. Check her Web site for helpful party tips and to see the list of possible themes.

New York City Fire Museum

278 Spring Street at Hudson Street
212-691-1303 Ext.15
www.nycfiremuseum.org

Is your child obsessed with fire trucks or has your child already decided to be a firefighter when he or she grows up? If so, book a party for your little red-engine driver and fifteen guests at the New York City Fire Museum. The museum's party package includes free play in the museum, storytelling, show-and-tell, an art project, a visit from a real-life firefighter, and a scavenger hunt. It also includes a fire truck–themed twelve-inch birthday cake, juice, fire-engine party decorations, and loot bags. Parties start at $650.

New York Transit Museum

Corner of Boerum Place and Schermerhorn Street
Brooklyn
718-694-1600
www.mta.info/mta/museum/#birthday

If your child loves riding the subway, plan a party at this decommissioned train station-turned-transit museum. The party package includes age-appropriate and hands-on workshops in their private party space. My daughter has attended several parties here and made lots of crafts, including decorating a subway tile. They also offer a kid-friendly guided tour of the museum, decorations, and cleanup. This is a drop-off type of party, so it's best for mature four- or five-year-olds. Packages start at $350 for twelve children and four adults, with a cost of $15 per additional child (maximum of twenty children). There is also an additional charge if adults stay.

Nature

Does your child seem more rural than urban? Do they point out poison ivy on hikes and love animals? If so, have your child's next birthday party at a zoo, working farm, or nature center.

*Alley Pond Park

228-06 Northern Boulevard at 72nd Street
Queens
718-229-4000
www.alleypond.com

A trip to Alley Pond, located in Douglaston, Queens, will remove your city kids from the urban sidewalks of the city and plant them on picturesque trails. Parties offered at Alley Pond are best suited for kids between the ages of four and twelve and include a discussion about nature and the handling of live animals. We went to a party at Alley Pond and especially loved walking around the nature center before the party and checking out the guinea pigs, rabbits, snakes, and other creatures. The spacious center has tables set up so kids can create nature-related craft projects, and, weather permitting, take a guided nature walk. Parent-supplied food and drink are served in the classroom area. Prices start at $190 for fifteen children for the two-hour party, and $10 for each additional child, with a maximum of twenty kids.

Audubon Nature Center

450 Flatbush Avenue at Empire Boulevard
Brooklyn
www.prospectpark.org
718-287-5252 ext. 102

Book a nature-inspired birthday with natural crafts and activities at the Audubon Nature Center in Prospect Park. If your child's birthday is between April and October, the center can also offer a narrated nature tour of the park, including a peek inside the electric boat *Independence*. Parties take place year-round on Saturdays and Sundays from 10 a.m. until 12 p.m. Parties run about $400 for twenty-eight kids.

* Greenbelt Nature Center

700 Rockland Avenue at Brielle Avenue
Staten Island
718-351-3450
www.sigreenbelt.org

Kids ages five and up can choose from various nature themes for their parties like Flying Fun, which is all about bats and other winged creatures, or Rugged Reptiles, where kids get a visit from the resident corn snake. All parties include an activity or craft, food, and paper party supplies. All you need to bring are the kids and the cake. Parties cost $15 per child with a ten-child minimum and a twenty-child maximum.

New York Botanical Garden

Bronx River Parkway at Fordham Road
Bronx
718-817-8687
www.nybg.org

If you are a member of the New York Botanical Garden, why not host a party at this historic garden, where the birthday party package includes a seasonal craft or activity, a party coordinator, pizza, drinks, and paper goods. There is a maximum of twenty kids per party.

Prospect Park Zoo

450 Flatbush Avenue at Empire Boulevard
Brooklyn
718-399-7321
www.prospectparkzoo.com

Choose from a variety of thematic parties at this Brooklyn zoo, like the Sea Lion Celebration, where kids learn all about sea lions and meet their keepers, or the Discovery Party, where kids learn all about the animals in the zoo's Discovery Center. Prices start at $500 for fifteen children and run about $650 for thirty kids. Members receive a discounted rate.

Queens County Farm Museum

73-50 Little Neck Parkway at 74th Avenue
Queens
718-347-3276
www.queensfarm.org

If you thought you couldn't have a birthday party on a farm in the city, then you haven't been to this little farm plot in Floral Park, Queens. Parties are held on the farm grounds from April through October and the package includes everything you will need from invitations to food (including the cake and goody bags). Two party hostesses lead the party, teaching kids how to feed the animals and tour the farm, and they assist the group on a tractor-drawn hayride. Prices for a party of twenty children run around $450, with $20 per additional child.

Queens Zoo

53-51 111th Street at 53rd Avenue
Queens
www.queenszoo.com
718-271-7361

Kids ages three through twelve can attend a fun birthday party at the Queens Zoo, where activities range from arts and crafts, up-close encounters with farm animals, a meet-and-greet with a zookeeper, and include guided tours of the zoo's animal exhibits. The package includes twenty-five admission passes as well as party bags. Parents must supply the paper products and food. The birthday child may choose from various themed parties like Domestic Animal Discoveries and Junior Zookeeper. Parties have a maximum group size of twenty-five people, including children and adults. Parties are held on select Saturdays and Sundays year-round from 10:30 a.m. until 2 p.m. Prices cost $330 for members and $350 for nonmembers.

Outdoor Venues, Parks, and Amusement Parks

It's always nice to have a party in a park because it's economical and fun. In order to throw a party at a city park like Central Park, Prospect Park, Forest Park, or any other NYC park, you will need to apply for a permit. Permits cost $25, and you can download a permit application or apply online at www.nycgovparks.org. You must send the application to the address specified on the form at least thirty days before the event. The application fee is nonrefundable, so if it rains or you must reschedule the party, you must reapply for a new permit.

If you're looking for a more structured event in an outdoor setting like an amusement park or a park, check out the locations that I've listed below. I've included the Historic House Trust in this section since many of the historic homes that are open for parties are located in a city park. Enjoy a fun park adventure for the big day, but don't forget to bring some sunscreen for the kids!

*Adventurers Park

1824 Shore Parkway at 25th Avenue
Brooklyn
718-975-2748
www.adventurerspark.com

Parties at this Brooklyn amusement park offer the birthday child a two-hour party with twelve rides, party goods, a slice of pizza or a hot dog, potato chips, a drink, and a party hostess. Packages start at $24 (plus tax) per child on weekends with a minimum of twelve kids. On weekdays, the price of admission per child drops to $22 (plus tax).

*Central Park Carousel

Central Park at East 65th Street
212-879-0244
www.centralparkcarousel.com

A perfect warm weather location for a party is at the lovely Central Park carousel. Parties include four spins on the historic carousel per child, as well as one hour in the picnic area, during which kids will have the choice of hot dog or a slice of pizza accompanied by apple juice. Each child will also receive a balloon and party favors. Party staffers provide a party hostess to set up, serve, and clean up. You can add on additional perks to the party at an additional cost like take-home photographs of each kid at the carousel, extra carousel rides, and other entertainment options, like a magician. Prices are $21.95 per child on weekdays and $27.95 per child on Saturdays and Sundays (minimum of twelve children).

*Historic House Trust

See Web site for locations through New York City.
212-360-8282
www.historichousetrust.org
Many of the historic homes in New York City are available for rental through the Historic House Trust, including the Van Cortlandt House, the Old Stone House, and Lefferts House. Although each house is rented out by various NYC parks organizations, the Historic Trust maintains a list of the homes available for rent and the rental prices. Most house rentals cost under $300 for a two-hour party and some, like the Van Cortlandt House, include staff-guided group activities. This is an interesting way to expose kids to New York City's historic past.

*Prospect Park Carousel

Prospect Park, Willink entrance at Ocean Avenue
Brooklyn
718-287-5252 ext. 102
www.prospectpark.org
Ever dream of having the Prospect Park Carousel all to yourselves? Well you can, if you book a private party at the carousel. From April through October, parties take place either before the carousel opens at 9:30 a.m. or after hours at 5:45 p.m. and run about two hours. Parties include unlimited rides of the carousel and two tables for food setup. Private parties cost $350. On Saturdays and Sundays, you

can also have a carousel party at 12:30 p.m. during public hours for a discounted rate of $175.

Victorian Gardens Amusement Park

Central Park at Wollman Rink
830 5th Avenue
212-982-2229
www.victoriangardensnyc.com
Spend your child's birthday at the amusement park at Wollman Rink. Victorian Gardens parties include unlimited rides all day for the children as well as free admission for each adult accompanying a child, an hour of private seating, a choice of chicken tenders or slice of pizza or hot dog, cookies, fruit, soda or juice boxes, paper goods, party favors, and the services of a party host to set up, serve, and clean up. Prices start at $38 per child on weekdays and $45 per child on weekends with a minimum of fifteen kids.

Science and Technology

Science isn't just something kids learn at school. Expose your children and their friends to the wonders of science and technology at these unique party locations.

Carmello the Science Fellow

300 Atlantic Avenue at Smith Street
Brooklyn
718-722-0000
www.carmelothesciencefellow.com
The enthusiastic and energetic Carmello the Science Fellow captivates kids with science activities tailored to the child's age and interest. Activities range from making glow-in-the-dark slime to experimenting with fake snow. The two-hour parties take place at

the Cosmic Cove (Carmello's storefront science classroom) in Brooklyn. There is a separate party room where food can be brought in and served. These parties are extremely popular, so you must book well in advance.

New York Hall of Science

47-01 111th Street at 47th Avenue
Queens
718-699-0301
www.nyscience.org

Choose from an extensive menu of party themes at this Queens science museum. From a junior chemist party, where your guests get to do hands-on experiments in the Pfizer Foundation Biochemistry Discovery Lab to an Out of This World party, where kids put on an "alien antennae" headband and discover how astronauts are trained to live in outer space. Packages include everything from food to loot bags, so all you have to bring is your family. Parties start at $575 for twelve kids, with a cost of $20 for each additional child.

Science Teacher Sarah

212-683-2010
www.scienceteachersarah.com

Science Teacher Sarah will host "awesome science birthday parties" at either your home or at her classroom. Parents and their kids can choose from a laundry list of themes including Blood, Bones and Bodies, and Reptile Safari. Parties run an hour and a half and are best for kids ages 4 through 9 years old. All packages include a science instructor and materials for the class.

Sony Wonder Technology Lab

550 Madison Avenue at West 55th Street
212-833-7858
www.sonywondertechlab.com

Is your child into gaming or animation? Book one of the many thematic parties at the Sony Wonder Technology Lab. From VIP tours of the museum to making a clay animation film, there are plenty of options for an amazing birthday celebration. Many parties are for children in third grade and above and start around $2,000. Gaming and animation parties run around three and half hours and cost $3,500 for up to a total of twenty people including adults. Parties should be booked at least six weeks in advance.

Sports

From cheering on your favorite New York team to participating in a game, a sports-themed birthday party is a sporty way to celebrate. Bowling pros and ice-skating fanatics should also check out the list of ice-skating rinks and bowling alleys that offer birthday party packages on pages 124–125.

Asphalt Green

555 East 90th Street at York Avenue
212-369-8890
www.asphaltgreen.org

You don't have to be in the suburbs to have a pool party. Kids ages five and up can splash away at an Asphalt Green pool party, which includes one hour of activity, and a half hour for refreshments in their private party room. The staff provides paper goods for the cake, along with helium balloons and a party host to set up, serve, and clean up. If your child would rather stay dry, Asphalt Green also hosts gymnastics parties and sports parties where kids can play a game of soccer. Prices for a gymnastic party start at $650; pool parties start at $800.

*Astoria Sports Complex

34-38 38th Street bet. 34th and 35th avenues
Queens
718-729-7163
www.ascsports1.com

You can choose from a variety of sports themes when you have your party at the Astoria Sports Complex in Queens. Parties include a choice of two sport activities, a party hostess, pizza, drinks, and party favors. Parties for up to fifteen kids start at $295.

*Aviator Sports and Recreation

Floyd Bennett Field at Flatbush Avenue
Brooklyn
718-758-7500
www.aviatorsports.com

The birthday child can choose a party theme based on ice-skating, rock climbing, gymnastics, basketball, or soccer parties at this sports complex located in an old airport hanger at the historic Floyd Bennett Field in Brooklyn. Party packages include everything but the cake.

The Baseball Center NYC

202 West 74th Street at Amsterdam Avenue
212-362-0344
www.thebaseballcenternyc.com

It doesn't have to be baseball season to have a baseball-themed birthday party in New York City. Parties at the Baseball Center include baseball or softball instruction, games, a decorated private party room, food, a party specialist, as well as a spe-

cial T-shirt for the birthday child—all in all, a hassle-free sports party.

Bounce U

6722 Fort Hamilton Parkway at 67th Street
Brooklyn
718-238-3288
www.bounceu.com

If your child is always the one at the front of the line for the bouncy castle at the ubiquitous NYC street fair, then you should plan a party at Bounce U, a playroom entirely devoted to bouncy structures (although they don't have a bouncy castle). Let your child burn off the inevitable birthday-cake-sugar high jumping around the "bounce room" and speeding down the big slide. Parties start at $635 on weekdays and $735 on weekends. Packages are all-inclusive for twenty-five kids.

Brooklyn Cyclones at Keyspan Park

1904 Surf Avenue at West 19th Street
Brooklyn
718-449-8497
www.brooklyncyclones.com

Celebrate a Brooklyn Cyclones–themed birthday party at this stadium by the sea with ten guests. Each child will receive a hot dog, soda, ice cream, bag of chips, and souvenir. To make the day even more special, the birthday boy or girl gets to stand on the field between innings while the entire ballpark sings "Happy Birthday!" as their name is emblazoned on the leader board. The party package includes invitations to send to all of your child's friends, as well as vouchers for one free game of speed pitch for each child. Prices start at $18 per child for bleacher seats.

Chelsea Piers Sports and Entertainment Complex

23rd Street at the Hudson River

212-336-6518

www.chelseapiers.com

Book an ultimate birthday challenge party at the Field House at Chelsea Piers, where guests can compete in games of tug-of-war, relay races, and dodge ball. Other party options include rock climbing, gymnastics, or team sports. You can also book golf, bowling, and ice-skating parties at Chelsea Piers. Parties start at $560 for ten kids.

Last Licks Ice Cream

245 East 93rd Street at 2nd Avenue

646-596-8566

www.lastlicksicecream.com

Have a party at this sports-themed ice cream parlor where kids get to engage in sports-related activities like decorating baseball caps and playing games for prizes. The walls are filled with sports memorabilia, making it feel more like a sports bar than a kids' ice cream parlor. Parties are ninety minutes in length and include a make-your-own sundae bar for dessert. Packages include everything from food to party favors and cost $45 per child for up to ten party guests and an additional cost of $25 per child beyond that. Their party room can accommodate up to thirty kids, but if you have an extensive guest list, inquire about renting out the entire ice cream parlor.

Sheridan Fencing Academy

2035 2nd Avenue at East 105th Street

212-831-0764

www.sheridanfencing.com

Have a unique party at this Upper East Side fencing academy. Parties will grant you and your guests exclusive access to the fencing academy as well as a lesson. Parties run ninety minutes in length.

*Staten Island Yankees

75 Richmond Terrace at Wall Street

Staten Island

718-720-9265

www.siyanks.com

Host a party at a Staten Island Yankees game. Bring your group to the Staten Island Yankee stadium and get the All-You-Can-Eat plan, which costs $16 per person and includes a limited-edition Staten Island Yankees hat, a program, group seating, the birthday child's name in lights on the video board, and unlimited ballpark food. The fun really starts after the game when kids are invited onto the field to run the bases.

Tennis Party at the Prospect Park Tennis Center

50 Parkside Avenue at Coney Island Avenue

Brooklyn

718-287-5252

www.prospectpark.org

Tennis anyone? If your child is a budding Serena Williams, book a party at the Prospect Park Tennis Center, where kids can participate in tennis-related games and instruction with the exclusive use of the courts. Parties are two hours in length and start at $400 for eight kids, with a maximum of sixteen kids.

Yankee Stadium

East 161st Street at Courtland Avenue

Bronx

718-508-3917

www.yankees.mlb.com

Have a birthday party at Yankee Stadium, where kids get to tour the stadium, followed by an exclusive party that includes food, beverages, and a Yankees promotional souvenir at the Hard Rock Cafe in the stadium. They also provide invitations. Birthday bashes take place daily except when the Yankees play at home on weekends or are scheduled to play a weekday game. Birthday bashes require advance booking of at least two weeks for twelve to thirty people, with a cost of $40 per person. They also provide invitations.

Theater

There are many ways you can enjoy the endless theatrical resources in the city and throw a drama- or musical theater–themed party. You can always throw a casual party where you invite a few children to a play and then grab a bite afterward or you can book a party package at one of the venues below. Check out the complete listing of theatrical venues on pages 54–59. I've also listed a few of the theaters that offer special birthday packages below:

*Galli Children's Theater
38 West 38th Street, 3rd floor bet. Fifth and Sixth avenues
212-810-6485
www.gallitheaterny.com
You have many options at this amazing children's theater, which will transport your children into a fairy wonderland, such as a fairy show that runs on Saturdays and Sundays at 3 p.m. Tickets for groups of twenty or more start at $12 each. You could also book the Show and a Party package that includes a private Galli's Fairytale Theater production, complete with a special birthday song tribute by the

characters from the show after the performance. The package includes the services of three staff members to help set up, serve, and clean up, but you must provide the food. The theater can accommodate up to seventy people and packages range from $800 to $1,500. The folks from Galli will also come to you, if you have access to a venue you prefer.

*Literally Alive Theater at The Players Theater
115 MacDougal Street at Minetta Lane
212-866-5170
www.literallyalive.com
Have your child's birthday at a show performed by this amazing and creative theater company. When we went to see *Treasure Island* here, a birthday party was occurring at the show. The girls at the party got to sit in reserved seats and participated in hands-on activities before the play. The ensemble even sang "Happy Birthday!" to her. The birthday child also receives a gift as well as a photo taken with the cast after the show. It costs $15 to $20 per child with a minimum of ten kids, and you can rent their party space for an additional fee.

Manhattan Children's Theater
52 White Street at Church Street
212-226-4085
www.mctny.org
If your child loves being on stage, book an acting-class party at this popular children's theater in New York City. At each party workshop, two teachers will engage the children in acting exercises and warm-ups as well as teach them how to bring a story to life on stage. At the end, the students perform a mini play for the parents. Parties take place from Sep-

tember to May and are held from 3:45 until 5:15 p.m. on Saturdays and Sundays. Parties cost $600 for twenty children and their families, with a limit of seventy-four people in attendance. There is an additional cost of $25 for each child beyond the twenty guests that are provided for.

Puppetworks

338 Sixth Avenue at 4th Street
Brooklyn
718-965-3391
www.puppetworks.org

Puppetworks is an extremely popular venue with Brooklyn families. This Park Slope puppet theater offers exclusive use of its puppet theater for birthday parties along with a viewing of its most current production. Puppet shows Saturdays and Sundays from 3:45 p.m. to 6:15 p.m. They perform the show that is currently in production. Parties are $400 for two and half hours and they accommodate fifty people.

Story Pirates at the Drama Book Shop

250 West 40th Street bet. Seventh and Eighth avenues
310-880-4725
www.storypirates.org

Not actually pirates, this theatrical troupe allows kids to become playwrights as they make up a play on-site to be performed by these energetic and extremely creative actors. Parties are held at the black box theater in the basement of the Drama Book Shop in Midtown or arranged as a Story Pirates house call in your very own home. In the theater, your birthday group will enjoy food and cake after the performance as well as the additional birthday child honor of his or her photo on the wall of the

shop alongside all the other kid playwrights. We've been to parties where the Story Pirates performed in a friend's living room and it was just as entertaining as the theater at the bookshop; the kids really got into writing the play and seeing something they created performed for them.

Swedish Marionette Theater in Central Park

Central Park at 79th Street
212-988-9093
www.cityparksfoundation.org

Plan a party at a unique marionette show at this historic theater in Central Park. Partygoers get to watch a puppet performance followed by a party in their private room with child-size furniture. The theater can accommodate up to a hundred people and the party room can seat thirty children.

*13th Street Repertory Company

50 West 13th Street at Sixth Avenue
212-675-6677
www.13thstreetrep.org

This old-school West Village theater hosts a kids theatrical performance every weekend. You have a choice of one of the three long–running and revolving plays, *Wiseacre Farm, Rumple Who?* and the *Imagination Show. Wiseacre Farm* is a great performance for a birthday party as it chronicles a group of farm animals searching for a birthday cake. The rental fee for the party room, which is really just a large table set up in the theater's intimate lobby, is $50, with, the additional admission ticket cost of $10 per child. The staff lets you set up your food and have the birthday about a half an hour prior to the curtain rising. We had Lucy's fourth birthday party here at the production of *Wiseacre Farm* and the kids loved participating in the show. I picked up some farm-themed goody bags, some pizza, and a cake, and we had a wonderful time—and it didn't cost a fortune.

Restaurants and Tea

A birthday celebration at one of these restaurants in New York City will ensure a good time—from darling tea parties to a restaurant that unleashes your wild western side.

*Alice's Tea Cup
102 West 73rd Street at Columbus Avenue
212-799-3006

156 East 64th Street at Lexington Avenue
212-486-9200

220 East 81st Street bet. Second and Third avenues
212-734-4832
www.alicesteacup.com
Partake in a traditional English tea party at this tea parlor with multiple locations in Manhattan. Parties start at $20 per child and include scones, sandwiches, chocolate mousse, and tisane tea. For an additional charge you can have a magician, a face painter, or someone dressed as Alice, who will read parts of *Alice in Wonderland* to the partygoers. Parties are offered all day, Mondays through Thursdays, as well as Fridays through Sundays after 3 p.m.

Cowgirl
519 Hudson Street at West 10th Street
212-633-1133
www.cowgirlnyc.com

Little cowgirls and cowboys can celebrate their birthday at this kitschy West Village restaurant. Parties take place in one of their designated party spaces and prices start at $13.50 per kid's meal. They have tons of add-ons like sand art with edible sugar sand, horseshoe painting, piñata smashing, and western-themed goody bags.

The Cupcake Café at Books of Wonder
18 West 18th Street bet. Fifth and Sixth avenues
212-465-1530
www.cupcakecafe-nyc.com
What can beat a party with cupcakes and children's books? Enjoy a party at this café located in Books of Wonder bookstore. The basic party package at the Cupcake Café is for twelve to fifteen children and costs $30 per child, with an additional charge of $10 for each child's admission after that. The party is generally two hours in length and costs $150 for each additional hour. The party package includes party supplies (party hats, balloons, etc), cupcakes, a small cake for the birthday child, and special gift for them, too. There are various activities that you can add on to the party like decorating cupcakes for an additional $10 a child, or you can add on the choice of pizza, sandwiches, or an open ice cream bar. The Cupcake Café needs at least two weeks notice for the party and there is an 18 percent gratuity fee.

Dylan's Candy Bar
1011 3rd Avenue at East 60th Street
646-735-0078
www.dylanscandybar.com
A party at Dylan's Candy Bar is like being in Willy Wonka's chocolate factory. Book a party at Dylan's and have a sweet experience that includes use of

their party room, a staff-led candy craft activity, pizza, juice, and party supplies. You can also arrange for kids to enjoy a candy spree as well as other party favors. The birthday child also gets to walk away sporting a cool Dylan's T-shirt. For older kids, Dylan's will also host Bar or Bat Mitzvahs and Sweet Sixteen parties.

Eli's Vinegar Factory

431 East 91st Street at York Avenue
212-717-9798
www.elizabar.com

You can throw a party on the second floor of this high-end Upper East Side market. Parties include food and the floor space, and they will give you a list of entertainment to choose from if you'd like to have some group-led activities. The food they provide is delicious and you get a choice of two meals, from mini hamburgers and pigs in a blanket to grilled cheese and other kid favorites. The two-hour party costs $25 per child with a minimum of twenty-five kids. There is an additional $300 cost for a staff of two to set up and breakdown the party.

Mars 2112

1633 Broadway bet. West 50th and 51st streets
212-582-2112
www.mars2112.com

You don't need a space suit to travel to Mars; just head to this themed restaurant in Midtown. Mars 2112 hosts all-inclusive parties that that feature food from their menu, a Martian meeting, a party host, balloon table decorations, and a $5 cyber-street game card for each child. Prices start at $18.95 per person, with a minimum of fifteen guests.

Cool Party Ideas on the Cheap

You don't have to take out a second mortgage to host a kid's birthday party. Here are some ideas for hosting without breaking the bank:

- **Outdoor concert series:** One of the best parties we've had was when we brought a bunch of my daughter's friends, a few blankets, and some pizza to a Laurie Berkner concert at the Celebrate Brooklyn Concert Series in Prospect Park. We even handed out mini accordions from Pearl River Mart (see p. 117) as party favors. This type of party can work for any kid's concert or outdoor concert series in the city.

- **A PJ Party:** This is quite a popular party option for six- to eight-year-old girls who might not be ready for a real sleepover. Invite a few girls over in PJs to decorate pillows, make popcorn, do each other's nails, and decorate cookies, and send your guests home before bedtime. Perfect for apartments, this small party idea is a cozy way to celebrate.

- **A Superhero Party:** Invite some kids over and have them run around in capes as they try to save the world. Thematic activities can include a scavenger hunt or decorating their own cape. If you keep the party small, this becomes a very apartment-friendly party idea.

- **Your local playground:** It seems like an obvious idea, but why not just order some pizzas and let the kids go crazy at the playground? You can do a variation of this party for older kids where you host the party at a skate park.

Decorations and Goody Bag Fillers

My kids walk away with serious swag bags at birthday parties these days. From puzzles to kites, they've gotten amazing treats over the years. If you need help figuring out what to give, check out the following list of places for some ideas beyond searching through the Oriental Trading Company Web site (www.orientaltrading.com) and ordering premade bags (I'll admit I've done this). Of course you can always check out Dylan's Candy Bar (see p. 114) for some sweet treats or Jack's 99 Cent store (see p. 191) for some inexpensive loot.

Balloon Saloon

133 West Broadway bet. Duane and Thomas streets

212-227-3838

www.balloonsaloon.com

If you are in need of balloons, you are in good hands at this TriBeCa balloon shop that has been making fantastic bouquets and displays for years (check out their Web site for examples of their work—it's stunning). The owner is very friendly and will work with you on your arrangement. You can even order a balloon bouquet for pickup later that day. Balloon Saloon also can prepare custom goody bags, but if you'd like to fill them yourselves, they have an entire section of the shop dedicated to loot bag accessories.

Economy Candy

108 Rivington Street bet. Essex and Ludlow streets

800-352-4544

www.economycandy.com

By far the city's best candy store, Economy Candy is filled with aisles of old-school candy available at incredibly low prices. This place has been on the Lower East Side for years and is jammed packed with candies that you may have even forgotten existed. We love to head over here and fill up a basket of Sweet Tarts, Runts, Nerds, and other candy. Personally, I love their selection of chocolate-covered treats—from pretzels to Oreos. You can fill up a generous goody bag at Economy Candy without ever going over budget.

Fill-R-Up

197 East 76th Street at Third Avenue

212-452-3026

www.fill-r-up.com

From personalized backpacks to children's beach chairs, you can get a wide variety of party favors for birthday parties at this Upper East Side gift basket shop. Fill-R-Up will work with you to create the perfect favors to suit your occasion.

Paramount Party Supplies

52 West 29th Street at Sixth Avenue

212-686-6747

For party supplies, balloons, and holiday-themed merchandise, stop by this Murray Hill party supply shop.

Party City

Check Web site for locations throughout New York City

www.partycity.com

Need a Dora the Explorer piñata? This moderately priced party store chain has all the goodies for throwing the ultimate bash—from paper plates to goody bag fillers. This is also a popular place to pick up a Halloween costume.

Pearl River Mart

477 Broadway bet. Broome and Grand streets
212-966-1010
www.pearlriver.com
I've gotten the most interesting goody bag items at this home décor shop in Chinatown. From cool plastic plates to mini robots, you'll find tons of novelty gifts that won't break the bank and will have the parents inquiring about your latest finds.

Random Accessories

77 East 4th Street at Second Avenue
212-358-0650
Looking for cute gifts for your guests like mini Ugly dolls or cool action figures? You'll find a wide assortment of kitschy accessories at this East Village shop.

Party Performers

If you're having the party at your apartment or a venue that doesn't provide entertainment and the thought of having to engage twenty kids in a craft project, breaking out the acoustic for a sing-along, or dressing up like a superhero doesn't sound appealing, think of hiring some outside entertainment.

King Henry Entertainment

8005 17th Avenue at 80th Street
Brooklyn
866-546-44367

www.kinghenryent.com
From costumed characters to clowns, you will find reliable party entertainment through King Henry. The staff is extremely friendly and will work with you to help choose the perfect entertainment for your party.

Kiki's Faces and Balloons

646-435-4739
www.kikisfacesandballoons.vox.com
From balloon sculptures to face painting, Kiki's Faces and Balloons is a great resource when planning a party. This service can also provide costumed actresses dressed as princesses that will perform a mini fairy tale show.

Liam the Magician

718-437-2887
This Brooklyn-based magician is quite a hit in the Brooklyn party scene. I hired him for my daughter's fifth birthday party and was shocked at how he captivated twenty-five kids without ever getting them riled up. He really has a knack with kids, and figures out a way to get them to all participate in the show. Parties include a magic show and balloon animals.

Looney Louie

212-533-7491
www.looneylouie.com
From juggling to magic tricks, Looney Louie will entertain the guests at your party. Friends of mine who have seen him at birthday parties rave about him. His shows run about forty-five minutes. He can also perform in Spanish and French.

117

Chapter Five. Time to Party: How to Throw an Unforgettable Bash for Your Kids

Mad Science

877-662-9926

www.madscience.com

Have a fun science-themed party with Mad Science. Parties run about an hour in length and are offered at 11:15 a.m., 1:45 p.m., and 4:15 p.m. on weekends. The folks at Mad Science can host a party at any location, and the party includes science demos, take-home chemistry experiments, and more depending on your package. Parties start at $375.

NYSketches

www.nysketches.com

From face painting to caricature artists, NYSketches is a one-stop shopping resource for all party entertainment. They have an extensive list of entertainment including mimes, magicians, and much more. If you are in need of party favors, they also make beautiful and tasty custom-designed cookies. They also do party invitations.

Cakes

Searching for a yummy ending to a perfect party? Pick up a cake at one of these New York City bakeries.

Baked

359 Van Brunt Street at Dikeman Street

Brooklyn

718-222-0345

www.bakednyc.com

The yummy birthday cakes at this Red Hook bakery range from the classic chocolate or butter-cream frosted to malted chocolate cakes, carrot cakes, and red velvet cakes, among many others. Baked sug-

gests that you order the cakes two days in advance and offers a delivery service if you cannot schedule a pickup.

Cupcake Café

545 Ninth Avenue at West 40th Street

212-465-1530

18 West 18th Street bet. Fifth and Sixth avenues, inside Books of Wonder

212-989-3270

www.cupcakecafe-nyc.com

The cakes at the Cupcake Café are so beautiful that I always feel guilty eating them. Of course once I have a bite, I quickly forget about the disappearing flower atop the cake, and instead focus completely on the buttery taste. The decorators at Cupcake Cafe will work with you on the cake's design and if you're interested in learning cake-decorating tips from the masters, they also offer cake-decorating classes. The Chelsea location is also available for parties (see p. 114).

Crumbs

Check Web site for locations throughout Manhattan.

www.crumbs.com

Known for their decadent cupcakes, Crumbs bakery also happens to be my husband's favorite in New York City. Needless to say, we order cakes and cupcakes for his birthday from this beloved bakery every year. With oversize cupcakes that come with names like the Blackout—a chocolate ganache–filled cupcake topped with a chocolate cream-cheese frosting—Crumbs does not disappoint.

Eleni's

75 Ninth Avenue at West 16th Street
888-435-3647
www.elenis.com

From birthday cupcakes to decorated cookies, Eleni's is known for elaborately decorated baked goods from Eleni's mom's scrumptious recipes. The cupcakes are as good as they look, and that's saying a lot. Check out their Chelsea Market location as well.

Fairway

Check Web site for locations throughout New York City.
www.fairwaymarket.com

This New York City supermarket chain has tasty and reasonably priced sheet cakes that are perfect for large parties.

JoMart Chocolates

2917 Avenue R at Nostrand Avenue
Brooklyn
718-375-1277
www.jomartchocolates.com

If you want to make a cake at home, stop by this old-school Brooklyn chocolate shop to pick up cake molds and specialty decorating supplies. They also have a large selection of chocolate molds if you'd like to make chocolate lollipops as take-home treats or if you'd like to make chocolate flowers with the kids as an activity at the party. JoMart hosts cake-decorating classes if you'd like to brush up on your decorating skills before you present your cake to the public. The homemade chocolate at JoMart is amazing and definitely worth the trip.

Magnolia Café

Check Web site for locations throughout Manhattan.
212-724-8101
www.magnoliacupcakes.com

I don't need to celebrate a birthday to take a cupcake break at Magnolia. In recent years this West Village bakery has added two new locations in Manhattan. The cupcakes are rich, buttery and just the perfect size for little hands. Every year we get my daughter Magnolia cupcakes for our family birthday party. Beyond cupcakes, they also offer tasty birthday cakes, puddings, and other goodies for your party.

Margaret Palca Bakes

191 Columbia Street at Degraw Street
Brooklyn
718-802-9771
www.margaretpalcabakes.com

This Brooklyn bakery will put any design on a cake. In fact I was shocked at how pretty (and tasty) their Thomas the Tank Engine birthday cake was at my son's birthday party. Just call in your order and the cake should be ready within forty-eight hours.

New York Cake & Baking Distributors

6 West 22nd Street at Sixth Avenue
212-675-CAKE
www.nycake.com

Want to bake your own cake? You'll definitely get inspired after a visit to this NYC baking supply shop. Filled with molds and all the accessories needed to make the perfect birthday cake, I cannot walk in the shop without walking out with a ton of baking supplies and cute decorations for cupcakes. Please note that this shop is closed on Sundays.

Sweet Melissa Patisserie

276 Court Street bet. Douglass and Butler streets
Brooklyn
718-858-3410
www.sweetmelissapatisserie.com
This fancy Brooklyn bakery offers folks fancy cakes that are both gorgeous and delectable and will appeal to adults and kids alike. If you are in search of cupcakes, Sweet Melissa's also has a nice selection of cupcakes and other treats. You can also have a birthday tea party at Sweet Melissa's; call for pricing.

Chapter Six

Family Outings:

Weekends In and Around the City

With the crazy world of family schedules, sometimes your family needs a break. If your weekend is filled with birthday parties, classes, and errands, then you're like every NYC parent trying to squeeze a lifetime in one weekend. Well, take a break from the daily grind and have some fun with the kids in and around New York City. I'm going to sound a little hokey, but our family tries to plan days where we do nothing but have fun—when we go out and do something as a family that doesn't include a side trip to the grocery store or another errand.

In this chapter, I'll give you the skinny on some fun activities to do with your city kids. From spending an afternoon ice-skating to a day trip upstate to pick your own pumpkin, you'll find many ways to create lasting family memories. With lots of weekend getaway ideas and a list of botanical gardens, there is so much to do in and around this kid-friendly city. With any of the opportunities described in two sections—In Town, which gives you the rundown on what to do in this amazing city, and Out of Town, which offers you the best places to go outside the city—you are certain to spend a memorable weekend with the kids. Have fun!

In Town

Stuck in the city on the weekend or looking for some fun after-school activities? From movies to nature preserves, there is so much to see beyond the "tourist" sites of the city.

Movies

You don't have to wait for Pixar to release a new film to get the kids to the theater; there are tons of kid-friendly film festivals and series offered year-round in New York City. Sure, you can always take your kids to see the latest kid-flick, but the opportunity to experience a film series at one of the following NYC theaters will expose your children to the exciting world of cinema and teach them to appreciate good films.

BAMKid's Film Festival

30 Lafayette Avenue at St. Felix Street
Brooklyn
718-636-4100
www.bam.org

This annual children's film festival is held in March at the Brooklyn Academy of Music and offers kids ages two and up the chance to view international films and shorts. There are many other events to experience throughout the festival, like concerts in the lobby and a "BAMmie" award ceremony where kids get to vote for their favorite film. My kids love the voting process and that we can check the results on the BAM Web site to see if the film they chose had won. We never miss seeing the shorts at this popular festival in Brooklyn. Word of advice—get tickets way in advance as the films sell out very quickly.

Big Movies for Little Kids

Cobble Hill Cinemas
265 Court Street at Butler Street
Brooklyn
718-596-9113
www.bigmoviesforlittlekids.blogspot.com

This bimonthly film series running throughout the school year offers kids a gentle introduction to the wide world of cinema. The films in this series are thoughtfully chosen by two local moms and are always a hit with the kids. From Wallace & Gromit shorts to *Pippi Longstocking*—the films will captivate your children. Films are shown on Mondays at 4 p.m. Be sure to get tickets early since shows sell out fast.

Top Ten New York City Kid Movies

Here's a list of the top ten New York City kid movies from Allison Prete and Teri Cunningham, the creators of the Big Movies for Little Kids series (see above).

❋ *Muppets Take Manhattan* Kermit, Miss Piggy, Gonzo, and the gang seek their name in lights on Broadway, leading to hilarity and a lesson in the power of friendship.

❋ *Ghostbusters* A team of zany, oddball scientists become heroes in this laugh-out-loud romp about supernatural pest control. "Who ya' gonna call?"

❋ *Enchanted* A classic fairy-tale princess begins a hopeful search for her true love to spend a happily-ever-after in gritty and chaotic modern-day Manhattan.

❋ *Speedy Awesome* vintage footage of New York City from 1928 including horse-drawn V trolleys and Babe Ruth playing at Yankee Stadium.

❋ *Little Manhattan* A touching tale of two eleven-year-old classmates who head downtown to explore and discover the greatest adventure of all.

❋ *A Night at the Museum* The American Museum of Natural History delightfully comes to life in the most wonderful, wacky way in this fun comedy.

❋ *Stuart Little* A sweet tale of a mouse with moxie who learns the true meaning of family when adopted by the Littles in Manhattan.

❋ *Curly Top* and *Little Miss Broadway* In *Curly Top*, spunky Shirley Temple hits the Hamptons with pluck and tap shoes. In *Little Miss Broadway*, the irresistible golden girl, as precocious as ever, finds her big break on the Great White Way.

❄ **The Little Fugitive** Endearing seven-year-old Joey runs off, wandering through Coney Island, and experiences adventures, tricks, mysteries, and wonders in this charming indie film.

❄ **Big** Be careful what you wish for! In this remarkable film with a lot of heart, Josh becomes an adult overnight, and begins working for a toy company and realizes that perhaps it's not so great to be a grown-up.

Jackson Heights Kid's Film Festival

Eagle Movie Theater
73-07 37th Road at 73rd Street
Queens
718-393-7711
www.jhfff.org
This locally run annual film festival lasts only one day and screens animated shorts from around the world. The Eagle Movie Theater in Jackson Heights is known for showing refresh releases from Bollywood (older kids might like a visit to the Eagle Movie Theater even when the festival isn't running since Bollywood movies are so lively).

New York International Children's Film Festival

See Web site for locations throughout Manhattan
212-349-0330
www.gkids.com

This annual children's film festival runs for a little over two weeks and screens both feature-length films and shorts from around the world. Founded in 1997, the festival is geared towards kids ages three through eighteen, although I'll admit I also liked many of the films. Get tickets early because these shows sell out quickly.

Tribeca Film Festival

See Web site for a list of locations throughout New York City.
212-965-2800
www.tribecafilm.com
This extremely popular annual downtown film festival hosts an outdoor "drive-in" kid-friendly screenings.

Tribeca Grand Film Series

2 Sixth Avenue at Walker Street
212-519-6600
www.tribecagrand.com
The Tribeca Grand offers kids the opportunity to see classic children's films for free in their posh screening room during their opulent Sunday brunch from 10 a.m. until 3 p.m. Parents can dine on an array of culinary delights while their children can chomp on complimentary popcorn as they take in memorable films like *The Wizard of Oz* and Disney classics.

Getting Active

City kids get exercise walking everywhere in the city, but that doesn't give them an excuse to sit in front of the TV or computer and not participate in sports. From climbing walls to bowling, kids and their parents can bond as they enjoy these athletic activities around the city.

Bowling

Kids can practice tying their laces on their cool rented bowling shoes as they attempt to hit some strikes at these atmospheric NYC bowling alleys. All of the venues below host kid's birthday parties as well.

AMF 34th Avenue Lanes

69-10 34th Avenue at 69th Street
Queens
718-651-0440
www.amf.com

This AMF bowling alley located in Woodside, Queens, attracts the locals as it's not far from the city and close to the bustling Jackson Heights neighborhood. It costs $5.75 per game and $5.50 for shoe rental. They also have youth leagues for kids ages five and up.

Big Apple Bowling & Fun Center at Whitestone Lanes

30-05 Whitestone Expressway at Lincoln Place
Queens
718-353-6300
www.whitestonebowling.com

If your family is dealing with a bout of insomnia or if you don't know what to do at 7 a.m. on a Saturday morning when everyone is awake, consider heading to Whitestone Bowling which is open 24 hours a day. Games range from $4.50 to $7.00, with an additional $4.50 for shoe rental.

Bowlmor

110 University Place bet. East 12th and 13th streets
212-255-8188
www.bowlmor.com

This popular Village bowling alley attracts a crowd, so try to go early in the afternoon to avoid a wait. The bowling alley opens at 11 a.m. on weekends. Games range from $9.45 to $12.95, depending on time of day, and you have to shell out $6 for shoe rental.

Gil Hodges Lanes

6161 Strickland Avenue at Mill Avenue
Brooklyn
718-763-6800
www.gilhodgeslanes.com

Gil Hodges Lanes offers an economical family fun pack in which families get two hours of bowling for up to six people, including shoe rental, for $49.99. They host Junior Leagues, and kids can also join their bowling club, where for $14 a week they get to bowl two games with free shoe rental.

Harlem Lanes

2116 7th Avenue at West 126th Street, 3rd floor
212-678-2695
www.harlemlanes.com

This bowling alley located in the heart of Harlem offers folks good family fun with twenty-four lanes of bowling. Games range from $5.50 to $7.50, depending on the time of day, and shoe rental costs $4.50 per pair. After honing your bowling form, take a walking tour of this historic NYC neighborhood. Just to note, you have to be twenty-one and older to enter the lanes after 8 p.m. on Saturday nights.

Leisure Time Bowl

625 Eighth Avenue at West 42nd Street, 2nd floor
212-268-6909
www.leisuretimebowl.com

Located in the Port Authority, this Midtown bowling alley has been recently renovated. Games range from $5.50 to $9.50, depending on time of day. You can also reserve a lane online. There is a six-person limit per lane.

Lucky Strike

624-660 West 42nd Street at Twelfth Avenue
646-829-0170
www.bowlluckystrike.com

This new bowling alley located right off the West Side Highway opens at noon every day. They have an interesting deal where they charge $55 per lane on weekdays for up to ten people or you can just pay $8.95 per person for a game. Parents with children have to be out of the alley by 5:30 p.m., because after that time the lanes are for people over twenty-one.

Melody Lanes Bowling Center

461 37th Street bet. Fourth and Fifth Avenues
Brooklyn
718-832-2695

Located in Sunset Park, Brooklyn, this alley is a popular place for birthday parties of children from neighboring Park Slope and Carroll Gardens. This is a real neighborhood bowling alley with a diverse crowd. Games cost $6 during the day and $7 for games after 5 p.m. Shoe rental only costs $4.

300 New York at the Chelsea Piers Sports and Entertainment Complex

23rd Street at the Hudson River
212-835-2695
www.3hundred.com

Enjoy bowling the day away at this uber-hip bowling alley located at the Chelsea Piers. After you bowl a game, you can sit by the water and watch the boats pass. Shoe rental is $6 and a game costs $8-10 per person depending on time of day or weekend rates.

Good Old-Fashioned Fun

Buzz-A-Rama 500
69 Church Avenue at Dahill Road
Brooklyn
718-853-1800

There was a time when there used to be a ton of places to race slot cars all over Manhattan, but today there is only one shop where kids can feel the thrill of racing small cars on a track. Make the trek out to Kensington, Brooklyn, to Buzz-A-Rama 500, if your kids feel the need for speed. Although it's usually open on Saturday afternoons, I'd advise calling ahead.

Ice Skating

Bundle up and skate around the city at the following NYC-area ice skating rinks. Don't forget to reward yourself with a hot cocoa, either. From outdoor ice-skating rinks at the American Museum of Natural History to public rinks located on the Coney Island boardwalk, you can skate all over this amazing city. Just to note, you can throw a birthday party at almost all of the skating venues below.

Abe Stark Ice

Coney Island Boardwalk at West 19th Street
Brooklyn
718-946-6536
www.nycgovparks.org

This Coney Island ice-skating rink, located on the boardwalk, is only open weekends from 1 p.m. until 4 p.m. during the months of October through the beginning of April. Admission to the rinks costs $8 per person for open skating and $5 for skate rental.

Aviator Sports and Recreation

Floyd Bennett Field at Flatbush Avenue
Brooklyn
718-758-7500
www.aviatorsports.com

Skate year-round at this Brooklyn sports complex. With two indoor rinks, you won't be kicked off the rink for hockey practice as one is designated for open skating. If your kid is a hockey fan, they have league hockey teams for kids ages five and up as well as figure-skating lessons. Admission costs $8 for adults and $6 for kids, and $4.50 for skate rental.

The Pond at Bryant Park

42nd Street bet. Fifth and Sixth avenues
212-768-4242
www.thepondatbryantpark.com

You know it's the holiday season when the ice-skating rink opens at Bryant Park. The best thing about the rink is that it's free! If you don't have skates you can rent them here. This rink tends to get quite crowded on the weekends, but it's a wonderful place to head to after school since it isn't too busy on weekday afternoons.

Chelsea Piers Sky Rink at the Chelsea Piers Sports and Entertainment Complex

23rd Street at the Hudson River
212-336-6100
www.chelseapiers.com

Kids can ice-skate in July at this year-round indoor skating rink that offers skating lessons and hosts hockey leagues. Open skate admission costs $13 for adults and $10.50 for kids with an additional $7.50 for skate rental. Chelsea Piers Sky Rink also hosts a popular skate camp in the summer.

City Ice Pavilion

47-23 32nd Place at 47th Avenue
Queens
718-505-6230
www.cityicepavilion.com

Make figure eights at this new rooftop ice-skating rink in Long Island City, Queens. The rink is only open seasonally and costs $5 for open skating admission on weekdays, and $8 on weekends with an additional $6 for skate rental. They also host parties and offer skating instruction.

Wollman Rink at Prospect Park

Prospect Park at Ocean Avenue entrance
Brooklyn
718-287-6431
www.prospectpark.org/wollman_rink

The sun always seems to shine at this outdoor Brooklyn ice-skating rink. The staff at Wollman rink provides skating lessons and also offers party packages if you'd like to celebrate a birthday here. Just to note, the Prospect Alliance is building a new ice-skating rink called the Lakeside to replace the aging Wollman Rink. Lakeside is scheduled to open in 2011, pending funding.

Seaport Ice Rink

Pier 17 at South Street and Fulton Street
212-661-6640
www.thenewseaport.com

Located on Pier 17 of the South Street Seaport, Seaport Ice offers a unique skating experience during New York City's winters. The rink first opened during the winter of 2008 and plans on returning each holiday season. You can skate from 12 p.m. until 8 p.m. on Sunday through Thursday and from 12 p.m. until 10 p.m. on Fridays and Saturdays. General admission costs $5 with an additional $7 to rent skates. You can also host birthday parties at the rink.

World Ice Arena in Flushing Meadows Corona Park

Corona Park at Avery Avenue
Queens
718-760-9001
www.worldice.pucksystems.com

The indoor skating rink in Flushing Meadows Corona Park offers open skating and a summer skate camp. In addition to camp, kids can take a skate lesson or have their birthday party at this local rink. Open skating costs $5 on weekdays and $8 on weekends with an additional $5 skate rental fee.

Roller Skating

Roller skating played such a large role in my childhood, and although many of the city's roller rinks have shut their doors, you can still a roll around these New York City rinks.

Dreamland Roller Rink

3052 West 21st Street at Surf Avenue
Brooklyn
800-362-5116
www.dreamlandrollerrink.com

Located inside the historical Childs Building in Coney Island, Brooklyn, this unique roller rink is the brainchild of the owner of the famous Lola Star shop (www.lolastar.com) on the Coney Island boardwalk. On Saturdays during the summer, Dreamland offers family skating at this funky roller rink from 2 p.m. until 6 p.m. Admission costs $10 per person and skate rental costs $5. Dreamland is also open for parties.

RollerJam USA

236 Richmond Valley Road at Page Avenue
Staten Island
718-605-6600
www.rollerjamusa.com

Family skate session is from 1 p.m. until 8 p.m. on Saturdays and 1 p.m. until 6 p.m. on Sundays at New York City's old school skating rink located in Tottenville, Staten Island. Admissions costs $9.50 plus the cost of the skate rental. After skating around the rink to pop music, head to Eggers Ice Cream Parlor (see p. 73) for a scoop.

Pools

It's hot in the city during the summer and you don't want to spend your days sitting in an air-conditioned apartment. Cool yourself down at some of New York City's pools. Some pools are free while others cost a small fee. Many branches of the YMCA and the Jewish Community Center have pools, but they are only open to members; consider joining one to sign your kid up for swimming lessons or take advantage of open swim sessions. Indoor or outdoor, splash your day away.

Astoria Sports Complex

3438 38th Street bet. 34th and 35th avenues

Queens

718-729-7163

www.ascsports1.com

Nonmembers can swim for $10 on weekdays and $15 on weekends. You must wear a swim cap while in the water but if you've forgotten yours, you can buy one from their shop on the premises. No children are allowed in the pool after 8 p.m.

The Floating Pool

www.floatingpool.org

www.nycgovparks.org

This floating pool barge is run by the NYC Department of Parks and Recreation and docks at a different New York City ports each summer. The barge has been stationed in Brooklyn and the Bronx in past summers, so check the schedule to see where it will travel next. Smartly designed, the pool offers folks the chance to escape the heat, and also hosts free swim classes for kids.

NYC Public Pools

www.nycgovparks.org

From the famed Astoria pool to the Red Hook pool, the city has many free public pools to beat the humidity. Check the city's Web site for a listing of area pools, both indoors and outdoors, at various recreation centers throughout the city. Please note that some recreation centers charge a small fee for use of the pool.

New York Spa Castle

131-10 Eleventh Avenue at 131st Street

Queens

718-939-6300

www.nyspacastle.com

Folks bring their kids of all ages to enjoy splashing and relaxing at the rooftop pools and saunas at this Korean spa. It costs $35 to enter the spa on weekdays and $45 on weekends. There is a discount for children under three feet tall.

Indoor Play Spaces and Arcades

Here are some fun places to get some energy out when it's too cold to head to the playground. Many of these play spaces also host birthday parties.

Bounce U

6722 Fort Hamilton Parkway at 67th Street

Brooklyn

718-238-3288

132-25 14th Avenue at 132nd Street

Queens

718-747-JUMP

www.bounceu.com

Kids will love expending energy while bouncing around this large space that is filled with bouncy structures. There are two locations, one in Brooklyn and one in College Point, Queens. An hour of bouncing in Brooklyn costs $15 per child and $13 per child in Queens. Check their Web site for both open bounce and family bounce times.

Chuck E. Cheese

Check Web site for locations throughout New York City.

www.chuckecheese.com

When I was growing up I used to beg my parents to go to the Chuck E. Cheese in Bay Ridge. Although this location no longer exists, there are still a bunch of Chuck E. Cheese restaurants around the city. At the arcades, kids have the option of jumping in a ball pit, playing video games, and eating pizza. The playroom is divided by age with a separate toddler space, so that parents don't have to worry about their little kids being trampled. The place tends to get very crowded, so try to visit between meals.

Kids 'n Action

1149 McDonald Avenue bet. avenues I and J
Brooklyn
718-377-1818
www.kidsnaction.com

This Brooklyn indoor play space boasts an enormous maze with a ball pit, roller coaster, go carts, and train ride. Kids 'n Action is a kosher establishment so you cannot bring outside food into the space, but they do have pizza available in their small café. This play space closes early on Fridays and is also closed on Saturdays. Admission costs $13 on weekdays and $14 on Sundays and includes unlimited rides and time on the play enormous indoor playground with slides and ball pits. Kids 'n Action also offers video games for older kids with an additional charge.

Mad Fun

303 Stanley Avenue at Snediker Avenue
Brooklyn
718-498-9402
www.maddfun.com

From laser tag and arts and crafts to bumper cars and a rock wall your kids will love a day at this Brooklyn indoor play center. An excellent choice for a birthday party venue, this play space is also extremely popular with camp groups, so it can get

quite crowded during the summer. Don't worry if you haven't packed a snack for the kids, Mad Fun has a food court on the premises.

Nature Preserves, Nature Centers, Nature Walks, and Farms

Learn about nature in the city at these urban nature centers, farms, and walks—all of which will make your kids feel as if they live in the country. If you want a listing of all nature-related events, consider getting a free subscription to the quarterly newspaper Outdoors in NYC. You can subscribe by calling 311 or going to www.nycgovparks.org.

Alley Pond Environmental Center

228-06 Northern Boulevard
Queens
718-229-4000
www.alleypond.com

This environmental center and park covers over six hundred acres and offers both bike and nature trails. The nature center on the premises houses many animals and offers classes for kids including family-oriented nature workshops. The center also hosts themed hikes, from haunted Halloween walks to educational nature walks. In the evenings they have astronomy classes for families where you can stargaze with your little ones. When my daughter and I participated in the family camping program through the parks department and spent the night sleeping at Alley Pond Park, she was shocked to see the abundance of stars in the night sky.

The Urban Ranger Program hosts many programs at Alley Pond Park and they have a large adventure course for families where you can try rope climbing and other challenging activities that you'd see on an episode of *Survivor*. The course is mainly for families with kids ages eight and up, and it is available for free—on a first come, first served basis—on Sundays at 10 a.m. and at 1:30 p.m. in May through November, as weather permits. Alley Pond also offers a day and overnight adventure program for kids to learn how to canoe, fish, and put up a tent; call the Urban Rangers for more information (718-846-2731).

The Audubon Center at Prospect Park
Prospect Park, at Lincoln Road/Ocean Avenue
entrance to Prospect Park
718-287-6215
www.prospectpark.org/audubon
Introduce your child to the world of nature in Prospect Park's boathouse-turned-nature-center. The Audubon Center hosts weekend events during which they educate kids about birds, bugs, and other parts of nature that appeal to kids. They also offer a free class for kids ages three and up every Friday at 3 p.m. On Saturdays at 1 p.m., the Audubon Center invites bird lovers to their free introduction to bird-watching class for all ages. Check the park's Web site for a list of weekly events.

Beyond classes, the amenities at the center include immaculate restrooms and the Songbird Café, which is a nice place to relax and look out onto the lake. On weekends from spring through early autumn, they also offer electric boat rides, which often have a seasonal theme or a focus on bird-watching.

Greenbelt Nature Center
700 Rockland Avenue at Brielle Avenue
Staten Island
718-351-3450
www.sigreenbelt.org

You'll have access to trails and amazing hikes for all levels at the Greenbelt Nature Center; just stop by the center and pick up a trail map—and go ahead and peruse their nature exhibits of creatures native to Staten Island, like raccoons. Don't forget to say hi to their live turtle and snake. The nature center also hosts events throughout the year—from family carnivals to nature workshops on ladybugs to hosting birthday parties and a summer camp for kids. This is a gentle place to introduce your kids to the world of nature; however, adults should feel welcome, too, as the center offers art classes for those who would like to learn to draw the natural surroundings.

If you're adventurous, take the kids on the "white" trail, which will lead you on an hour-long hike to their carousel. You can also just drive to the beautiful carousel; the staff is extremely friendly and helpful and will provide you with driving directions.

The Henry Luce Nature Observatory
Central Park at 79th Street
212-772-0210
www.centralparknyc.org
My kids and I love heading to the Henry Luce Observatory in Belvedere Castle at Central Park and afterward walking along the scenic ramble just outside the observatory grounds. This gorgeous building offers stunning views of the park as well as a collection of nature-related items like skeletons of small animals and stuffed birds. Young bird-watchers and nature lovers can borrow binoculars from the center to explore the wildlife. A cool fact about the nature center is that it's also an operational weather station.

Jamaica Bay Wildlife Refuge

Cross Bay Boulevard at Broad Channel

Brooklyn

718-318-4340

www.nps.gov/gate; www.nyharborparks.org

If you have a car or can rent one, visit both the Salt Marsh Nature Center and the Jamaica Bay Wildlife Refuge on the same day since they are both easily accessible from the Belt Parkway. After a trip to each of these nature centers you can compare the different marshlands and the various forms of wildlife you see on the trails. The Wildlife Refuge trail covers over nine thousand acres, but the main trail at the refuge is just a mile and a half loop around the water. My kids loved exploring the nature exhibits in the center. For tired parents, there are many benches where you can sit and watch the birds, and the bathrooms are immaculate.

Queens County Farm Museum

73-50 Little Neck Parkway at 74th Avenue

Queens

718-347-3276

www.queensfarm.org

We make an annual trek to this unique farm museum in the middle of Queens to partake in one of their many festivals that range from apple fests to Indian powwows. There is so much to see at this 47-acre working farm museum: you can go on hayrides, feed sheep and goats, even tour a historic farmhouse. At the Queens County Farm Museum you can expose your child to a farm that is both free *and* reachable by public transportation. Their popular Farm Fest in May when they shear sheep is not to be missed!

Salt Marsh Nature Center

3302 Avenue U at East 33rd Street

Brooklyn

718-421-2021

www.saltmarshalliance.org

You'll feel far removed from the world of hipster Brooklyn when you venture to this nature center and stroll on the pleasant and extremely easy trail behind the center. The trail will take you around the marshlands, where you can see the remnants of one of the first working mills in North America. Since the walk isn't challenging, it can be enjoyed by all and can take anywhere from fifteen minutes to an hour, depending on your pace.

The Salt Marsh also offers bike trails and a large park across the street. The nature center hosts nature classes for kids and also shows kid-friendly movies at night during the summer; check their schedule on their Web site. The nature center also offers canoeing programs for kids ages eight and up; we saw them on our walk having a great time.

Camping in the City

Family Camping Program: New York Parks and Recreations

Check the Web site for participating parks.

311

www.nycgovparks.org

This free program run by the Urban Park Rangers introduces New Yorkers to the beauty of the outdoors. All you need to bring is a sleeping bag on this unique city adventure and you get to spend the night camping in a city park. The family-friendly evening begins with a cookout, followed by a lesson for city folks on how to pitch a tent. Other evening activities include guided nature walks, night hikes, stargazing, and making s'mores by a campfire. The family camping session ends early the following morning, when participants are offered breakfast and help dissembling the tent (I'll admit I was alone with my daughter and asked for help).

The program runs on Friday and Saturday nights throughout the summer alternating between various parks throughout the five boroughs. You can only sign up for one camping night each summer, which was much to my daughter's dismay since she had the best time camping in the park. Just to note, although some people brought younger kids, the program was really suited for kids ages five and up. The median age of the kids on our trip was seven years old.

Spots fill up quickly, and you must call at 9 a.m. on the Monday before the weekend you'd like to camp in order to reserve a spot.

Camping in an Old Airport at Floyd Bennett Field

Floyd Bennett Field at Flatbush Avenue
718-338-3799
www.nyharborparks.org/visit/flbe.html
If you're really adventurous and want to camp on your own, head to the defunct city airport-turned-park, where you can take your bike on the runways. For $50, you can apply for a permit to camp at one of the four public campsites for three days—the only campsites in New York City where you can camp without an accompanying ranger. Accommoda-

tions include a barbecue pit and public bathrooms. Many people choose to rent the space for large family get-togethers and don't actually stay the night. If you want to have a fun night doing cool coastal camping at an airport that once hosted historic flights from Amelia Earhart and Charles Lindbergh, this is a unique experience. Perhaps you'll feel haunted by the ghosts of these legendary aviators.

NYC Parks and Gardens

Spend the day engaging in children's activities in city parks and gardens. Even if you live in a walk-up without any light, with these family programs and classes available, your children can learn how to nurture their green thumbs.

Brooklyn Botanical Garden

1000 Washington Avenue at Crown Street
Brooklyn
718-623-7200
www.bbg.org
This 52-acre garden in Brooklyn boasts magnificent roses, a children's garden, the wonderful Steinhardt Conservatory, as well as my personal favorite, the Japanese Hill–and-Pond Garden, among other gardens. The children's garden offers drop-in activities like classes and family programs throughout the day. On Tuesdays the garden is free, which makes for a nice midweek day trip when school is not in session.

Conservatory Garden at Central Park

105th Street and Fifth Avenue at Vanderbilt Gate
311
www.centralparknyc.org

This six-acre garden in Central Park offers Saturday morning tours at 11 a.m. from April through October. Access to the garden is free and its blooming flowers are a true pleasure to walk through with kids.

Forest Park

Myrtle Avenue at Union Turnpike
Queens
311
www.nycgovparks.org

This Queens park is over five hundred acres in size and boasts a horseback-riding academy, a beautiful carousel, and a band shell where they offer free seasonal concerts. The park is a lovely place to take the kids on a pony ride, a spin on the carousel, or to have a picnic.

The High Line

Gansevoort Street to 34th Street bet. Tenth and Eleventh Avenues
212-206-9922
www.thehighline.org

I've been waiting for this elevated to park to open for years and was so excited to visit when it became available to the public in June 2009. Located on an old elevated train line, the park offers family programs that focus on gardening as well as craft workshops and other activities. Stroll at this unique new addition to the NYC parks program.

Narrows Botanical Gardens

Shore Road bet. Bay Ridge Avenue and 72nd Street
Brooklyn
718-238-1692
www.narrowsbg.org

Stroll through this four-and-a-half-acre garden created by volunteers, who transformed this stretch of waterfront property into a gorgeous area with a lovely rose garden. I like to take my kids to this garden to show them that if a community gets together they can accomplish beautiful things.

New York Botanical Garden

Bronx River Parkway at Fordham Road
Bronx
718-817-8700
www.nybg.org

This 250-acre Bronx garden will satisfy any nature lover, especially with the added plus that the garden is free from 10 a.m. until 12 p.m. on Saturdays. The gardens offer two family-friendly places to visit, the Everett Children's Adventure Garden and the Ruth Rea Howell Family Garden, both of which are specifically designed with hands-on activities for kids. The gardens offer children's programs for kids between the ages of three through twelve, as well as activities for the entire family. We love to visit in the winter when they host their popular annual holiday train show, where you can see model trains ride around replicas of NYC landmarks. You can even picnic in their designated picnic area. These gardens are a true paradise, less than a half hour from Manhattan.

Queens Botanical Gardens

43-50 Main Street at Dahlia Avenue
Queens
718-886-3800
www.queensbotanical.org

The Queens Botanical Gardens are free and open year-round, making it a lovely place for a nice stroll or to take the kids for an afternoon at their children's garden. The garden offers hands-on classes for children ages five through twelve to teach them about plants, gardens, and nature, while they enjoy playing in a beautiful environment. Check their Web site for a full schedule of events.

Staten Island Botanical Garden

1000 Richmond Terrace at Snug Harbor
Staten Island
718-448-2500
www.snug-harbor.org

Every New York City kid must take a ferry across the river to see the beauty of Snug Harbor, where they can visit the treasured New York Chinese Scholar's Garden. There it's hard not to find both peace and tranquility as you sit on a bench in the Moon Viewing Pavilion. Your kids can also take a romp through the scenic Secret Garden located on the grounds. There is a minimal charge to enter the two specialty gardens, but the rest of the grounds are without charge. The garden offers educational programs for kids and hosts events throughout the year.

You can easily spend the entire day in Staten Island with a trip to the botanical garden as well as a visit to any one of the neighboring museums nearby like the Staten Island Children's Museum (see p. 50) or the **Snug Harbor Cultural Center** (www.snug-harbor.org), which are both part of the Snug Harbor complex. This is the perfect afternoon for families who want to participate in activities for both adults and kids.

Wave Hill

West 249th Street at Independence Avenue
Bronx
718-549-3200
www.wavehill.org

This 28-acre public garden in the Bronx has a wide variety of weekend family programs that combine both art and nature, from making a bird's nest to designing T-shirts. You can also tour the galleries on Saturdays at 2:15 p.m. and the lush gardens on Sundays at 2:15 p.m.

Outdoor Kids Festivals and Events in NYC

From concert series to festivals, check out the abundance of free children's events in the city.

Carroll Park Kids' Concerts Series
www.carrollparkbrooklyn.org
June–August
The organization Friends of Carroll Park offers this popular concert series held at a local playground in Carroll Gardens. The concerts are free and afterward your kids can run in the park sprinkler or at the playground.

Children's Day at the South Street Seaport
www.childrensdaynyc.com
June
Children's Day was created in 1993 and originally held at the World Trade Center after the first tragedy at the Towers. After 9/11, the festival was moved to the South Street Seaport and attracts families from around the city with a full day of activities from musical performances to arts and crafts.

City Parks Foundation
www.cityparksfoundation.org

Spring and summer
The City Parks Foundation hosts a ton of free kid-friendly activities, from traveling puppet shows to musical performances throughout the various city Parks. Check out their Web site for a full schedule.

Governors Island Family Festival
www.governorsislandalliance.org
May
Held annually during the opening weekend for Governors Island, this festival includes live music and other family-friendly activities.

Madison Square Park Conservancy
www.madisonsquarepark.org
Spring and summer
This organization hosts a popular annual kid fest in the spring at Madison Square Park as well as a free summer-long kids' concert series.

NYC KidsFest in Morningside Park
www.nyckidsfest.com
June
Held in Morningside Park, this free uptown children's festival attracts many local families who come to participate in arts and craft projects and to watch everything from double dutch teams to musical performances.

Macy's Fishing Contest
Prospect Park, Brooklyn
www.prospectpark.org/calendar/event/fishingcontest
July

Go Fish!
Battery Park, Manhattan
www.bpcparks.org/bpcp/events/events.php
October

Out of Town

Escape the city streets for a day trip to a farm. From a family-friendly weekend away to a day trip, there is a lot to see right outside the city.

Local Farms

Pick your own fruit off the vine rather than at your local bodega at the following area farms that are within an hour and a half from Manhattan:

Alstede Farms
84 Route 513 (Old Route 24)
Chester, NJ
908-879-7189
www.alstedefarms.com
Pick strawberries and cut your own flowers at this New Jersey Farm. Alstede also offers pony rides and a bouncy castle on weekends, which makes it quite a hit with the kids. I love that you can cut fresh flowers as well as pick red, black, and purple raspberries, and currants, blackberries, peaches, peppers, tomatoes, eggplants, and apples. You can also feed the animals at the farm or crawl through their famed hay tunnel in the autumn; see their Web site for a list of seasonal events. We like to combine a strawberry-picking trip at Alstede with a visit to the **Valley Shepherd Creamery** (50 Fairmount Road, Long Valley, NJ; 908-876-3200; www.valleyshepherd.com) where you can watch dairy farmers making cheese.

Applewood Orchards

82 Four Corners Road
Warwick, NY
845-986-1684
www.applewoodorchards.com

Warwick is known for its many orchards, and although we've been to most of them, Applewood is a nice, quiet orchard that offers a petting zoo, puppet shows, and other kid-friendly activities. We like to combine a trip here with a visit to the **Warwick Drive-in** as well as to my personal favorite, **Bellvale Farms** (385 Route 17A, Warwick, NY; 845-988-1818; www.bellvalefarms.com), which sells the best homemade ice cream around atop Mt. Peter. This is to the perfect place take in the view after a day picking apples and before you head to the movies.

Lawrence Farms Orchards

39 Colandrea Road
Newburgh, NY
845-562-4268
www.lawrencefarmsorchards.com

You can pick a lot more than apples at this Newburgh Farm. In the summer you can pick strawberries, apricots, and peaches as well as vegetables like broccoli and eggplant. If you don't want to pick fruits or veggies, visit their large shop filled with their locally grown goodies. In the fall, you can try to escape from their fun corn maze, which (I have to admit) took me longer than I thought it would. Lawrence Farms Orchards also offers a kid-size village, where my kids love hanging out in the little homes, the small church, and jail.

The Orchards of Concklin

2 South Mountain Road
Pomona, NY
www.theorchardsofconcklin.com

Located right outside the city in Westchester, these orchards give folks the chance to pick everything from strawberries and apples to flowers. Sometimes they even offer apple cider, which you can sip on while your kids bounce around the bouncy castle. The Orchards of Concklin host many seasonal events, so check the schedule on their Web site.

Stone Barns Center for Food and Agriculture

630 Bedford Road
Pocantico, NY
914-366-6200
www.stonebarnscenter.org

Stone Barns Center for Food and Agriculture offers farm education programs on weekends. One of their family programs allows families to feed chickens and then collect their own eggs.

Terhune Orchards

330 Cold Soil Road
Princeton, NJ
609-924-2310
www.terhuneorchards.com

Located in Princeton, New Jersey, Terhune Orchards lets folks pick their own apples and pumpkins. One of the reasons why this orchard is great for kids is that the apples are grown on dwarf trees so they are easy to pick, unlike the standard variety of trees where you often need a stick to remove the apples from high branches. This orchard requires very little work and you can catch a hayride or visit the petting zoo with the kids. In addition to apples, you can pick a variety of fruit including strawberries and cherries. Don't forget to grab some cider and tasty doughnuts for the ride home!

Summer Fun:

Camp and Other Summertime Adventures

School's out and you don't know what to do with your kids? Don't worry, there are tons of amazing camps in and around the city where kids can enjoy a range of activities from learning about the *Intrepid* to heading out on the water at a sailing camp. Of course summer isn't the only time when kids are off from school, and since most people can't take off work during every break that their kids get, there are many fun places for kids to spend midwinter recess and spring breaks; I've placed a star next to the following camps that offer a week of activities for kids on school breaks. It's also okay if you envy your kid's summer plans now that they're signed up for a truly one-of-a-kind summer break—I'll admit that I found myself wishing that I could go back to camp while working on this chapter.

Although I have an extensive list of camps, many of which came highly recommended, I feel that choosing a camp is an extremely personal process in serving your own child's needs. When I was a child, my main priority was finding a camp that didn't require that you go swimming, and I ended up choosing an art camp that had a mandatory classical music assembly. Although I loved it, many kids would shudder at the thought of attending that camp. I've recommended camps to friends that my daughter loved and their kids weren't thrilled with. Talk to your child and make a list with them about what they'd like to do for the summer. You should also tour the camp and ask questions—and don't be afraid to ask for references.

Since there is a myriad of camps in the city to choose from, I tried to break down this chapter by theme to make it easy for you to use. I've also high-lighted camp fairs, camp associations, and organizations that host camps.

Camp Fairs

The New York Family and American Camp Association holds the Blackboard Camp Fair at various locations in New York City in November and January. The fairs have representatives from many area camps (over forty camps participate), from sleep-away to day camps. This is a great way to research a bunch of camps at once. There are also many suburban camps that attend the fair as well. Check out the Blackboard Camp Fair's Web site for more information on the camps that are represented (www.blackboardcamps.com).

Camp Associations

Many camps are affiliated or accredited through different organizations. I've listed many organizations that have a Web site with a user-friendly database of regional camps. Just type in the age of your child, their interests, and desired location into the search bar and you'll find a ton of camps that are appropriate for your camper.

American Camp Association

800-777-CAMP

www.acacamps.org

Lists all accredited camps through the American Camp Association.

Jewish Summer Camp

www.jewishsummercamp.com

Lists Jewish camps around the NYC area, from sleepaway to day camps.

Summer Camps on College Campuses

www.summeroncampus.com

Lists all area colleges that host summer camps for kids ages eight through eighteen.

Organizations Offering Summer Camps

From the Y to the JCC, there are many organizations that offer summer camps.

*JCC Manhattan

334 Amsterdam Avenue at West 76th Street

646-981-1665

www.jccmanhattan.org

JCC Staten Island

Joan & Alan Bernikow JCC

1466 Manor Road

Staten Island

718-475-5200

www.sijcc.org

Park Summer Camps

Check Web site for participating parks in New York City.

www.nycgovparks.org

Many NYC parks run summer camp programs in city recreation centers for kids ages six through thirteen. The camp is free and they fill up quite quickly. Registration usually happens at the beginning of March.

Samuel Field Y

58-20 Little Neck Parkway

Little Neck, NY

718-225-6750

www.sfy.org

The Samuel Field Y in Little Neck hosts many camps throughout the NYC area, from a camp at the Queens County Farm Museum to a camp at the Y facilities. They also run a popular camp at the Henry Kaufman Campgrounds in Huntington, New York, in Suffolk County, with pickup buses leaving from all over the city. They have a complete list of camps on their Web site, including a camp for special-needs children.

YMCA

Check Web site for locations throughout New York City.

www.ymcanyc.org

The branches of the YMCA offer economical camps;

check their Web pages, accessed from the YMCA site above, for registration information.

School Camps

Many schools offer summer programs. For instance every summer my daughter attends a camp at a local Montessori school. Check out your local private school to see if they offer a summer program. Obviously if I listed all the programs offered at New York City's private schools, this chapter would be bursting at the seams. So it's best to investigate your local schools to see what they offer.

Museums, Gardens, and Farms With Camps

Here are some museums, gardens, and farms that offer summer camps for kids:

American Museum of Natural History and The Rose Center for Earth and Space
Central Park West at 79th Street
212-769-5100
www.amnh.org

Children's Museum of the Arts
182 Lafayette Street at Broome Street
212-274-0986
www.cmany.org

Intrepid Sea-Air-Space Museum
Pier 86 at West 46th Street
877-957-SHIP
www.intrepidmuseum.org

New York Botanical Garden
Bronx River Parkway at Fordham Road
Bronx
718-817-8700
www.nybg.org

New York Hall of Science
47-01 111th Street at 47th Avenue
Queens
718-699-0005
www.nyhallsci.org

Queens County Farm Museum
73-50 Little Neck Parkway
Queens
718-347-3276
www.queensfarm.org

Traditional Day Camps

Remember making lanyard bracelets and having an all-out color war? Here is a list of traditional camp programs around the city:

Camp Henry at the Henry Street Settlement

265 Henry Street at Montgomery Street
212-254-3100
www.henrystreet.org

This accredited American Camp Association camp at the Henry Street Settlement is for kids ages five through thirteen and runs for seven weeks. Campers go on trips to city museums and amusement parks and also engage in daily activities like arts and crafts, sports, swimming, and other fun activities. This is an extremely economical camp with an entire summer of classes and activities costing less that $1,500.

Camp Riverdale at the Riverdale Country School

5250 Fieldston Road at West 253rd Street
Bronx
718-432-4787
www.riverdale.edu

For almost fifty years, Camp Riverdale at Riverdale Country Day School has offered kids days filled with swimming instruction, arts and crafts, nature study, and other enjoyable activities. No need to pack a lunch since campers eat meals cooked by the Riverdale Country School chef.

*Central Queens YM & YWHA

67-09 108th Street bet. 67th Avenue and 67th Road
Queens
718-268-5011
www.cqyjcc.org

Located in Forest Hills, this YM and YMHA offers a range of summer camp programs for all ages. They have half-day programs at the Y for kids in kindergarten and first grade and a full time camp for kids two and a half to five year old. Grade-school-age children can also attend the YMHA camp at the Henry Kaufman Campgrounds in Huntington, New York. They offer a teen travel camp for kids entering sixth grade through ninth grade.

Downtown Day Camp

20 Warren Street at Columbia Street
Brooklyn
212-766-1104, ext. 250
www.downtowndaycamp.com

For over eighteen years, this TriBeCa day camp has offered swimming, art, dance, and other activities at their Downtown Community Center for kids entering kindergarten through the sixth grade. They also host Belleayre Mountain Nature Camp, a one-week sleepaway camp session in upstate New York, for kids in fifth grade through eighth grade. The Belleayre program also has a camp session during spring break.

Ethical Culture Fieldston School Summer Programs

33 Central Park West at West 64th Street
212-712-6237
www.ecfs.org/summer/programs.aspx

The summer programs at Fieldston offer a wide variety of options for kids in kindergarten through twelfth grade. For a traditional day camp experience, sign your kids up for Fieldston Outdoors, where they will swim, study nature, play sports, and engage in other activities, including music. There is a focus on the environment in this program.

Long Island City Kids Camp at the YMCA

5-02 50th Avenue at 5th Street
Queens
718-392-KIDS
www.lickids.com/camps

Long Island City Kids has a camp for kids ages two and a half through nine years old. The summerlong camp offers activities including yoga and martial arts. The camp offers a flexible schedule, but there is a two-week minimum for campers.

Mill Basin Day Camp

5945 Strickland Avenue at 56th Drive
Brooklyn
718-251-6200
www.millbasindaycamp.com

Since 1998, this Brooklyn camp for kids in pre-K through ninth grade has filled campers' days with swimming, arts and crafts, magic, and other fun activities.

New Country Day Camp at the 14th Street Y

344 East 14th Street bet. First and Second avenues
212-780-0800, ext. 248
www.14streety.org

Kids entering kindergarten can enjoy a summer at this Staten Island camp run by the 14th Street Y at the Henry Kaufman Campgrounds in Staten Island. Campers get to swim, go on hiking trails, perform in theater workshops, along with many other activities. If you need extended hours, campers will be supervised until 6 p.m. They have buses picking kids up from all around the city.

Oasis Children's Services Summer Programs

20 Jay Street at John Street
Brooklyn
800-317-1392
www.oasischildren.com

Oasis Children's Services runs camps throughout the city for kids ages five and up. In Manhattan they host a camp in Central Park as well as a teen field trip program with flexible enrollment, which is great when planning summer vacations.

Park Explorers Summer Day Camp

407 10th Street bet. Fifth and Sixth avenues
Brooklyn
718-788-3620
www.parkexplorers.com

This camp, which originally started as a playgroup in 1983, has many fans. In 2000, the playgroup became a fully listed camp for kids ages four through fourteen. Park Explorers utilizes Prospect Park for outdoor fun and activities and has a flexible schedule so that your child doesn't have to attend for the entire summer. They also have an extended-day option for working parents.

*The Park Slope Day Camp

241 Prospect Park West at Windsor Place
Brooklyn
718-788-7732
www.parkslopedaycamp.com

This popular Brooklyn camp is for kids ages three and half years through fourteen years old. They have locations in Bay Ridge, Park Slope, and Windsor Terrace, and each camp is designed around a different theme. Campers spend most of their days outdoors in Prospect Park. Park Slope Day Camp offers flexible scheduling so that your child doesn't have to attend for an entire summer. Kids Orbit, which is affiliated with Park Slope Day Camp, runs a camp during school breaks.

Poly Prep

Dyker Heights Campus

9216 Seventh Avenue at 92nd Street

Brooklyn

718-836-9800

www.polyprep.org

Campers from three and a half to thirteen years old can enjoy the summer program at Poly Prep. Kids will enjoy their 25-acre campus, where they can participate in a host of activities such as arts, athletics, swimming, and many other fun activities.

*Richmond County Day Camp

3555 Victory Boulevard at Crane Street

Staten Island

718-761-1492

www.rcdaycamp.com

An accredited camp through the American Camp Association, this Staten Island camp for kids ages five through fifteen years old is located in a 40,000-square-foot air-conditioned facility that offers kids a summer of art, swimming, field trips, and other fun activities. The camp offers a flexible schedule and a sibling discount.

Staten Island Day Camp

2800 Victory Boulevard at Loop Road

Staten Island

800-301-CAMP

www.statenislanddaycamp.com

Since 1979, this camp has been entertaining kids ages five through thirteen with arts, swimming, and a host of other activities.

Specialty Camps

Many of the after-school programs in chapter 2 offer summer programs as well, where kids can specialize in science, art, or even spend the summer perfecting a stand-up routine. Call or check their Web sites to find out if a summer camp is offered. Below I've highlighted other specialty camp programs throughout the city:

Computers

Apple Store

Check Web site for locations throughout New York City.

www.apple.com

Kids ages eight through twelve and their parents can participate in free camps held at Apple stores around the country. Choose from movie, music, photo, or presentation workshops. This isn't really a camp, but an interesting few hour workshop. The New York City camps fill up quickly, so sign up early. They also have youth programs throughout the year at various Apple stores.

Pony Club at Kensington Stables

51 Caton Place at East 8th Street

Brooklyn

718-972-4588

www.kensingtonstables.com

Kids ages six through eleven can spend their summer at this Brooklyn stable learning how to care for a horse. There are horseback rides and lessons available every day.

Sailing

NYC Summer Sailing Camp at Atlantic Yachting

79th Street Boat Basin, Riverside Park

212-518-4604

www.atlanticyachting.org

At this camp, kids get to spend the summer learning how to sail a yacht. Camp is held at the Boat Basin, and campers get to experience manning the helm and learn how much teamwork goes into sailing a boat.

Family Camps:

Tag along with your kids on these fantastic summer adventures:

❄ **Club Getaway:** This club offers weeklong and weekend family camps where parents enjoy some alone time as well as family bonding while their children attend a camp program. (59 South Kent Road, Kent, CT; 877-7GO-PLAY; 800-6GETAWAY; 860-927-3664; www.clubgetaway.com)

❄ **Family Adventure Camps through the Appalachian Mountain Club:** These all-inclusive family camps have an emphasis on the outdoors and nature education. (Locations in New Hampshire and Maine; 603-466-2727; www.outdoors.org)

❄ **Family Nature Camp at College of the Atlantic:** Located between the Atlantic Ocean and the mountains of Acadia National Park, this camp focuses on nature exploration. (Bar Harbor, ME; 800-597-9500; www.coa.edu/html/famnatcamp.htm)

❄ **Great Camp Sagamore:** Spend some time outdoors at the weekend family camp offered by one of the last Adirondacks Great Camps. (Sagamore Road, Raquette Lake, NY; 315-351-5311; www.greatcampsagamore.org)

❄ **Medomak Camp:** This 250-acre family camp in Maine has all the amenities of a family camp plus massages that are available for the adults. (Washington, ME; 866-MEDO-MAK; www.medomakcamp.com)

❄ **Tyler Place Family Resort:** This family resort in Vermont has a host of outdoor activities and classes for the family, as well as a supervised program for kids. (Highgate Springs, VT; 802-868-4000; www.tylerplace.com)

❄ **YMCA Camp Mason:** There are weekend family camps throughout the year at this Y campground. (23 Birch Ridge Road, Hardwick, NJ; 908-362-8217; www.campmason.org)

❄ **Frost Valley YMCA:** This camp hosts weeklong summer family camps and family camp weekend programs throughout the year. (2000 Frost Valley Road, Claryville, NY; 845-985-2291; www.frostvalley.org)

The City as a Camp

These camps travel around the city of field trips instead of being centrally located on a campus.

Kim's Kids Summer Camp

378 3rd Street at Fifth Avenue
Brooklyn
718-768-6419
www.kimskidscamp.com

This Park Slope–based camp takes kids on daily field trips all over the NYC metro area, from swimming in lakes outside of the city to a trip to Sesame Place. The program utilizes both the city and the surrounding area as the camp's classroom.

*New York City Explorers

110 Schermerhorn Street at Boerum Place
Brooklyn
718-797-3707
www.nycityexplorers.com

The New York Explorers takes campers on daily trips all around the big apple.

Theater and Arts Camps

If your child is obsessed with the theater or the movie *High School Musical*, you should sign them up for these theater camps. I've also highlighted theaters below that offer drama and musical theater camps.

Camp Broadway

336 West 37th Street bet. Seventh and Eighth avenues, Suite 460

212-575-2929
www.campbroadway.com

This theater camp has programs for kids age five through eight and up that are taught by experienced Broadway actors, performers, and directors. The camp is a great theater experience for Broadway-loving kids.

Create-A-Play Summer Camp

Manhattan School for Children
West 93rd Street bet. Amsterdam and Columbus avenues
646-485-5123
www.kidscreative.org

Your children can enjoy spending the summer at the Create-A-Play summer camp run by Kids Creative and the popular kids' band, the Dirty Sock Funtime Band. Days at Create-A-Play involve engaging in creative activities like art, songwriting, set design, acting, dance, and video creation. The camp goes on field trips to inspire kids' creativity.

Curtain Up Kids

119 Sullivan Street at Prince Street
917-494-7620
www.curtainupkids.com

Kids ages six through sixteen can spend their summer at the Players Theatre in the West Village. Camp sessions run for three weeks and focus on a single musical production. On the last day of camp campers perform the musical. Past camp performances have included *The Sound of Music* and *Annie*. They also have after-school theater classes throughout the year.

The Peanut Gallery at the Gallery Players

199 14th Street bet. Fourth and Fifth avenues
Brooklyn
718-595-0547
www.galleryplayers.com

This Park Slope theater camp runs weeklong programs for kids in first grade through sixth grade. By the end of each week, the kids create a show and perform it for family and friends.

Cool Arty Camps Outside the City

From sleepaway camps to day camps, here are some serious art camps worth checking out:

French Woods Festival of the Performing Arts Summer Camp

350 Bouchoux Brook Road
Hancock, NY
800-634-1703
www.frenchwoods.com

Kids ages seven and up can head to this upstate sleepaway camp to engage in a variety of performing arts. Campers can study music, filmmaking, theater, circus arts, magic, and many other subjects.

Stagedoor Manor Performing Arts Camp

116 Karmel Road
Loch Sheldrake, NY
888-STAGE88
www.stagedoormanor.com

Located in the Catskills, this sleepaway camp offers campers a summer of total theater immersion. Kids ages ten and up can sign up to spend their summer putting together a production. This camp is ideal for kids who take theater seriously.

Usdan Center for the Creative and Performing Arts

185 Colonial Springs Road
Huntington, New York
631-643-7900
www.usdan.com

This Long Island art camp attracts a ton of city kids and I should know, because not only did I attend as a kid, I also taught creative writing here as an adult. The camp's buses pick up kids throughout the five boroughs to bring them to this amazing art center that offers theater, dance, music, art, chess, and writing. There are also daily assemblies where children are exposed to top-rate performers. It's a great place to expose your child to the arts or for children who want to pursue their art seriously (there are some programs that require an audition). Children are asked to pick a major and a minor at the camp, which they will study in structured classes. The camp is for children who have completed kindergarten and up until high school. Kids in kindergarten and first grade are in the Discovery Program where they are introduced to a variety of arts.

Chapter Eight

Getting Dressed:

Shopping for Clothing, Shoes, and More

New York City kids are fashionistas. When I drop my daughter and son off at school, I am always surprised at how well dressed their classmates are. The good news is that it doesn't take a lot of money to dress your child in cool clothes. You can go wild with color and get them clothes that you only wish you could wear to work. Covering shopping for the under-twelve set in New York City is a big job, and although many major department stores like Macy's and Lord & Taylor sell kids' clothes, I've limited my picks to mainly independent shops, but I did list a few department stores.

From secondhand stores to high-end boutiques, I've listed the best places to score some threads for your little ones. Enjoy your shopping spree!

Abercrombie & Fitch

720 Fifth Avenue at West 56th Street
212-306-0936

199 Water Street bet. Fulton and John streets
212-809-9000
www.abercrombiekids.com
Return Policy: Full refund for unworn items with receipt. Merchandise credit if you don't have a receipt.

Tweens love this shop that sells basics like jeans, shorts, and tees. The store has a location on Long Island just for kids' clothes, but Abercomie shops also carry sizes for tweens that many adults can squeeze into.

Barneys New York

660 Madison Avenue at East 61st Street
212-826-8900
www.barneys.com
Return Policy: Full refund within 30 days with receipt and tag. Store credit if it's a gift.
City kids know that Barney is not just a purple dinosaur on a preschool show, but a New York City retail institution. The children's department at this swank store is small and is best suited for the under-eight set. Filled with brands like Kid by Phillip Lim and Vilebrequin, Barneys also has a good selection of toys by Plan Toys and Kid Kraft.

Berkley Girl

1418 Second Avenue bet. 73rd and 74th streets
212-744-9507

410 Columbus Avenue bet. 79th and 80th Streets
212-877-4770

www.berkleygirl.com

Return Policy: Store credit within ten days of purchase.

This popular clothing store specializes in clothes for the tween girl set. Every few months Berkley Girl hosts a "Friends of Berkeley Girl Focus Group" at their shop, giving tween girls a place to get together, meet new friends, and chat about fashion, creating their own designs and giving their feedback on the store. The store hosts a report card program; if your child scores all As, he or she receives 15 percent off all purchases—but don't worry if she scores below an A because she'll still get a discount. The shop carries a varied selection of clothes like pj's by Skivvy Doodles, cute T-shirts, and accessories; this is a shop that will appeal to girls and their parents.

Bombalulus

101 West 10th Street at Sixth Avenue

212-463-0897

www.bombalulus.com

Return Policy: Store credit within three weeks of purchase with receipt.

This West Village children's clothing store carries cool threads for kids under twelve. The shop also stocks a small amount of educational toys and puzzles. From tutus and funky T-shirts to sequin shoes, you'll find it at this beloved shop. Pick up one of the T-shirts with an image of Miles Davis or Bob Dylan, and you'll have the ultimate city kid hipster.

Bonpoint

392 Bleecker Street at West 11th Street

212-647-1700

1269 Madison Avenue at 91st Street

212-722-7720

811 Madison Avenue at 68th Street

212-879-0900

www.bonpoint.com

Return Policy: Store credit within thirty days with receipt.

This French clothing chain has three Manhattan boutiques. Bonpoint caters to kids twelve and under with classic clothing like cardigans, simple dresses, and khakis. The clothing at this high-end shop is absolutely beautiful but is also on the pricey side. Keep an eye out for their amazing sales, where you'll find that most of the clothing has been marked down between 30 and 50 percent. Bonpoint also has sample sales throughout the year.

Bloomingdale's

59th Street at Lexington Avenue

212-705-2000

www.bloomingdales.com

Return Policy: Return within six months with receipt.

Shopping with parents at Bloomingdale's is something every NYC kid should experience. This East Side department store carries luxury brands like Burberry, Diesel Kid, Juicy Couture, and other high-end labels. They have a large children's department, which makes it the place to find an outfit for a special occasion or just pick up some casual wear. They also carry shoes.

Bu and the Duck

106 Franklin Street at Church Street

212-431-9226

www.buandtheduck.com

Return Policy: Store credit with receipt.

This timeless TriBeCa shop carries clothing for kids

eight and under. The owner designs all the outfits in her studio located at the back of the shop. She also designs gorgeous knit stuffed animals. My daughter was fascinated with the mannequin of a little boy in the shop (apparently all the kids who shop there head over to him). The friendly owner has been out-fitting the kids of TriBeCa for over eleven years, and it's definitely worth a trip downtown. If you're on a budget, Bu and the Duck has two big sales each year, in January and June. Get on the mailing list to receive information about sales.

Catimini

1284 Madison Avenue at 92nd Street
212-987-0688
www.catimini.com
Return Policy: Store credit within ten days. After ten days, exchange only.

You'll secretly wish some of these clothes came in your size at this Upper East Side boutique. Catimini is a part of a French clothing chain that outfits kids from newborns to teens. One step into the shop and you'll embrace a world of colorful and fun French fashion. From brightly colored shirts and dresses for girls to more traditional clothes for boys, you'll find many unique items at Catimini—but like all high fashion, these children's clothes come at a price.

The Children's Place

Check Web site for locations throughout New York City.
877-PLACE-USA
www.childrensplace.com
Return Policy: Full refund within ninety days of purchase with receipt. After ninety days, store credit.

For sturdy, fashionable children's wear, check out this clothing store chain that carries clothing for kids ages fourteen and under. They often have amazing sales where you can get items of clothing for only $2! This is a great place to pick up some outfits for camp and school since the materials wear well and aren't pricey.

Crembebe

68 Second Avenue at East 4th Street
212-979-6848
www.crembebe.com
Return Policy: Store credit within two weeks of purchase.

Owned by local parents, this East Village shop car-ries clothing for newborns through preteens. Crembebe's collection will have your child dress-ing like an East Village hipster. With cool skirts for girls and rock star T-shirts for the boys, you might envy their wardrobe and ask, "Doesn't this come in my size?" The store also carries a small selection of wooden toys.

Crewcuts at J. Crew

99 Prince Street bet. Greene and Mercer streets
212-966-2739
www.jcrew.com
Return Policy: Full refund within sixty days of original purchase with receipt. Store credit after sixty days.

If it's good enough for the President's kids, shouldn't it be good enough for yours? Kids can dress like mini versions of preppie adults at this shop that sells mostly casual wear. Crewcuts is currently only housed in the Soho location of J. Crew, but I'm sure it won't be long before it pops up somewhere else.

Ed Hardy
49 Mercer Street at Broome Street
212-431-4500

425 West 13th Street at Washington Street
212-488-3131
www.edhardyshop.com
Return Policy: Exchange or store credit within 30 days.
Is your child hip and fashionable? Head downtown to Ed Hardy where kids can sport the latest trendy fashion. From hoodies to T-shirts, Ed Hardy carries an entire line of hip kids' wear.

Firefly Children's Boutique
225 Front Street at Beekman Street
646-416-6560

240 7th Avenue at 4th Street
Brooklyn
718-965-3535
www.fireflychildrensboutique.com
Return Policy: Exchange or store credit within two weeks of purchase.
Firefly boutiques are packed with European designer outfits at discounted prices. The staff is extremely friendly and helpful, and they have a great selection of clothing for girls and boys. Firefly is the perfect place to pick up an outfit for a special event and is also known for its amazing end-of-season sales.

Flora and Henri
1023 Lexington Avenue (bet. 73rd and 74th streets)
212-249-1695
www.florahenri.com
Return Policy: Store credit within two weeks of purchase.

An Upper East Side boutique that specializes in European-made casual clothing and shoes for newborns as well as kids up to age ten. Although the designs are quite simple and minimally embellished, the looks are classic and timeless.

Flowers by Zoe
1070 Madison Avenue at East 81st Street
212-535-3777
www.flowersbyzoeclothes.com
Return Policy: Return or exchange within fourteen days of purchase.
This Upper East Side boutique carries the popular girls brand Flowers by Zoe. The colorful collection includes cotton dresses, shirts, and leggings for the under-twelve set. The clothes are a bit pricey, but if you check out the second floor—the small loft area—the racks are filled with real deals on clothes.

GapKids
Check Web site for locations throughout New York City
800-427-7895
www.gap.com
Return Policy: All refunds and exchanges within thirty days of purchase.
This popular chain store carries all of the everyday basics for kids. My family also takes advantage of the large sales rack in every store. Beyond being fashionable and reasonable, GapKids clothing is a worthwhile purchase because it is sturdy enough to withstand multiple washings.

H&M

Check Web site for locations throughout New York City.

212-564-9922

www.hm.com

Return Policy: Refund within 30 days with receipt.

Funky and inexpensive are my two favorite words, and they just happen to best describe the children's department at this trendy European clothing store. H&M's clothing has a cool edge and is also quite durable. Beyond clothing, they also carry funky hats and other seasonal accessories (as well as a collection of Hello Kitty hair clips). This is a good place to pick up a hip outfit for your little one to wear to a birthday party or to find a ballet outfit for dance class.

Hollister

600 Broadway at West Houston Street

212-334-1922

www.hollisterco.com

Return Policy: Lenient—any exchange or return with receipt.

Tweens go mad for these threads that are inspired by the carefree California surf lifestyle. Your kids can shop in either the "Betty" or the "Dude" section where they will find vintage-inspired jeans and other stylized clothes.

Jacadi

1841 Broadway at 60th Street

212-246-2753

1281 Madison Avenue at 89th Street

212-369-1616

1260 Third Avenue at 72nd Street

212-717-9292

5005 16th Avenue at 50th Street

Brooklyn

718-871-9402

Return Policy: Refund within fourteen days, after fourteen days store credit.

This French clothing store has several boutiques in New York City and carries gorgeous clothes for kids. If you're looking for an outfit to wear to a special event, you'll be sure to find it here. They also have classic casual clothes for kids like beautiful knit sweaters and nice cords for boys. The shop tends to be on the pricey side, but they have great sales.

Jane's Exchange

191 East 3rd Street at Avenue B

212-677-0380

www.janesexchangenyc.com

Return Policy: No exchanges or returns.

This East Village consignment shop has a large collection of inexpensive clothes for kids as well as toys. If you have clothes to sell, Jane's Exchange accepts merchandise on consignment and shares the selling price with the owner. Consignors receive thirty percent on all items under $100 and forty percent on items over $100. The money you earn at Jane's Exchange is only good at the shop. You can also sell gently used highchairs and toddler toys that have been cluttering your closets.

Kico Kids

75 Ninth Avenue at West 16th Street

212-675-5426

www.kicokids.com

Return Policy: Refund within two weeks with receipt. Store credit within thirty days with receipt.

Many shops in the city sell Kico Kids, but if you'd like

to see the entire collection, head to the Kico shop in Chelsea Market. These cool threads are for kids ages twelve and under, but you'll wish you could squeeze into one of their cute sweaters or funky dresses.

Lesters

1534 Second Avenue at East 80th Street
212-734-9292

2411 Coney Island Avenue at Avenue U
Brooklyn
718-375-7337
www.lestersnyc.com
Return Policy: Full refund within seven days. Store credit within fourteen days of purchase.

Although the Upper East Side has a Lester's, the original location is in Brooklyn and takes up almost two city blocks with shops for kids of various ages. The Brooklyn location also has a shoe shop across the street with an amazing selection of kids' shoes. Head to the Upper East Side location to purchase high-end kids' clothes at discount prices. Lester's has enough inventory to fill your kids' closet until they're teenagers. They also sell high-quality casual wear, so if you want your child to sport a Juicy Couture sweat outfit for a good price, you have come to the right place.

Loehmann's

Check Web site for locations throughout New York City.
www.loehmanns.com
Return Policy: Full refund within two weeks. Store credit within thirty days.

This chain store sells off-price merchandise by major brand names. Several locations, including the one on the Upper West Side, carry children's clothes.

Lucky Kid

127 Prince Street bet. West Broadway and Wooster Street
212-466-0849
www.luckybrand.com
Return Policy: Full refund within thirty days with receipt. Store Credit or exchange without receipt.

Want a cool T-shirt and a pair of jeans for your kid? Head to the famed jean's company that now has a line of clothes for kids. I've picked up some of my favorite kids' casual wear at Lucky, like a T-shirt with "Rocket Scientist" emblazoned on the front that my son literally wore all summer. This location only carries kids' clothes, but other Lucky shops, like on the Upper West Side, have adult apparel, too. Inside tip: Check the sales rack.

Lucky Wang

799 Broadway at East 11th Street
212-353-2850

82 Seventh Avenue South at West 15th Street
212-229-9200
www.luckywang.com
Return Policy: Exchange only within ten days of purchase.

Although Lucky Wang only outfits kids ages eight and under, smaller children they can squeeze into some of these outfits even if they're a bit older. Lucky Wang carries very fashionable and comfortable clothes for kids, like kimonos and lightweight pants. If you happen to have friends that have young babies, the company offers a great selection of baby clothes that would make amazing gifts. The stores also have a small selection of toys that appeal to kids under eight.

Monnalisa

1050 Third Avenue at East 62nd Street

212-758-2669

www.monnalisa.eu

Return Policy: Store credit within two weeks of purchase.

This Upper East Side boutique carries gorgeous Italian designer dresses, sweaters, shoes and accessories. The shop tends to be on the pricey side, but they have beautiful well-made clothes.

Oilily's

465 West Broadway at Houston Street

212-871-0201

www.oililyusa.com

Return Policy: Store credit within fourteen days of purchase.

This Dutch shop carries clothes for girls of all ages, including their moms (sorry, boys, they only have clothes for you from newborns up to twelve months). Get a matching outfit with your daughter at this Soho shop.

Old Navy

Check the Web site for locations throughout New York City.

800-OLD-NAVY

www.oldnavy.com

Return Policy: Refunds and exchanges within thirty days of purchase.

This clothing chain carries staple items for kids, including bathing suits and Halloween costumes. This is the perfect place to pick up school clothes that often get worn out at recess. The clothing is extremely economical, and you can stock up on essentials without breaking the bank.

Patagonia

426 Columbus Avenue at 80th Street

917-441-0011

101 Wooster Street at Prince Street

212-343-1776

www.patagonia.com

Return Policy: Lenient—full refund with receipt. Store credit for unworn items without receipt.

From fleece jackets to T-shirts, you can find it at Patagonia. Stock up on outerwear and other staples to brave the New York City winter. The clothes are high quality and aren't too expensive.

Petit Bateau

1094 Madison Avenue at 82nd Street

212-988-8884

www.petit-bateau.com

Return Policy: Exchange or store credit only within ninety days.

Fans of French casual wear should head to Petit Bateau to pick up soft T-shirts and other cotton clothes for kids. They also make really soft leggings and dresses. From newborn to adult apparel, there is something for everything at this boutique. They also have a selection of baby blankets and onesies if you are in search of a nice gift.

Prince & Princess

41 East 78th Street at Madison Avenue

212-879-8989

www.princeandprincess.com

Return Policy: No returns.

For those who like to dress their child in formal wear or need an outfit for a special event, Prince & Princess is your one-stop shop. This Upper East

Side shop carries formal wear for kids and knows that there is nothing cuter than a child in suspenders and a suit.

Scoop NYC

473-475 Broadway bet. Broome and Grand Streets
212-925-3539
www.scoopnyc.com
Return Policy: Exchange or refund within two weeks of purchase.

This popular shop has a large children's section that carries brands like Alice & Olivia and Zac Posen. If you want your daughters to become little fashionistas and your sons to look like the hippest kid on the playground, head to this shop. Don't forget to pick something up for yourself while you're there, since they do carry adult sizes.

Space Kiddets

26 East 22nd Street bet. Broadway and Park Avenue South
212-420-9878
www.spacekiddets.com
Return Policy: Store credit or exchange within ten days of purchase.

From rain boots to dresses, you'll find it at this East Side kids' shop. Carrying clothes for newborns through preteens, Space Kiddets offers unique T-shirts, bags, dresses, and everything else you need to dress your kid in funky garb from lines like Small Paul and Petit Bateau. They have a separate shop for preteens upstairs.

A Time for Children

506 Amsterdam Avenue bet. 84th and 85th streets
212-580-8202
Return Policy: Store credit within seven days of purchase.
www.atimeforchildren.org

Owned and operated by the Children's Aid Society—with all proceeds going to the society, this store carries clothing from brands like Small Paul and Splendid for newborns to kids up to size 12. If you are in search of a cool kid-size T-shirt, they have shelves filled with an assortment of superhero logos. The shop also carries an interesting selection of toys like plush pigeons from Mo Willems's best-selling Pigeon children's book series and Paddington Bear dolls. If you want to score some cool threads for your kids while your money goes to a good cause, you must shop at this Upper West Side store.

Tribeca Girls

171 Duane Street at Staple Street
212-925-0049
www.tribecagirls.com
Return Policy: Refund or store credit within seven days with receipt.

Tucked away on Duane Street, Tribeca Girls carries cute clothes for your trendy girls ages one to twelve years old. With Paul Frank T-shirts and cute pj sets, the shop has all the clothes a girl would want to buy. I was surprised to see a bunch of very well-made corduroys on sale for $15 when I visited the shop. The clothing ranges in price, but they do have an extensive sale section.

Trico Field

65 West Houston Street at Wooster Street
212-358-8484
www.fith-usa.com
Return Policy: Store credit or exchange within two

weeks with receipt.

This high-end Soho shop sells Japanese clothes for the under-twelve set with a great collection of tees, pants, hats, and other items. It's fun to browse in the shop and check out the interesting selection of clothes that they stock.

Zaba Kids Boutique

85 Franklin Street bet. Broadway and Church Street
212-226-6355
www.zababoutique.com
Return Policy: Exchange, refund, or store credit within thirty days of purchase with receipt.

This TriBeCa boutique carries a wide range of kids' clothes. Although the shop does carry baby and toddler clothes, you can find nice items for the four-and-up crowd from brands like Appaman, C.P Company, and many others.

Brooklyn

Area Kids

Check Web site for locations throughout Brooklyn.
www.areakids.com
Return Policy: Store credit within thirty days with receipt.

Dress your city kid in Star Wars tees, hip Appaman clothes, and other cool finds at this local Brooklyn chain that carries clothes up to a kid's size 10. Area Kids also carries the hard-to-find Salt-Water sandals, as well as a selection of toys.

Blue Bass Vintage

431 Dekalb Avenue at Classon Avenue
Brooklyn
347-750-8935

www.bluebassvintage.com
Return Policy: No exchanges or refunds.

You don't have to be thrifty to want some cool vintage clothes. Kids love wearing one-of-a-kind pieces and you'll find them at this hip Clinton Hill vintage clothing shop, where you can also score some threads for yourself as you browse for your kids.

Brooklyn Industries

Check Web site for locations throughout New York City
www.brooklynindustries.com
Return Policy: Store credit or exchange only within 30 days of original purchase with receipt.

Older kids can probably wear some of the smaller adult sizes at this popular Brooklyn-based chain that is perfect for gifts for out-of-towners. They have a wide selection of kids' T-shirts and jackets to choose from—my kids always wear their "Brooklyn" sweat jackets from Brooklyn Industries. Also, moms will love their roomy, fashionable, machine-washable handbags that are great for carrying the additional items moms have to bring along like SIGGS cups and snacks.

Corduroy Kids

613 Vanderbilt Avenue at Bergen Street
Brooklyn
718-622-4145

231 5th Avenue at President Street
Brooklyn
718-789-2044
www.corduroykid.com
Return Policy: Store credit within a month of purchase.

Owned by two Brooklyn parents, these Brooklyn boutiques carry clothes for newborns to kids age seven. Stop by the shop to pick up everything from a rocket ship T-shirt to a peasant dress to toys. The staff at these neighborhood shops are extremely friendly.

Diva

1409 Avenue M at East 14th Street
Brooklyn
718-645-9797
www.divagirlfashion.com
Return Policy: Exchange or credit within one week. This is the shop for hip girls and their fashion-forward moms. The outfits are far from cheap, but if you have a special event or just have an urge to dress your baby girl to the nines, this is the place to do it. Diva carries Miss Blumarine, Simonetta, Loredana, Pampolina, Pappa Ciccia, and Verde Mela, and the shoe selection includes brands like Moschino and Dolce & Gabbana. The staff is very helpful and accommodating, which is exactly what you'd expect at a funky little shop like Diva.

Flying Squirrel

96 North 6th Street at Wythe Avenue
Brooklyn
718-218-7775
www.flyingsquirrelbaby.com
Return Policy: Exchange or store credit within one week of purchase.
Flying Squirrel sells gently used children's clothing, as well as strollers and other baby accessories like swings and highchairs. The clothing is all in good shape, and unbelievably well priced. They also buy children's clothes, so if you have tubs of clothes that are crowding up your cramped apartment, you should take them to the Flying Squirrel. The shop also sells a few new items like diaper bags, books, and toys, and the extremely cute Flying Squirrel T-shirt (which is produced by a sweatshop-free manufacturer) for your hipster tot.

4 Play BK

360 Seventh Avenue at 10th Street
Brooklyn
718-369-4086
Return Policy: Full refund within seven days with receipt. Store credit within fourteen days with receipt. You can't return hats or shoes.
Hip, skateboarding preteens will want everything in this popular Park Slope boutique that appeals to both preteens and adults. Take your child shopping here and you'll wish you were in high school again to buy all the clothes for yourself. Although the clothing is really for older teens and twenty-somethings, most preteens can fit into the smaller sizes.

The Green Onion

274 Smith Street bet. Sackett and Degraw streets
Brooklyn
718-246-2804
Return Policy: Full refund with receipt within 14 days. Store credit only after two weeks.
This cute Cobble Hill shop sells clothes and toys for kids ages ten and under. From cool pj sets to hand-knit sweaters, the Green Onion carries a wonderful selection of clothes. Whether you want lunchboxes by Crocodile Creek or Salt-Water sandals, you'll find it all at this Brooklyn boutique.

Gumbo

493 Atlantic Avenue at Third Avenue
Brooklyn
718-855-7808
Return Policy: Store credit only.

This cool kids' clothing shop, with its very funky clothing that ranges from hip to hippie for babies and kids, fits in perfectly with Brooklyn. Gumbo also carries clothes designed by local artists and hosts music classes in the shop for kids ages five and up.

Happy Days Children's Wear

4802 Fifth Avenue at 48th Street
Brooklyn
718-567-3900
Return Policy: Full refund within seven days if items are unused and in original packaging. Store credit within 30 days with receipt.

The lower level of this Sunset Park superstore boasts an enormous children's department, which carries everything from pj's to outerwear. The clothing is moderately priced, and parents could stock up on a ton of essentials here without spending their life savings. The store also carries school uniforms.

The Melting Pot

492 Atlantic Avenue at Nevins Street
Brooklyn
718-596-6849
www.nancybatik.com
Return policy: Lenient, open return policy.

If you are a fan of batik, you must head over to the Melting Pot. This shop has an entire line of kids' clothing with amazing batik designs, like the one I saw with an image of the Brooklyn Bridge. Other designs include clouds, dragons, and peace signs.

They have a line of adult clothing as well, so you and your child can wear matching T-shirts.

Sprout Kidz

849 A Union Street bet. Sixth and Seventh avenues
Brooklyn
718-398-2280
www.sproutkidz.net
Return Policy: Full refund within seven days with receipt and tags. Store credit for all other returns.

This Park Slope kids' clothing shop sells organic clothes for kids ages eight and under. The owners describe their collection as fun, and the brightly colored long-sleeve shirts and dresses are just that.

Still Hip Brooklyn

283 Grand Avenue at Clifton Place
Brooklyn
718-398-0008
www.www.stillhipbrooklyn.com
Refund Policy: No exchanges or returns.

Still Hip Brooklyn is a gem, selling second-hand children's clothes for newborns to a children's size 7 as well as kids' shoes, books, toys, and other accessories. Run by two local Brooklyn moms, this Clinton Hill shop is extremely inviting. In a neighborhood with a dearth of shops for kids, you'll find a general store chockful of a wide variety of merchandise as well as an oversize bulletin board filled with ads for nannies, classes, and other local parenting information, all of which make the shop a neighborhood resource. If you have gently used items that your children have outgrown, set up an appointment to sell them to the shop. Keep in mind that the owners are very discriminating in selecting the gently used merchandise and that most of the outfits for sale can pass for new garments. In addition to selling cool threads, the shop has a space to host kids' classes and birthday parties. Check the Web site for party pricing and the list of the classes offered.

Tuesday's Child Boutique

1904 Avenue M at East 19th Street
Brooklyn
718-375-1790
www.tuesdayschild.com
Return Policy: Store credit only.

Operating for almost thirty years, this small shop on Ave M in Midwood is the place for fashion-savvy parents. Tuesday's Child is an exclusive retailer that carries high-end European labels such as Armani, Catamini, La Perla, and Petit Bateau. The shop is stocked with all of the finest clothes, from layette to preteen clothes, and the sales staff is extremely helpful. This is a good option if you're searching for special outfits for a baby or toddler of either sex, since they carry both gowns and suits.

Queens

Denny's Children's Wear

254-45 Horace Harding Boulevard at 94th Street
Queens
718-225-8833
www.dennyschildrenswear.com
Return Policy: Full refund within fourteen days.
Store credit within thirty days.

Not the restaurant chain, Denny's Children's Wear is actually my mother-in-law's favorite place to shop for my kids. This kids' clothing store has a biannual 90 percent-off sale where you can pick up brand-name jackets at heavily discounted prices. Denny's stocks high-end clothing for boys and girls, and it specializes in getting your kids ready for camp with their stock of sleep-away essentials.

Domsey's Express

1609 Palmetto Street at Wykoff Avenue
Queens
718-386-7661
Return Policy: No exchanges or returns.

Years ago I would make the pilgrimage from the West Village to visit the former location of Domsey's Express like many other hip folks trying to score one-of-a-kind outfits. Now you can make the trip to Ridgewood, Queens, where you can get second-hand kids' clothes at extremely reasonable prices.

Kid City

Check Web site for locations throughout New York City.
www.kidcitystores.com
Return Policy: Refund within thirty days with tags and receipt.

In search of a school uniform? With locations in the outer boroughs, Kid City is the place to get ready for school and pick up inexpensive kids' essentials. You can also find backpacks here.

Piccolo Mondo

71-21 Austin Street at 71st Avenue
Queens
718-261-6771
www.boutiqueforchildren.com
Return Policy: Exchange or store credit within ten days.

If you like to dress your child in Hugo Boss, Roberto Cavalli, and other high-end clothing brands, then stop by this Forest Hills boutique. Piccolo Mondo has all the brands to make your child look like a mini adult.

Street Fairs, Holiday Markets, Flea Markets and Other Places to Shop in NYC

Some of the best clothing can be found at these area flea markets and seasonal fairs around the city:

❄ **Artists and Fleas:** A popular Williamsburg flea market, Artists and Fleas is only open on weekends (129 North 6th Street, Brooklyn; www.artistsandfleas.com).

❄ **Brooklyn Flea:** This weekly flea market is housed in Fort Greene during the warmer months and indoors in DUMBO during the winter. Check the Web site for the schedule (176 Lafayette Avenue, Brooklyn; 718-935-1052; www.brooklynflea.com).

❄ **BUST Magazine Craftacular:** This biannual craft fair sponsored by BUST magazine features artisans selling silk-screened kids' T-shirts and handmade dresses (The Warsaw, 261 Driggs Avenue, Brooklyn; www.bust.com/craftacular).

❄ **Grand Central Terminal Holiday Fair:** We make an annual trip to check out both the holiday fair and train show at Grand Central Terminal. Run during the holiday season, this indoor market has many interesting vendors, including plenty who sell children's clothes (Grand Central Terminal at Lexington Avenue and 42nd Street; www.grandcentral-terminal.com).

❄ **Holiday Market at Columbus Circle:** This annual holiday fair at Columbus Circle lasts from November through December and has a unique selection of kids' clothes and toys for sale (southwest entrance to Central Park at Columbus Circle; www.nycgovparks.org).

❄ **Holiday Market at Union Square:** You know it's holiday season in New York City when you see the vendors at Union Square. There are tons of eclectic kid clothing vendors at this market (south end of Union Square; www.nycgovparks.org).

❄ **The Holiday Shops at Bryant Park:** Run between November and December, this holiday market has unique kids' clothes. (Bryant Park at Sixth Avenue; www.thepondatbryant-park.com).

❄ **Renegade Craft Fair:** Each year the Renegade Craft Fair comes to McCarren Park in Brooklyn for a weekend fair. The fair usually happens in June and vendors sell everything from crafts to toys, clothing, and other goods. The fair is quite festive, and bands even perform (McCarren Park, Brooklyn; www.renegadecraft.com).

Shoe Stores

City kids walk a lot. Instead of seeing the world from the backseat of a minivan, a city kid walks to school and the subway, and spends countless hours running around at the playground. This means it's important to provide your city kid with comfortable shoes. Honestly, this is my only big splurge when it comes to shopping for my kids. Luckily, you can find many quality shoe brands at designer discount stores like Century 21 (see p. 188) and Daffy's (see p. 188), but it's also important to get your child's foot measured properly to ensure a good fit.

Some of the following boutiques also sell adult shoes, so you can grab a pair, too. Of course you can find shoes at all major department stores—Macy's, Lord & Taylor, Barneys (see p. 147), and Bloomingdale's (my favorite shoe department in the city), but here are some independent and chain shoe stores that specialize in growing feet.

Blue Elephant

10721 71st Road at Queens Boulevard
Queens
718-261-3222
www.blueelephantonline.com
Return Policy: Store credit or exchange within seven days.
This Forest Hills shoe store has a nice selection of shoes for kids of all ages. They carry brands like Ecco, Geox, Naturino, and many others. The staff is very friendly and knowledgeable about kids' shoes sizes.

East Side Kids Shoes

1298 Madison Avenue at East 92nd Street
212-360-5000
www.eastsidekidsshoes.com
Return Policy: Store credit within fourteen days.
This family-owned shop carries a wide range of shoes imported from Europe as well as American brands like Nike. Whether you need shoes for a formal event or just for everyday wear, you will be sure to find a pair at this beloved Upper East Side shoe store. The friendly staff will happily measure your child's feet and recommend shoes for various occasions.

Harry's Shoes

2315 Broadway at West 83rd Street
212-874-2034
www.harrys-shoes.com
Return Policy: Store credit or exchange within ten days.
For years this Upper West Side boutique has been sizing the city's kids and supplying them with reliable, fashionable, and comfortable shoes from brands like Merrell, Geox, and many others. They have a separate shop for kids, down the block from their original location.

Lisa Polansky

121 Seventh Avenue at President Street
Brooklyn
718-622-8071; 866-432-0595
www.lisapolanskyinc.com
Return Policy: Store credit within seven days.
This cramped Brooklyn shop carries a good selection of kids' shoes. If you don't see what you're looking for, just ask Lisa and she'll find it or order just what you're looking for. Lisa is great at recommending shoes for kids—and moms, too.

Little Eric Shoes

1118 Madison Avenue at 83rd Street
212-717-1513
Return Policy: Store credit or exchange only.
This Upper East Side shoe store is a neighborhood staple and a good place to pick up everything from sandals to snow boots. It carries Italian and other European imported shoes, and offers a toy section.

Naturino

1185 Madison Avenue at East 86th Street
212-427-0679
www.naturino.com
Return Policy: Exchange or store credit.
Fans of these extremely well-made Italian shoes will love the selection at the Naturino shop on the Upper East Side. They specialize in shoes for kids up to twelve years of age. The shoes vary in style from casual and sporty to formal wear.

Payless Shoe Source

Check Web site for locations throughout New York City.
www.payless.com
Return Policy: Refund with receipt.
Payless has good shoes at reasonable prices. Here's a tip: Don't head to a Payless shop; instead go to the Web site to check out the entire collection. Then order the shoes you want, they'll be delivered to your local Payless store free of charge. You can find nice Airwalk sneakers for kids as well as tap and ballet shoes, if your child is taking dance lessons. They also offer a selection of slippers and socks.

Peek-a-Boo Kids

90 Seventh Avenue at Union Street
Brooklyn
718-638-1060

333 Court Street at Sackett Street
Brooklyn
718-643-0306
Return Policy: Exchange or store credit only.
With locations in Park Slope and Carroll Gardens, this Brooklyn shoe shop is a local favorite. Peek-a-Boo Kids carries shoes for newborns and toddlers, with brands like Umi and Ecco. The staff is extremely friendly and the sales are amazing. At the end of the winter they have a buy-one-get-one-free sale, which is very popular with the locals.

The Shoe Garden

152 West 10th Street at Waverly
212-989-4320
www.shoegardennyc.com
Return Policy: Exchange or store credit within seven days with receipt.
Started by two local moms, this West Village shop has an amazing collection of shoes for kids. From ballet flats to snow boots, with brands like Naturino and Ecco, you will be able to find a fashionable and comfortable pair of shoes for your child.

Shoofly

42 Hudson Street at Thomas Street
212-406-3270
www.shooflynyc.com
Return Policy: Exchange or store credit only.
Head to TriBeCa to pick out shoes for your kids from a large collection of European imports and popular

brands like Sketchers. The staff is very friendly and patient when measuring feet. In addition to scoring a cute pair of shoes, you can also find tons of girl's hair accessories. My daughter wanted about ten different barrettes from this shop. Inside tip: Shoofly has amazing seasonal sales, like a big half-off sale. Check their Web site for upcoming sales.

Soula Shoes

185 Smith Street at Warren Street
Brooklyn
718-834-8423

184 Fifth Avenue at Sackett Street
Brooklyn
718-230-0038
www.soulashoes.com
Return Policy: Exchange or store credit only.
Head to Brooklyn for some shoe shopping at Soula. Parents might be tempted to purchase a pair of shoes for themselves at this hip shoe store that is primarily for adults but has a nice children's section, which includes Pumas and other hip sneakers.

Stride Rite

Check Web site for locations throughout New York City.
www.striderite.com
Return Policy: Return within thirty days with receipt for refund.
This kids shoe store sells reliable and well-made footwear that won't break the bank. Many shops carry Stride Rite, but Stride Rite shops house a larger collection.

Tip Top Kids

149 West 72nd Street bet. Amsterdam and Columbus avenues
212-787-4960
www.tiptopshoes.com
Return Policy: Return within ten days for store credit or exchange.
For over forty years Tip Top has been selling shoes to local families. If you are looking for Heelys (the sneakers that have roller skates on the bottom), you can get a pair at this reliable Upper West Side shoe store. Tip Top also carries brands like Teva, Saucony, Merrill, and many others, including a selection of adult shoes, so you can get a pair for yourself.

Windsor Shoes Too

227 Prospect Park West at 16th Street
Brooklyn
718-499-5755
Return Policy: Thirty days with receipt for store credit.
Located in Windsor Terrace, Brooklyn, just blocks from Prospect Park, this kids-only shop stocks reliable brands like Stride Rite, Merrill, Crocs, and more. The shop also has a large collection of Jibbitz, so kids can decorate their Crocs.

The Malls

When you think of the mall, you may not think of New York City, but the Big Apple has its share of malls. From high-end malls in Queens to a big suburban-style mall on Staten Island, here are some worth checking out.

Kings Plaza

5100 Flatbush Avenue at Avenue U

Brooklyn

718-253-6844

www.kingsplazaonline.com

This large mall has tons of kids' stores and hosts events for little ones like Radio Disney days and other cultural events. If you have smaller kids in tow, they will enjoy the indoor rides like pretending to drive a car with Sesame Street characters for just fifty cents. I grew up going to this mall and still love to head there to pick up a chocolate chip cookie at the Cookie House (www.cookiehouse.com). This is a nice place to spend a rainy day since there is a large movie theater in the mall.

Stores:

American Eagle Outfitter * Finish Line * Foot Action USA * Gamestop * GapKids * H&M * Kids Footlocker * Morning Glory * Old Navy * Payless Shoe Source * The Children's Place

Queens Center

90-15 Queens Boulevard at Woodhaven Boulevard

Queens

718-592-3900

www.shopqueenscenter.com

This popular Queens mall is accessible by public transportation. There is also a play area for kids.

Stores:

As Seen On TV * The Children's Place * Disney Store * Gamestop * Glamour Shots * H&M * Kids Foot Locker * Lid's Kids * Macy's * Morning Glory * Rave Girl * Spencer's Gifts * Stride Rite * Urban Outfitters

The Shops at Atlas Park

8000 Cooper Avenue at 80th Street

Glendale, NY

718-326-3300

www.theshopsatatlaspark.com

Just minutes from Forest Hills, this mall is more L.A. or Boca Raton than Queens. The outdoor mall boasts a seasonal farmer's market. With large chain restaurants like a Johnny Rocket's and a fondue restaurant, this mall attracts a family crowd. It also houses a large movie theater.

Stores:

Gymboree * Frankie's Playce

Staten Island Mall

2655 Richmond Avenue at Platinum Avenue

Staten Island

718-761-6666

www.statenisland-mall.com

This is the closest you'll get to a suburban mall in New York City.

Stores:

Build-A-Bear Workshop * The Children's Place * Crazy 8 * Disney Store * Gamestop * Gymboree * Justice * Kids Foot Locker * Macy's * Morning Glory * Old Navy * Rave Girl * S & L's Children's Design * Spencer's Gifts * Stride Rite

Suburban Malls

Some of these are reachable by mass transit, but if you have a car you will have access to many other places that carry children's clothing.

Long Island

Roosevelt Field Mall

630 Old Country Road
Carle Place, NY
516-742-8000
Stores:
United Colors of Benetton * Build-A-Bear Workshop * Club Libby Lu * GapKids * Gymboree * H&M * Janie and Jack * Stride Rite * The Children's Place * Disney Store * The Limited Too * Bloomingdale's * JCPenney * Macy's * Nordstrom * Pottery Barn Kids

The Mall at The Source

1504 Old Country Road
Westbury, NY
516-228-0303
Literally a half a mile down the road from Roosevelt Field Mall is a personal favorite of mine, the Source Mall. Although a lot smaller than Roosevelt Field, the Source is filled with shops like Old Navy, and there's even a Gymboree outlet.
Stores:
* The Children's Place Outlet * GapKids * Gymboree * H&M * Old Navy * Old School Games * Surprise Toys * Rave Girl

Westchester and Rockland

Palisades Center

1000 Palisades Center Drive
West Nyack, NY
914-348-1000
This mall is insanely large. There is even a New York Sports Club inside, so one of you can work out while the other shops!
Stores:
babyGap * Build-A-Bear Workshop * The Children's Place * Discovery Channel Store * Disney Store * GapKids * Gymboree * H&M * Hammett's Learning World * Kids Foot Locker * LEGO Store * Old Navy * Stride Rite * Target

The Westchester

125 Westchester Avenue
White Plains, NY
914-683-8600
A lot of the stores at this mall are high-end, but many, like Hanna Andersson, have amazing sales. The kids' clothing stores are all bunched together, so you can sort through the stores quickly without having to trek all over the mall. The mall also offers a kid-friendly restaurant called City Limits, as well as a food court and a Ben & Jerry's.
Stores:
* babyGap * Build-A-Bear Workshop * GapKids * Gymboree * Hanna Andersson * J. Jill * Jacadi * Janie and Jack * Kids Foot Locker * Neiman Marcus * Oilily * The Children's Place * Stride Rite * Talbots Kids & Babies

Outlets

Every spring and fall, we make a pilgrimage to one of these three New York outlets to stock up on seasonal essentials for the whole family. All of these outlet malls have plenty of bathrooms with diaper decks.

Tanger Outlet Centers: Deer Park

152 The Arches Circle
Deer Park, NY

631-242-0239

www.tangeroutlet.com

Stores:

Gap * Big Dogs * Carter's * The Children's Place * Cool Brands 4 Kids * Disney Store* Little Me * Old Navy * OshKosh B'Gosh * Pepperidge Farm * Stride Rite

Tanger Outlet Centers: Riverhead

1770 West Main Street

Riverhead, NY

631-369-2732

www.tangeroutlet.com

Stores:

Gap * Big Dogs * Carter's * The Children's Place * Cool Brands 4 Kids * Disney Store * Little Me * Old Navy * OshKosh B'Gosh * Pepperidge Farm * Pottery Barn Kids * Stride Rite

Woodbury Common Premium Outlets

498 Red Apple Court

Central Valley, NY

845-928-4000

Stores:

Carter's * The Children's Place * Danskin * Gap Outlet * Little Me * Nautica Kids * Oilily * OshKosh B'Gosh * Petit Bateau * Stride Rite * Keds * World of Fun

Books, Comics, Literary Landmarks, Book Festivals, and Other Adventures in Reading

After a long day exploring this big city, kids and their parents like to unwind with a good book. New York City is a literary city and is filled with many independent bookstores and chains that have amazing sections devoted to kids. Introduce your little ones to the world of children's literature in these homey bookstores.

New York City is chuck full of options; you can spend your afternoon palling around with Clifford at the Scholastic Store in Soho (see p. 173) or spend a weekend at the annual New York Comic Con, a world-famous comic convention. With bookstores, literary landmarks, book festivals, and children's reading rooms at various branches of the New York Public Library (www.nypl.com), there is no better time to expose your child to New York's literary scene.

A Baker's Dozen of NYC Books for Young Readers

Looking for a book that will appeal to your city kid? Here are some NYC-themed books from Peter Glassman, owner of Books of Wonder (see p. 170), a children's bookstore in Chelsea:

Ages Four through Seven

* *Eloise* by Kay Thompson, illustrated by Hilary Knight
* *The Escape of Marvin the Ape* by Caralyn Buehner, illustrated by Mark Buehner
* *The House on East 88th Street* by Bernard Waber
* *How Little Lori Visited Times Square* by Amos Vogel, illustrated by Maurice Sendak
* *Knuffle Bunny: A Cautionary Tale* by Mo Willems
* *The Little Red Lighthouse and the Great Gray Bridge* by Hildegarde H. Swift, illustrated by Lynd Ward
* *Little Toot* by Hardie Gramatky
* *The Man Who Walked Between the Towers* by Mordicai Gerstein
* *My New York* by Kathy Jakobsen Hallquist
* *Old Penn Station* by William Low
* *Pet of the Met* by Lydia and Don Freeman
* *This Is New York* by Miroslav Sasek
* *Uptown* by Bryan Collier

Ages Seven through Twelve

❊ *All-of-a-Kind Family* by Sydney Taylor
❊ *The Cricket in Times Square* by
   George Selden
❊ *Dave at Night* by Gail Carson Levine
❊ *From the Mixed-up Files of Mrs. Basil E.
   Frankweiler* by E.L. Konigsburg
❊ *Gods of Manhattan* by Scott Mebus
❊ *Harriet the Spy* by Louise Fitzhugh
❊ *The Night Tourist* by Katherine Marsh
❊ *The Pushcart War* by Jean Merrill
❊ *The Saturdays* by Elizabeth Enright
❊ *Scooter* by Vera B. Williams
❊ *So You Want to Be a Wizard* by Diane Duane
❊ *A Tree Grows in Brooklyn* by Betty Smith
❊ *The Young Unicorns* by Madeleine L'Engle

Bookstores

Stop by any one of these bookstores located throughout the city and introduce your child to the joys of reading. Many of these bookstores offer story-time hours and other kid-friendly activities. Also remember that books make an ideal birthday gift; after receiving a slew of toys, parents are often grateful for books because they offer so much to kids and are extremely apartment friendly since they don't take up much room.

While researching this book, I was both shocked and saddened by the diminishing number of independent city bookshops, so if you have the opportunity, please support your local bookstore. Many of the shops that have closed over the years had a huge influence on me as a kid growing up in the city, and I hope our city kids will be able to enjoy these treasures.

Babbos Books

242 Prospect Park West bet. Prospect Avenue and Windsor Place
Brooklyn
718-788-3475
www.babbosbooks.com

This Windsor Terrace used bookstore has a good selection of used children's books. Kids will love choosing a book for their home library. You can also sell books to Babbo's for store credit, but they only accept book sales on Sundays and they request that you bring in less than twenty books. They also have a small section of new books.

Bank Street Books

610 West 112th Street at Broadway
212-687-1654
www.bankstreetbooks.com

Bank Street Books is a NYC gem. If you are looking for books for your kids or books about child development, this is the place to go. Since 1970 this bookshop has been carrying the classics as well as up-to-date books on parenting subjects. It's an ideal stop if you are in the Morningside Heights area. The store also has a good list of recommended reads for kids on the shop's Web site. The upstairs has educational toys as well as unique items like T-shirts based on Mo Willems's Pigeon series and literary-inspired posters for your child's bedroom walls. The staff is incredibly knowledgeable, so ask them about any book and they will be sure to find it.

Barnes & Noble

Check Web site for locations throughout New York City

www.barnesandnoble.com

This chain bookstore has many superstores in the city where kids can spend hours browsing around their children's section. Many of these children's corners offer amenities like a stage and a play area and allow kids read the books before purchasing them. They are also really good when it comes to special orders. The Barnes & Noble children's section is a nice spot to spend a rainy day, but be aware that city locations tend to get crowded with nannies and toddlers during the weekdays. Most stores also offer story times; just call ahead for times. It's good to note that the B&N location on Fifth Avenue and 18th Street carries a large selection of textbooks and educational books for kids. You can also order from their Web site, and if you live in Manhattan, they offer same-day delivery.

Bookberries

983 Lexington Avenue at 71st Street
212-794-9400

If you are on the Upper East Side, you must check out the children's section of this incredible independent bookstore for a good read. Kids will find a variety of books from princess-themed books to children's classics. The children's area is separate from the adult area, giving them some privacy while they look for the perfect book.

Bookbook

277 Bleecker Street at Morton Street
212-807-0180

When the beloved West Village Biography Bookstore shut its doors in the fall of 2009, the owners opened a new outpost on Bleecker Street. Upon entering the shop, you'll notice a wall filled with children's classics from Tin Tin books to the entire collection of Roald Dahl books.

BookCourt

163 Court Street at Dean Street
Brooklyn
718-875-3677
www.bookcourt.org

This beloved Brooklyn bookstore had kids in mind when the owners recently renovated their space with a rather large children's section at the front of the store. Filled with the classics like *The Phantom Tollbooth* and an extensive section of early readers and middle-reader series books, this Cobble Hill staple is the place to pick up a good book. The store also provides kid-size seats for little readers, so they can leaf through their purchases. In fact it's hard to drag my kids out of the seats and away from the display of mini sticker books in the children's area. If you don't see a book you're looking for, the staff is extremely friendly and always willing to put in a special order. If you are picking up book for a gift, they always have funky kid-friendly wrapping paper. For the parents, this bookshop has an amazing selection of quality fiction and nonfiction, as well as a large selection of parenting books. Check the events schedule for children's book authors that might be reading as well as for story times.

The Bookmark Shoppe

8415 3rd Avenue between 84th and 85th Street
Brooklyn
718-833-5115
www.bookmarkshoppe.com

The Bookmark Shoppe has moved from Dyker Heights to Bay Ridge and is still a wonderful independent bookstore that hosts a variety of kid-friendly events. The kids' section is filled with children's classics, series books, and many early readers.

Books of Wonder

18 West 18th Street bet. Fifth and Sixth avenues
212-989-3270
www.booksofwonder.com

This Chelsea bookstore specializes in children's books, but kids and adults can spend a day perusing the shop's shelves filled with everything from classic kid's books to the latest best sellers. The bookstore is carefully divided by reading level and theme. If you have any questions, just ask the friendly staff. Honestly, I could get lost in this bookstore as I relive my childhood reading, like the All-of-a-Kind Family series and the Frog and Toad books. They also have a section devoted to New York City–themed reads. If you find yourself in need of a decadent treat, the Cupcake Café is attached to the bookstore. Kids can sip hot chocolate and parents can relax with a latte as their children read their new books. The store also hosts birthday parties (see p. 114). Books of Wonder has many events at the shop, where kids can get to meet some of their favorite authors. Check their Web site for a list of events, which happen quite regularly.

Borders

Check Web site for locations throughout New York City.
www.borders.com

This bookstore chain, with locations throughout the city, has large children's sections in its stores that often host story hours. Borders also has a nice selection of discounted books for kids as well as kids' craft books. My daughter is hopelessly obsessed with their magazine section, which has a large variety of kid-focused magazines.

Community Bookstore

143 Seventh Avenue at Carroll Street
Brooklyn
718-783-3075
www.communitybookstore.net

Park Slope's only independent bookstore, Community Bookstore is a treasure to the neighborhood and has a wonderful children's selection tucked away in the back of the shop. The shop carries a wide variety of thoughtfully selected children's literature as well as a nice selection of parenting books. Every time I enter the kid's section, even if I don't intend to purchase a book I inevitably find a book that I feel my kids must read or I rediscover an old classic. Right beyond the children's section is a quiet backyard garden. The shop hosts many readings; check the schedule to see if there are children's book authors scheduled to read.

The Corner Bookstore

1313 Madison Avenue near 93rd Street
212-831-3554

This Upper East Side bookstore seems as if it's straight out of Old Manhattan. It's a classic shop with a nice selection of quality adult books and a section for kids. The staff is very friendly and will recommend reads and order books if necessary. It's a nice place to stop in for a book when you're exploring Museum Mile (see p. 47).

Drama Book Shop

250 West 40th Street bet. Seventh and Eighth avenues

212-944-0595

www.dramabookshop.com

If your children want to act or love the theater, this is the store for them. Filled with tons of plays and theater-related books, Drama book Shop has a diverse selection of kids books. My daughter loved the fact that they had a *Wizard of Oz* cutout book. The basement of the shop houses a black box theater, where the incredibly talented and energetic Story Pirates host weekend shows and birthday parties (see p. 113).

Everything Goes Book Café and Neighborhood Stage

208 Bay Street near Victory Boulevard

Staten Island

718-447-8256

www.etgstores.com

After you take a ride on the Staten Island Ferry, walk a few blocks to Everything Goes to pick up a used children's book and relax at their café. This bookstore and café also hosts events, so be sure to check their Web site to see what is happening.

Freebird Books & Goods

123 Columbia Street at Kane Street

Brooklyn

718-643-8484

www.freebirdbooks.com

Housed on the other side of the Brooklyn-Queens Expressway in Brooklyn's Cobble Hill, this used bookstore has a vibe that will make you think you've just walked into a bookstore in a small college town rather than Brooklyn. They have a selection of kids'

books, and their stock rotates quite regularly. The shop also hosts events and classes.

Greenlight Bookstore

686 Fulton Street at South Portland Avenue

Brooklyn

www.greenlightbookstore.com

In Fall 2009, this 2000-square-foot independent bookstore opened in the heart of trendy Ft. Greene, Brooklyn. The store was much needed in the area since there was a dearth of bookstores. The shop offers a weekly storytime at 10:30 a.m. for all ages.

Heights Books

120 Smith Street bet. Hicks and Henry streets

Brooklyn

718-624-4876

www.heightsbooks.com

Okay, Heights Books is no longer located in Brooklyn Heights but in Boerum Hill. For years this used bookstore sat on Montague Street, but in its new digs on the lively Smith Street, this shop has gotten a bit larger. Although the children's section isn't that large, you can still find books for older kids. Heights Books also buys books, so if you have old what-to-do-with-a-baby books crowding your shelves, you should stop by and trade them in for a good novel.

Hue-Man Bookstore & Cafe

2319 Frederick Douglass Boulevard at 124th Street

212-665-7400

www.huemanbookstore.com

This Harlem bookstore has a large children's section, story hours on the weekends, and other kid-friendly events to offer. The store also carries a large section of African American literature and books.

Idlewild Books

12 West 19th Street bet. Fifth and Sixth avenues

212-414-8888

www.idlewildbooks.com

If you're a fan of travel, you must take your child to this unique bookshop devoted to the savvy traveler. Even if you aren't off to explore the world, take your child here to see the many books about foreign lands. The kid's section has a bunch of books on visiting various countries and cultures. They carry pictures books, early readers, and books for older kids.

Kinokuniya Bookstore

1073 Avenue of the Americas at West 41st Street

212-242-9040

www.kinokuniya.com

If you have an anime-obsessed child, you must take them to this Japanese bookshop across the street from Bryant Park, which has an extensive collection of anime books. The downstairs has the best selection of Japanese and French school supplies, even erasers that are shaped like sushi. If your child wants to learn the art of origami, they have many books on the subject as well as origami paper to get started. The bookstore also houses a nice café that overlooks Bryant Park.

Logos Bookstore

1575 York Avenue at East 84th Street

212-517-7292

www.logosbookstorenyc.com

This Upper East Side neighborhood bookstore has a good selection of kids' books in their children's area. The bookstore also has a large selection of Judeo-Christian books, so if you are searching for a chil-

dren's Bible this is a great place to find one. The shop also has special events for kids and hosts birthday parties. On Mondays at 3 p.m., they have a storyteller or puppeteer perform at the shop.

McNally Jackson Books

52 Prince Street bet. Lafayette and Mulberry streets

212-274-1160

www.mcnallyjackson.com

A gem in Soho, McNally Jackson's children's section offers readers of all ages a good selection of quality books as well as a slice of cake and a glass of milk in their café. Parents will love the diverse fiction and nonfiction in this modern and sleekly designed shop that also carries a small amount of toys. The shop has a weekly story hour on Saturdays at noon, with themes varying from teatime to travel.

Penn Books

Penn Station, LIRR Level

212-239-0311

Penn Station, NJ Transit Level

212-239-3109

www.pennbooksny.com

Heading to Amtrak or the LIRR and left all your family's reading materials at home? You're not alone; packing for a family is hard work. Just head to one of these bookstores located in Penn Station. They have a lot of series books, popular kids books, and children's classics.

Posman Books at Grand Central Terminal

9 Grand Central Terminal at Vanderbilt and 42nd Street

212-983-1111

www.posmanbooks.com

Are your kids heading for a long train ride and need a good read? Stop by Posman and pick out book from the last remaining location of this NYC-based independent bookstore. They have a good selection of reads so your child won't be disappointed as he or she boards the train out of the city. My family also likes to stop here when we go to the holiday fair and train show at Grand Central during the holiday season.

The PowerHouse Arena

37 Main Street at Water Street
Brooklyn
718-666-3049

www.powerhousearena.com

Attention all cool kids! This independent bookstore located in Brooklyn's super hip DUMBO is a funky place to score an art book. The store has a selection of kid's books with a focus on picture books.

P.S. Bookshop

145A Front Street at Pearl Street
Brooklyn
718-222-3340

This used bookstore located in DUMBO, Brooklyn, carries books for infants to adults. Booklovers can spend hours walking down the aisles browsing through the reads.

Rizzoli Bookstore

31 West 57th Street bet. Fifth and Sixth avenues
212-759-2424

www.rizzoliusa.com

This classic art bookshop has a nice selection of kids' books and is a great place to pick up a gift. If your children are into art, they might like browsing through the many coffee-table art books in the shop.

St. Marks Bookshop

31 Third Avenue at East 9th Street
212-260-7853

www.stmarksbookshop.com

The East Village bookstore isn't located on St. Marks anymore, but has moved to Third Avenue and 9th Street. They have a children's area where you can find classic kids' books for varying ages and levels of readers. If you have an older child who's into literary magazines and zines, this store has a large collection in the back of the shop. They also have a few tables of discounted books.

Scholastic Store

557 Broadway at Prince Street
212-343-6166

www2.scholastic.com

Harry Potter and Clifford fans must visit this Soho superstore that brings you up close and personal with the Scholastic books we've all grown to love. If you're a fan of the Magic School Bus, they have an entire area surrounded by a large yellow bus that houses Magic School Bus books and puzzles. There are also many good academic books for kids, like primers and writing journals, as well as walls filled with popular Scholastic series for middle and teen readers. The shop hosts events every month; they have a calendar of events available upon entry and on their Web site. The Scholastic store also hosts parties (see p. 104).

Shakespeare & Co.

See Web site for locations throughout New York City

www.shakeandco.com

This New York City–based independent chain bookstore has a kids' section with a wide variety of books for kids of all ages. They also have a large selection of parenting books. If you don't see a book that you're looking for, ask the staff to order it. My family often stops by the shop on lower Broadway to pick up a good book to read on the F train.

Spoonbill & Sugartown Books

218 Bedford Avenue at North 6th Street
Brooklyn
718-387-7322

www.spoonbillbooks.com

Located on Williamsburg's main drag, Spoonbill & Sugartown is a very unique bookstore with an eclectic selection of books. In an area dedicated to children's books for various levels of readers, they have comfy chairs so you and your children can sit and read a book. After picking up some new reads, head for a walk along lively Bedford Avenue. Older kids will like browsing through the shops or playing in nearby McCarren Park (www.mccarrenpark.com).

Strand Book Store

828 Broadway at East 13th Street
212-473-1452

www.strandbooks.com

A part of New York history, this family-owned bookstore is the home of "18 miles of new, used, rare, and out of print books," and has one of the best children's sections in the city. On the second floor of the shop, kids and their parents can spend hours looking through the large shelves filled with books for kids. They even have a table of good NYC-themed kids' books as well as cute Strand T-shirts and bags that they keep by the registers. This is a definite stop for city kids looking to stock up on some summer reading. When we were there, we scored a new copy of Chitty Chitty Bang Bang for under $2.

Unoppressive Non-Imperialist Bargain Books

34 Carmine Street bet. Sixth Avenue and Bedford Street
212-229-0079

www.unoppressivebooks.blogspot.com

This West Village bookstore has been stocked with discounted books for years and is perfect for getting goody bag presents or gifts. The children's bookshop has an extensive selection of various kids' books so you can pick up classics on the cheap.

WORD

126 Franklin Street at Milton Street
718-383-0096

www.wordbrooklyn.wordpress.com

A Greenpoint, Brooklyn, favorite and located across the street from the America Playground, Word has a large children's section that takes up the back of the store and carries a varied selection of kids' books along with educational toys. WORD also hosts kid-friendly book events like a celebration of Children's Book Week (www.bookweekonline.com) and readings by children's book authors. WORD also offers folks the opportunity to join their Book-a-Month Club, for which you'll get one book per month with a $65 six-month subscription; selections vary by age.

The Book-a-Month Club makes a fun birthday present for a little reader or an adult.

Libraries

Your local library might be your own second home, but the main branches of these public libraries also have large children's sections and often host literary events for kids. Check the Web sites for events at each location. You may find that an outing to one of the main branches makes a nice day trip.

New York Public Library

Check Web site for locations throughout New York City.

www.nypl.org

This library system includes libraries in Manhattan, the Bronx, and Staten Island. The famed Central Research Library on Fifth Avenue in Manhattan has two extremely notable stone lions at the steps of the grand building. The building is quite large and has a gift shop on the first floor with tons of toys and books for kids of all ages. Children will love a visit to the Central Children's Room that was recently relocated to the main branch after years at the Donnell Library. In the colorful room located on the ground floor, kids can see displayed the original stuffed animals that were the inspiration for the Winnie-the-Pooh books and participate in tons of kid-friendly activities. The New York Public Library offers programs for kids of all ages at branches throughout the city. Although the Central Library is located in Manhattan, the Bronx and Staten Island have main hubs in their boroughs; visit the **Bronx Library Center** (310 East Kingsbridge Road, Bronx; 718-579-4244) and on Staten Island, **The St. George** (5 Central Avenue, Staten Island; 718- 442-8560).

Brooklyn Public Library

Central Branch, Grand Army Plaza at Eastern Parkway
Brooklyn
718-230-2100

www.brooklynpubliclibrary.org

The Brooklyn Public Library system offers an enormous children's book section and many free kid-friendly events throughout the year, including a film series, workshops, and readings. They also have exhibits in the lobby, many of which would appeal to kids. They have computers available for kids to use, as well as an extensive collection of films and CDs. Check the Web site for branches throughout Brooklyn and listings of events.

Queens Library

89-11 Merrick Boulevard bet. 89th and 90th avenues
Queens
718-990-0700

www.queenslibrary.org

This was my library system growing up, and I still have memories of heading to the Central Library in Jamaica to do research for all my term papers. The central branch has a large children's area and hosts many kid-friendly events, offering everything from knitting classes to science workshops where kids can participate in experiments. If you're looking for books on Asian culture, you should plan a visit to the Flushing branch. This impressive library with a sleek design (an interesting glass structure) is a uniquely multicultural library that is host to events from dance to musical performances. It also offers a large collection of foreign language books.

Book Festivals

Enjoy an outing beyond the local bookstore and library. These book festivals are a great way to meet your child's favorite authors, create exciting book-related craft projects, and spend the day with the family. From annual festivals to on-going series, here are some suggestions for enjoying books as a family:

Brooklyn Book Festival

September

www.brooklynbookfestival.org

Brooklyn is teeming with writers, so it's no wonder that they host their own book festival. Located outside Brooklyn's Borough Hall, the festival includes a children's area with scheduled activities for kids and readings by children's book authors. Local shops, presses, and various literacy organizations set up booths where you can pick up books for kids. Get there early as it soon becomes crowded, but don't let that discourage you—it's always fun and gets kids excited about reading and meeting local authors.

Word for Word Series at Bryant Park

May–August

www.bryantpark.org

On Saturdays throughout the late spring and summer, families can listen to this popular children's reading and writing series run out of Midtown oasis Bryant Park. Located in the Bryant Park Reading room, Word for Word lets kids hear stories from the Frog and Toad series, meet familiar storybook characters like Clifford, engage in scavenger hunts, and take a family writing workshop. In addition to Word for Word, the park also has a free book cart, so if you want to have lunch with your children in the park and relax with a good book, you can borrow a book from the cart for the duration of your stay; just remember to return it. Check the Bryant Park Web site for the Word for Word schedule.

The Little Red Lighthouse Festival

September

www.nycgovparks.org

This annual festival is held in Fort Washington Park by the historic Little Red Lighthouse, which was immortalized in the famous children's book *The Little Red Lighthouse and the Great Gray Bridge* (see p. 167). To celebrate the festival, a local celebrity reads the book aloud, and there are booths with craft projects as well as hayrides, musical performances, and other kid-friendly entertainment. The year we went there were reptiles on display that the kids could touch. The Little Red Lighthouse is open for scheduled tours, but get there early for tickets since they run out quickly. The park and the Little Red Lighthouse are a bit of a trek from the subway, so be prepared for a walk. Bring food and have a picnic, since it's an ideal picnic spot, with tables and amazing views of the water.

New York Is Book Country Fair

September

www.newyorkisbookcountry.com

One of my earliest memories as a kid was heading to Manhattan to attend the New York Is Book Country fair and seeing folks dressed like my favorite storybook characters and picking up some new books. The fair used to be held on Fifth Avenue, but is now held in Central Park. There are tons of kid-friendly activities and many local bookshops and publishers set up booths with displays of their new titles.

The New York Times Great Children's Read

October

www.nytimes.whsites.net/greatread

This New York Times children's book festival takes place at the Columbia University campus. The festival has a large bookshop set up underneath a tent as well as various tables filled with free book-related craft projects and scheduled readings throughout the day. Celebrities read children's classics, authors read their own books, and musical guests perform. When we went, They Might Be Giants performed and kids rocked out on Columbia's lawn.

Literary Landmarks

New York City is the inspiration for so many works of literature. Be sure to check out these literary landmarks from popular children's books and have the books come to life for your kids.

❈ **Edgar Allan Poe Cottage** Older children who are into Edgar Allen Poe can visit the cottage where Poe wrote the famed "Annabel Lee." The cottage just underwent extensive renovations, and there will be a new visitor center opening on the property. (3309 Bainbridge Avenue, Bronx; 212-881-8900; www.bronxhistoricalsociety.org)

❈ **The Portrait of Eloise at The Plaza** The lobby of this famed hotel houses a large painting of Eloise, their most famous fictional resident. You can also head over to the Palm Court to see where Eloise drank her tea. (Fifth Avenue at Central Park South; www.theplaza.com)

❈ **Alice in Wonderland statue in Central Park** Kids will get a kick out of seeing the statue of beloved Alice in Central Park, located near East 74th Street. Kids can climb on the larger-than-life statue of Alice, the White Rabbit, and the Mad Hatter. (www.nycgovparks.org)

❈ **The boats from Stuart Little** Stop by the Kreb's boathouse on the eastern side of the park between 72nd and 75th streets, and rent a model boat like the one Stuart Little, the famed NYC mouse, rode on in the classic children's tale Stuart Little. (www.centralparknyc.org)

❈ **The Little Red Lighthouse and the Great Gray Bridge** Visit the Little Red Lighthouse and the Great Gray Bridge (the GW) and see a part of NYC children's literary history. The book they inspired, written by Hildegarde H. Swift and illustrated by Lynd Ward, is one of my kids' favorite books, The Lighthouse is located in Fort Washington Park in Washington Heights. It's open to the public at various times throughout the year through the Urban Park Rangers (www.historichousetrust.org; 212-304-2365).

❈ **Period rooms at the Metropolitan Museum of Art** Once your child reads From the Mixed-up Files of Basil E. Frankweiler, by W. L. Konigsburg, they will have a greater appreciation for the Met. Enjoy seeing the antique beds where Claudia and her brother Jamie slept and the fountain where they bathed. (1000 Fifth Avenue at 82nd Street; 212-535-7710; www.metmuseum.org)

❄ **The Lower East Side Tenement Museum**
Although this isn't the tenement where the family from the Sydney Taylor's *All-of-a-Kind Family* lived, the tenement is quite similar to the one described in the book, and the neighboring area and its charm still remain. Kids reading the series will enjoy walking down Hester and Rivington streets and seeing where these fictional children grew up. (108 Orchard Street; 212-982-8420; www.tenement.org)

Comic Shops

This section was written and researched by my husband, Peter Isaacs, our family comic expert who has been collecting comics for over thirty years and has introduced our family to the world of superheroes. Now we know that every Wednesday is the day when the new comic books come out and that real collectors bag and board their books. Here's a look at NYC's comic book stores. Although a few of our family's favorite shops have recently shut down, there is still a bunch to explore.

New York City has also been the setting for many comic books, like Spiderman, who grew up in Forest Hills, or Daredevil, who lived in Hell's Kitchen. So take your kids out and explore this city of comic book stardom.

Bergen Street Comics
470 Bergen Street at Flatbush Avenue
Brooklyn
718-230-5600
www.bergenstreetcomics.com

A new addition to the local comic book scene, Bergen Street Comics has a really good catalog of independent comics and graphic novels including well-known and obscure titles. Of course, they also carry all of the latest and greatest Marvel and DC comics, too. With more sophisticated comics and seating available to customers for reading, this is the perfect store for precocious kids. Bergen has quickly cultivated a strong following with a variety of signings and workshops.

Brooklyn Superhero Supply Company
372 5th Avenue at 5th Street
Brooklyn
718-499-9884
www.superherosupplies.com
This isn't a comic shop, but a storefront for the amazing 826 NYC, a nonprofit organization that encourages literacy and writing. The shop is filled with superhero capes, masks, and fake potions that promise to make you invisible along with tons of other stuff that would appeal to both comic book readers and non-comic book readers. Behind a wall of books is the secret entrance to the classrooms for 826 NYC. This place is unique and definitely worth a visit.

Comic Den
8062 Lefferts Boulevard at Austin Street
Queens
718-805-3789
www.comicden.com
This is a classic neighborhood comic book store—exactly the kind of place where I spent

my allowance while I was growing up. They do a nice job of fitting a ton of stuff into a small space.

Cosmic Comics

10 East 23rd Street at Broadway, 2nd floor
212-460-5322
www.cosmiccomics.com
Cosmic has a great selection of back issues for most mainstream comics. However, what stands out for me is how months and months of recent comics are displayed across and along the entire wall of the store. This is an easy way for kids to have a good comic book store experience without having to thumb through boxes of comics and risk the ire of collectors who want their back issues to remain in pristine condition.

Forbidden Planet

840 Broadway at East 13th Street
212-473-1576
www.fpnyc.com
This is a well-organized store with a good layout of current comics, graphic novels, and comic book–themed toys. A plus for the older kids is the second floor with an incredible selection of anime books and movies, as well as a good selection of materials for role-playing games.

Galaxy Comics

429 5th Avenue at 8th Street
Brooklyn
718-499-3222

123 Seventh Avenue at Carroll Street
Brooklyn
718-623-1234

6823 5th Avenue at 68th Street
Brooklyn
718-921-1236
This Brooklyn-based local comic book chain offers kid-friendly comic book shopping. Their shop on Fifth Avenue in Park Slope with superhero posters on the ceiling is my son, Max's, favorite. Instead of focusing on expensive (and delicate) back issues and collectibles, the store has a lot of newer action figures and comic book–inspired toys. They also sell a wide variety of kids' T-shirts with pictures of comic book characters.

Jim Hanley's Universe

4 West 33rd Street bet. Broadway and Fifth Avenue
212-268-7088

325 New Dorp Lane at Clawson Street
Staten Island
718-351-6299
www.jhuniverse.com
This is a comic book superstore. The Manhattan location is a really large space that has everything you could want. Comic book–loving kids can keep themselves busy for hours. I am a big fan of their array of comic book–themed T-shirts that are displayed along one wall of the store.

Midtown Comics

200 West 40th Street at Seventh Avenue
212-302-8192

459 Lexington Avenue at East 45th Street
212-302-8192

www.midtowncomics.com

The Westside store, in particular, stands out, with one floor of comics and another floor of toys. However, what truly separates Midtown Comics from other stores is their collection of high-end back issues. When I was younger, I was always looking for those hard-to-find collector items. If I had known the store existed when I was a kid, this is where I would have gone to buy the special comics.

Rocketship

208 Smith Street at Baltic Street
Brooklyn
718-797-1348
www.rocketshipstore.blogspot.com

More of a high-end comic book store than an old-fashioned mom-and-pop shop, Rocketship focuses on independent comics with really interesting comic book art. They have a large collection of graphic novels that range from the obscure to the mainstream. It is also a good store for new comic book readers, with a rack of kids' comics by the cash register and a large selection of Marvel and DC graphic novels for those that are just getting familiar with the characters.

St. Mark's Comics

11 St. Mark's Place at Third Avenue
Brooklyn
212-598-9439

148 Montague Street at Henry Street
Brooklyn
718-935-0911

www.stmarkscomics.com

This shop looks and feels like my idea of a comic book store. There is a focus on the mainstream titles and displayed on the wall as you enter are the most recent issues of Marvel and DC comics. There are literally dozens of the usual large, white comic book boxes filled with years and years of back issues. There are sales on back issues a few times each year, so your kids can catch up on story lines from before they were born at a very reasonable price. The staff has always been incredibly friendly and helpful when I have brought my children to the store.

Silver Age Comics

2255 31st Street bet. 23rd Avenue and Ditmars Boulevard
Queens
718-721-9691
www.silveragecomics.com

The store is located in the Ditmars-Astoria subway station on the N and W lines. From the outside it does not look like much, but when you enter you can tell that it is helmed by comic book lovers, as every inch of the store is covered in comics. The store has some excellent sales on back issues that would have made this a favorite place for me when I was growing up.

Graphic Novel Museums and Comic Conventions

Check out this comic art museum and these annual conventions that are kid friendly.

Museum of Comic & Cartoon Art

594 Broadway at West Houston Street
212-254-3511

www.moccany.org

MoCCA is a nonprofit organization that focuses on promoting comic and cartoon art. The exhibits are changed regularly and there are a variety of lectures and signings. Located in a loft in Soho, it is a nice way to introduce children to the art world and get them comfortable in a gallery environment. The comic book themes are extremely kid friendly and the museum is free for kids twelve and under.

Big Apple Convention

www.bigapplecon.com

I wish this convention had existed when I was a kid, as the place is packed with comic book vendors from all over the country. It is a good way for new fans or regular comic readers to get all the back issues that they could ever dream of. Additionally, there are always a variety of celebrities from TV, movies, and popular culture on hand to sign autographs.

New York Comic Con

www.nycomiccon.com

You do not have to be a comic book fan to enjoy this spectacle. Held in the Jacob Javits Center on West 34th Street, they have had more than 75,000 attendees in a single convention. Comic fans will love walking the aisles checking out the books set up by a variety of comic stores. However, what stands out for me is all of the comic book companies that are represented. Both DC and Marvel have large booths, along with many independent comic book publishers.

Chapter Ten

Toys, Crafts, Games, and Magic

Finally your house isn't filled with brightly colored Fisher-Price plastic baby and toddler toys anymore, but is instead filled with board games like Monopoly, one-hundred-piece puzzles, and science kits. You may be at a loss about which toys your child needs (if any). You may also be upset that your once-very-active child who spent hours playing with their toys is now fixated on TV, the Internet, and portable gaming devices. Just because you have a savvy city kid doesn't mean they are too old for toys. Board games are a great way to get in some old-fashioned family bonding. I know that this will sound hokey, but I've heard of many families that have family game nights. I also believe that the hours my daughter and I spent playing Scrabble Junior have made her a better speller and that my son developed exceptional motors skills mastering Perfection.

Head to the toyshop and pick up cool toys like chemistry sets, magic kits, and fun board games. You may be surprised at how many toys you'll actually want for yourself. I'll admit on a recent trip to the toy store I almost bought myself a kit for making lip balm. Your kids are at the age when toys start becoming fun as well as being an important part of their learning process. I mean, didn't we all learn to cook using our Easy-Bake Oven?

This section will also give you inside tips on scoring discounted toys, which come in handy during the holiday season and also for stocking up on presents for the never-ending stream of birthday parties. Additionally, if your child likes crafts, check out the list of craft shops and stores that offer in-store craft activities, so you always have instant plans for a rainy day or a day-off from school. If your child is more Harry Potter than craft queen, I've listed unique magic shops and amazing magic shows performed throughout the city, often without the cost of admission!

Toy recommendations from the owner of the Manhattan toy store, Kidding Around

We've all walked into a toy shop and found ourselves wondering what to buy. Here are some suggestions from Christina Clark, who owns Kidding Around, a Manhattan toy store, with her husband, Paul Nippes. Christina says to children, "The best toys are always the ones that your parents will play with you. Marble runs, with their wonderful blend of building and cause-and-effect definitely fall into that category. Haba makes a fabulous wooden one with tons of exciting accessories to add to a basic set. There are also great ones in plastic made by Quercetti, Taurus Toy, and a grand motorized one by Learning Journey that uses gears and creates a continuous loop."

Christina shares her complete list of toy suggestions for city parents below, listing her favorite categories of toys for children in between the ages of four and twelve.

Pretend play: Pretend play is how children learn to become the adults they see in the world around them. Mimicking their parents, teachers, construction workers, and doctors is how children learn about the world, and how to resolve conflicts, share, cooperate, and get along. Recommended toys include:

✳ Tools: Battat makes a set of vehicles that can be taken apart and put together again using a power drill.

✳ Tea sets, plastic or wooden food, and food preparation sets: PlanToys makes beautiful wooden tea sets.

✳ Dolls: We tend to underestimate the value of nurturing and caring for others in children's play. Corolle makes beautiful dolls that will last for the next generation to love.

Fantasy Play: Fantasy play helps to spark imaginations and creative thinking. Having a variety of toys and accessories around will help in this process. Note for parents: Take out a notebook and unobtrusively jot down the overheard conversations while your kids are engaging in creative play—you will cherish them later! Recommended toys include:

✳ Capes for action heroes, kings, knights, queens, princesses, or wizards.

✳ Tutus, princess attire, boas, tiaras, handbags, and wands.

✳ Fire fighter and astronaut costumes—Aeromax makes the toy-industry standard.

✳ An assortment of fireman, cowboy, construction, and police hats.

Creative Play: When I was a child I often said, "I'm bored. What can I make?" So this category really appeals to me. Recommended toys include:

✳ Harrisville Designs has a beautiful potholder-making loom that is better than the ones I had when I was a child.

✳ Kits by Creativity for Kids and Alex cover everything from beads and pottery wheels to easels and clay, with a range of mediums like paint, yarn, and wood.

* Uberstix is a new kind of construction set in which the pieces are engineered to connect with most major building systems: Lego, K'NEX, and Erector Set. They also have a recycling component that works with straws, Popsicle sticks, paper cups, and paper clips.

* Action Products makes a Dinosaur Dig kit in which the child, as a paleontologist, chips away at a sand block with a hefty steel chisel and hammer (protective goggles included) to uncover dinosaur bones, which he or she can then construct and paint to make a complete skeleton.

* Train sets by Learning Curve (makers of Thomas the Tank Engine) and Brio are terrific building toys. Young engineers have to solve constructive problems and figure out how to complete a loop over various terrains so that the trains can continue their travels.

Games: In a time of isolating activities like television watching, computer tinkering, and video game playing, I love games that bring family and friends together. Recommended toys include:

* Zingo (ages four to eight). It's a matching game with a gizmo that drops two tiles that players must try to match to their own boards. Bilingual versions are also available in Spanish, French, and Hebrew.

* Kids on Stage (ages three to eight). Younger players love this game because they don't

have to be able to read to get used to taking turns, sequencing, and moving along a board in order to act out the pictures on the cards they draw. Get out your video equipment for the first time they play—it can be a hoot!

* Rat-A-Tat-Cat (ages six and up). Among the very few games that older kids don't mind playing with their younger siblings, Rat-A-Tat-Cat is a card game that involves getting the lowest possible score. With cards numbered from zero to nine, no major adding is required.

* Go Fish for Letters (ages six and up). This is a great variation on the classic card game that uses letters instead of numbers for early readers.

* Maze Ways Cat and Mouse (ages six and up). These logic games by Smart Games really live up to their name. In this particular game one must build a path from one object (or several) to another along a framed game board that holds nine tiles. The spiral-bound challenge book begins with easy problems and progresses to more difficult ones. The whole game is easily stored within the box for easy cleanup.

* Gobblet and Blokus and Quarto (ages five and up). Don't be fooled by the early ages listed for these great strategy games; adults will be just as happy to play.

* SET (ages six and up). This is arguably the best game out there. SET is an attribute-

matching card game and stands alone in its ability to capture the attention of anyone from six to sixty-six years old.

❋ Take Off! (ages ten and up). The laminated map for this board game is almost four feet by two feet and serves as the playing board. The players must get their fleet of four jets from one end to the other by following flight paths or drawing cards that send them to particular destinations.

Toy Stores

Acorn Toy Shop
323 Atlantic Avenue bet. Smith and Hoyt streets
Brooklyn
718-522-3760
www.acorntoyshop.com
Local artisans make many of the unique toys that are sold at this Brooklyn toy shop. If you are looking for an inventive private play space for your child, they have a selection of gorgeous handmade play tents that look like tepees. Located in downtown Brooklyn on a once-underutilized Atlantic Avenue, the shop is a Brooklyn gem and a symbol of the neighborhood's transformation.

American Girl Place
609 Fifth Avenue at 49th Street
877-247-5223
www.americangirl.com
Girls from the metro area flock to the three-story shop on Fifth Avenue where you can purchase all the dolls from the American Girl collection along with their accessories. At this shop, the American Girl catalog is brought to life on the shelves. My daughter kept pointing everything out that she had seen in the catalog and had a good sense of what she wanted before we even stepped into the store.

Besides purchasing American Girl products, the shop offers many services for girls and their dolls. Your child can get a professional photograph taken with their doll and can choose from a variety of packages. She can also spend the day at the salon getting the doll's hair done or getting the doll's ears pierced. If you want a simpler day, just walk through the floor of historical dolls and start up a discussion on American history with your child. The ground floor also has a large collection of American Girl books.

Annie's Blue Ribbon General Store
365 State Street at Bond Street
Brooklyn
718-522-9848
www.blueribbongeneralstore.net
This eclectic general store located in Boerum Hill, Brooklyn is full of unique toys and books, which makes it the ideal stop for an off-beat birthday gift or stocking stuffer. From mini Buddhas to balloon making kits, the shop has goods that will appeal to kids of all ages. Annie's Blue Ribbon General Store also has a great collection of home goods like funky picture frames and piggy banks to spruce up your kid's room.

Area Play
331 Smith Street bet. Baltic and Douglass streets
Brooklyn

718-624-2411

www.areakids.com

The window of this Carroll Gardens toy shop is filled with sleekly designed toys. Area Play carries toy essentials, from scooters to sea monkeys. They carry brands like Eeboo, Kid Robot, Melissa & Doug, Plan-Toys, and many other favorites. This shop is owned and operated by a local mom who knows what kind of toys that city kids like. They also gift wrap for no additional charge. Additionally they have a small selection of books; my daughter loves sorting through their collection of the Little Miss and Mr. Men book series.

Balloon Saloon

133 West Broadway at Duane Street

212-227-3838

www.balloonsaloon.com

For years this corner shop in TriBeCa has been supplying New Yorkers with bouquets of balloons (see p. 116), but their shop also has a great supply of toys like Shrinky Dinks, board games, and the best selection of goody bag stuffers that you'll find in the city. Their business cards are designed to look like a twenty-dollar bill, which really adds to the ultimate kitsch appeal of this NYC staple.

Boomerang Toys

173 West Broadway bet. Leonard and Worth streets

212-226-7650

World Financial Center, Wintergarden Level

225 Liberty Street at South End Avenue

212-786-3011

www.boomerangtoys.com

Visit both locations of this popular downtown toyshop to pick up a variety of toys from brands like Playmobil, Lego, Alex Toys, and many others. Kids can play with their train table set up in the store. Boomerang has a good selection of toys for older kids like science sets. I almost bought my kids a clear plastic pot, so they can see their plants' roots grow, but since I don't have a green thumb I thought I'd be setting them up for a big disappointment. If you're in downtown on a rainy day with the kids, spend the afternoon walking around the Wintergarden level of the World Financial Center.

Build-A-Bear Workshop

565 Fifth Avenue at 46th Street

212-871-7080

Staten Island Mall

2655 Richmond Avenue

Staten Island

718-698-1477

www.buildabear.com

What can I say about Build-A-Bear? First of all, kids get to make their own personalized stuffed animal. In the Manhattan shop, you can dress your new stuffed buddy in a series of touristy NYC-inspired outfits, which is kind of cute. Kids choose from a variety of animals to stuff, choose which sounds to add to the animal, and finally also get to print out a birth certificate for their furry friend. These toys are ideal for city kids. If you buy one, your child can keep all the bear's clothes and accessories in the space-saving cardboard carrying case that he or she totes them home in. My daughter loves her bear and it has tons of clothes (and even a pair of underwear and slippers). Both locations host parties and various events throughout the year, so check their Web sites for their schedules.

Century 21
22 Cortlandt Street at Maiden Lane
212-227-9092

472 86th Street at York Avenue
718-748-3266
Brooklyn
www.c21stores.com

A New York City secret, this discount clothing shop also has a large selection of discounted kids' toys. The Brooklyn location has a separate home store across from the department store, which carries a larger selection of craft projects, Melissa & Doug toys, board games, and other toys at deep discounts. This is an economical place to stock up on birthday presents, since the minute your child starts attending school, you will start to receive a steady stream of invites.

The Children's General Store
168 East 91st Street bet. Lexington and Third avenues
212-426-4479

The Children's General Store is a neighborhood toy store that is stocked with a variety of toys for all ages. From craft kits to puppets, there is much in this small shop to spark a child's imagination. They also offer free gift wrapping.

Cozy's Cuts for Kids
1416 Second Avenue at 74th Street
212-585-2699

448 Amsterdam Avenue at 81st Street
212-579-2600
www.cozyscutsforkids.com

In addition to getting your child's hair cut at this salon, your kid can also choose from a wide variety of toys, like Zingo and Webkinz, at their toy boutique.

Daffy's
Check Web site for locations throughout Manhattan
www.daffys.com

Like Century 21, this discount designer shop also carries toys. The toy area varies in size at each location, but all carry a bunch of quality toys at discounted prices. I purchased a Dorothy Barbie doll from the 34th Street location and it was one of the biggest hits with my daughter. Daffy's carries everything from licensed products like Spiderman toys to art kits.

Dinosaur Hill
306 East 9th Street at Second Avenue
212-473-5850
www.dinosaurhill.com

This East Village staple has been selling toys and clothes to city kids since the eighties. Although a large section of the shop caters to younger kids, they have an amazing selection of puppets and marionettes for the budding puppeteers in your family. The staff is extremely friendly and the shop is particularly inviting. Find a funky gift for a picky NYC kid at this wonderful shop.

Disney Store
Staten Island Mall
2655 Richmond Avenue
Staten Island
718-494-1032

Queens Center
90–15 Queens Boulevard
Queens
718-271-1036
www.disneystore.com
If your child is asking for a trip to Disney World, try to appease them with a visit to the Disney Store, a chain that sells Disney-themed merchandise. This is the spot to find a Disney Princess doll or toy based on any Disney movie. Of course you'll have to travel out to one of these malls to visit, which makes it a fun rainy-day excursion for families.

Playing Chess in the West Village

Chess is more than a board game and is extremely popular with school-age children. Most schools offer after-school chess clubs and classes. If your child dreams of being a grandmaster, you must visit these NYC shops:

Chess Forum
219 Thompson Street at Great Jones Street
212-475-2369
www.chessforum.com
Located in the West Village, the Chess Forum has a wide variety of boards to choose from, including sets with pieces that carved to look like popular TV characters like the *Simpsons*. Chess Forum recommends that you purchase for your kids the set that schools and tournaments use, with the numbers and letters on the board. Next door, they have tables where you can play both chess and Scrabble. They also offer chess lessons and host a chess camp.

New York Chess & Game Shop
192 Flatbush Avenue at Dean Street
Brooklyn
718-398-3727
www.newyorkchessandgameshop.com
This Brooklyn chess shop offers classes for kids of all levels as well as private lessons and summer camps. They have a good selection of chessboards and accessories, like a padded carrying case for your child's chessboard. The shop has open play during business hours when you and your child can pick up a game of chess, Scrabble, or backgammon.

Village Chess Shop
230 Thompson Street at Great Jones Street
212-475-9580
www.chess-shop.com
This classic West Village chess shop located across the street from the Chess Forum is a great place to spend the day playing chess. They have tables set up inside the shop available on a first come, first serve basis. If you have any questions about chess, just ask the friendly staff. Village Chess Shop also offers lessons and camps.

Want to travel around the city playing chess? Here is a list of public chess tables in NYC that are usually filled with skilled chess players, so you might pick up a tip or two:

❋ The Chess and Checkers House in Central Park (inside park on 65th Street, just west of the dairy; www.centralpark.com)

✳ Consider joining the Marshall Chess Club in the West Village. They offer chess lessons, camps, and of course, tables for drop-in games. (23 West 10th Street; 212-477-3716; www.marshallchessclub.org)

✳ Washington Square Park chess tables (www.nycgovparks.org)

✳ At Bryant Park, chess games are set up on green folding tables; sometimes they offer free lessons through the NYC parks department (www.bryantpark.org)

E.A.T. Gifts

1062 Madison Avenue, near 80th Street
212-861-2544

E.A.T. carries tons of kitschy gifts for kids and adults. Get everything from placemats to retro Snoopy and Lucy statues at this toy and gift shop. The staff is very friendly and is eager to help you choose a present for a child of any age and will offer suggestions. Personally I love browsing through the shop and taking a trip down memory lane with some of their retro-themed gifts. They have a good selection of smaller toys, which makes it an ideal place to get a present or party favor.

Enchanted Toys

1179 Lexington Avenue bet. East 80th and 81st streets
212-288-3383
www.enchanted-toys.com

This shop is filled with gorgeous handcrafted wooden toys. From stunning wooden castles to other toys that spark imaginative play, the shop's focus is on natural toys and so it doesn't carry video games and other commercial toys. It's nice to browse around looking at all the beautiful and unique items that they have in the store.

Exotiqa

280 City Island Avenue at Hawkins Street
Bronx
718-885-3090
www.themagicofgifts.com

Located on City Island's main street, which feels more like a small New England seaside town than a Bronx neighborhood, Exotiqa has toys and gifts for kids. Filled with puzzles, arts and crafts, Ugly dolls and other toys, they try to rotate the inventory so you'll never know what you may find at this local shop.

FAO Schwarz

767 5th Avenue at West 59th Street
212-644-9400
www.fao.com
See party section, pages 102–103.

Frankie's Playce

The Shops at Atlas Park
8000 Cooper Avenue
Queens
www.frankiesplayce.com

Located at a chic outdoor Queens mall that seems more L.A. than NYC, this independently owned toy store has a large selection of toys that I hadn't seen in other shops. They also have a large party room and a children's hair salon on the premises. From barrettes to board games, you'll find it at this Queens toy store.

Heights Kids & Toy Box

85 Pineapple Walk at Henry Street
Brooklyn
718-246-5440

This beloved Brooklyn Heights shop carries a large variety of European toys like Playmobil and Lego. Even older kids will appreciate the train table setup in the shop. This is a nice place to pick up a gift since they offer suggestions and free gift wrapping. From traditional board games to specialty toys, this shop will appeal to kids of all ages (although don't look for video games here, you won't find them). The store is attached to Heights Kids, a Brooklyn superstore that caters to the Brooklyn baby-boom crowd.

Ibiza Kidz

61 Fourth Avenue bet. 9th and 10th Streets
212-228-7990
www.ibizakidz.com

This Village toy and shoe shop sells toys for all ages, like Alex art kits, dolls, and wooden subway cars so kids can build the New York City subway line in their apartment. At Ibiza you can pick up a toy or possibly a new pair of shoes. They also carry kid's clothes.

Jack's 99 Cent Store

110 West 32nd Street bet. Sixth and Seventh avenues
212-268-9962

16 East 40th Street bet. Madison and Fifth Avenues
212-696-5767

My family is addicted to 99-cent stores. We just love the bazaar-like atmosphere of junk shops. Although Jack's is a discount store and not an actual 99-cent store, there are bargains to be found at this NYC staple. In addition to picking up inexpensive goody bag items and stocking stuffers, you can walk away with a lot of toys without breaking the bank because the toy area carries so many reputable brands. The toys aren't 99 cents, but they aren't very expensive either. I purchased a DVD version of Thomas the Tank Engine bingo here, which has been a hit with my family. They change the merchandise regularly, so check in when you're near one of the two stores. If you need a gift for a younger child, they have a lot of Fisher-Price toys on hand.

It's Magic: Magic Shops and Shows Around the City

Want your kid to be the next Houdini or David Blaine? If your child is a budding magician, they will love a trip to one of these magic shops. Some offer free magic shows and others offer magic camps. All carry starter magic sets for kids, so you can have your child perform a magic show just for you.

Abracadabra Superstore

19 West 21st Street at Sixth Avenue
212-627-7523
www.abracadabrasuperstore.com

You can find a variety of magic tricks at this Chelsea costume and magic shop. On Sundays at 3 p.m., you can also enjoy a free magic show. The staff is friendly and will help you navigate your way through the shop and pick out the right magic tricks for your little magician.

Fantasma Magic
421 Seventh Avenue at 33rd Street, 2nd floor
212-244-3633
www.fantasmamagic.com
Kids will have fun on a visit to this magic shop located on the second floor of a Midtown building. The shop carries magic sets for kids and has information on local magic shows if you're looking to take in a performance.

Magic Brunch at Cercle Rouge Restaurant
241 West Broadway bet. Walker and White streets
212-226-6252
www.cerclerougeresto.com
Every Saturday and Sunday from noon until 2 p.m., Ragidy Supreme performs a magic show at this Tribeca restaurant. In addition to the magic show and good eats, your child will also bring home free balloons.

Tannen's Magic
45 34th Street at Sixth Avenue, Suite 608
212-929-4500
www.tannens.com
Magic lovers must visit Tannen's, a magic shop that has been stocking professional magicians with the latest tricks since 1925. The shop carries magic sets and tricks for kids and also offers a magic camp for kids ages twelve and up. The site has info on magic shows like the popular Manhattan Magic Show (www.manhattan-magicshow.com), which is better suited for older kids. If you decide to get tickets, mention Tannen's and you'll receive a discount.

Rogue Magic and Fun Shop
85-08 Queens Boulevard at 67th Avenue
Queens
718-505-0316
www.roguefunshop.com
Head to Queens to check out this magic shop stocked with tricks. The folks from the shop host a weekly magic show on Saturdays from 9 p.m. until 11 p.m. They also have family shows, so call ahead for updates on shows or check their Web site. If you and your child want to sharpen your magical abilities, they also offer classes.

Jan's Hobby Shop
1435 Lexington Avenue bet. 93rd and 94th Streets
212-861-5075
Jan's Hobby Shop is a part of NYC history. For over thirty years Jan's has been on the Upper East Side selling kits for making model airplanes and cars. The shop moved to bigger digs in the same neighborhood to fit its large selection of material for hobby enthusiasts. The owner knows a ton about these kits, so ask him which kit is best to start your child off on a lifetime of model building.

Kidding Around
60 West 15th Street, near Sixth Avenue
212-645-6337
www.kiddingaroundnyc.com
A personal favorite, Kidding Around has a large selection of toys for all ages. Carrying brands like Brio and Playmobil, Kidding Around also stocks educational toys like microscopes and musical instru-

ments. Many of the toys they sell are European imports and all of them are of the highest quality. You can find interesting board games at the shop, like Blokus. The shop has a large section of smaller yet substantial toys that are perfect for goody bags and stocking stuffers. With free gift wrapping and a nice staff, there isn't much more to ask from this homey Manhattan toy shop.

Kidrobot

118 Prince Street bet. Wooster and Greene streets
212-966-6688
www.kidrobot.com

This uber-hip Soho shop sells both toys and clothing. Browse through the white shelves filled with an assortment of small robots, doughnut key chains in funky packages, as well as other unique toys. The small store feels more like a Soho gallery than a toy shop and is often crowded with kids and adults checking out the many figurines. Some of the toy robot figures are collectibles since only a small number of those figurines were produced.

Little Things

145 7th Avenue at Carroll Street
Brooklyn
718-783-4733

Located in the heart of Park Slope, this shop is crammed full of toys—everything from educational toys to art supplies. This is a neighborhood staple and folks come here to pick up a variety of toys and crafts from Alex craft kits to old-school board games. They offer free gift-wrapping.

Lulu's Cuts and Toys

48 Fifth Avenue at Bergen Street
Brooklyn
718-832-3732
www.luluscuts.com

Lulu's has a wide selection of Playmobil toys and Thomas the Tank Engine trains. In addition they have a wall of smaller toys that make great stocking stuffers or goody bag fillers. They also cut children's hair and sell cute barrettes.

Macy's Herald Square

151 West 34th Street bet. Broadway and Seventh Avenue
212-695-4400

The toy section on the eighth floor of this historic NYC shop is only open during the holiday season when it is transformed into a winter wonderland. Kids can get their picture taken with Santa or see a puppet show at Santaland. The toy section carries many notable brands of toys.

Madame Alexander Doll Factory

615 West 131st Street at Broadway
212-283-5900

If you're shopping for a doll, you must stop by the Madame Alexander Shop, where you can pick up one of their classics. Madame Alexander sells dolls based on children's books like *Eloise* and *Fancy Nancy*. My daughter was quite taken with their *Wizard of Oz* doll collection. The dolls are extremely well made and if they happen to break you can send them to their on-site doll hospital. They also offer tours of the doll factory.

Tours of the Madame Alexander Doll Factory

Visitors are welcome to tour this historic doll factory seven days a week from 9:30 a.m. to 4:15 p.m. The tours are free and take place every forty-five minutes. Kids and collectors will love walking through the collection of Madame Alexander dolls, and the tour includes a video on their history. They have the original dolls on display and the tour guide will explain the history of the doll collection. If you'd like a behind-the-scenes tour to see the designers working on the dolls and also visit the doll hospital, schedule a private walk-through (212-283-5900).

After the tour you can spend some time picking out your own Madame Alexander doll at their shop that is filled with collectible dolls. I especially loved the *Desperate Housewives* dolls for sale. My daughter loved the tour and afterward we were able to find a reasonably priced baby doll for just $3. The factory also hosts birthday parties where kids can make their own dolls (see p. 104).

The Manhattan Dollhouse Shop in FAO Schwarz

236 Third Avenue at 20th Street
212-253-9549
www.manhattandollhouse.com

This Manhattan shop sells completed dollhouse sets for kids who are interested in a "starter home." Dollhouse fans will have fun on a visit to the shop where they can stock up on accessories and miniatures. They also sell dollhouses that fit Barbie dolls.

Mary Arnold Toys

1010 Lexington Avenue at 72nd Street
212-744-8510

Mary Arnold has been providing toys for city kids since the 1930s. This shop is a classic Upper East Side toy store and is definitely worth a visit to see their selection of toys. Mary Arnold carries everything from Fisher-Price to art supplies. Additionally, if you live on the Upper East Side they offer a free delivery service. They also offer free gift wrapping.

Mini Max Toys and Cuts

152 Atlantic Street near Clinton Street
Brooklyn
718-222-TOYS
www.minimaxnyc.com

Opened by local moms, the shop carries educational toys and crafts by brands like Plan Toys and Alex. They also have a line of action figures of Virginia Woolf, Barack Obama, Albert Einstein, and other notables by Jailbreak Toys. In the back of the shop is a small hair salon for kids. The shop hosts many kid events and programs like drop-in art projects and story time with a focus on local authors.

Nairobi's Knapsack

744 Franklin Avenue at Sterling Place
Brooklyn
347-295-2011
www.nairobisknapsack.com

With an emphasis on multicultural products, this Crown Heights kids' shop sells toys, books, and room décor. They also carry a nice selection of toys from brands like Eeboo, Karito Kids, and others that offer children the opportunity to learn about other cultures. Nairobi's Knapsack also hosts birthday parties and offers violin lessons for kids ages four and up.

Nintendo World Store

10 Rockefeller Plaza (West 48th Street) bet. Fifth and Sixth avenues
646-459-0800
www.nintendoworldstore.com
Adults and kids alike are addicted to the Nintendo Wii—I know my family loves playing Wii bowling in our living room. Stock up on Wii games and accessories at this Midtown mega store, where you and your child get the chance to try the latest gaming devices and games from Nintendo. One word of warning: It may be hard to drag your husband from this shop.

Pizzazz Toyz and Kidz

281 Court Street bet. Butler and Douglass streets
Brooklyn
718-797-3177
This neighborhood favorite supplies the Cobble Hill and Carroll Gardens community with everything from Thomas Trains to Shrinky Dinks. The shop is bursting at the seams with toys and carries both educational toys like craft sets and commercial toys like Disney Princess play cell phones. They also have a large selection of scooters. Pizzazz Toyz and Kidz provides free gift wrapping.

Pumpkin Toys & Hobbies

334 Bleecker Street at Christopher Street
212-352-0109
This West Village toy shop stocks tons of offbeat

and interesting toys that you wouldn't find at your local toy store chain, like cool science kits. They also carry clothing and I was particularly taken by their collection of funny T-shirts. Most of the clothes are for the younger set and if you're looking for a nice baby gift you'll be sure to find it here.

The Red Caboose

23 West 45th Street bet. Fifth and Sixth avenues
212-575-0155
www.theredcaboose.com
Every hobby enthusiast should check out this shop located in the basement of a Midtown building. They have a large assortment of hobby kits for building model airplanes, cars, or subway cars. They also sell a ton of books on trains, model cars, and other hobby-related subjects.

Scholastic Store

557 Broadway at Prince Street
212-343-6166
www2.scholastic.com
This book and toy store carries a large selection of educational toys. In addition to Melissa & Doug toys and interesting dress-up clothing like a NASA space outfit for the over-four set, the shop carries a ton of Harry Potter merchandise. Have your children's favorite Scholastic tales come alive with games and toys based on Scholastic books.

State News—The Toy Store

112 East 86th Street at Park Avenue
212-831-8010
This large Upper East Side toyshop carries everything from Lego to Playmobil. The aisles are jam-packed with toys so you won't be disappointed with

their selection. They have a separate area where you can purchase books and art supplies. Since State News owns it, this quirky shop has an extensive magazine aisle where you can check out magazines for kids and their parents.

Tah-Poozie

50 Greenwich Avenue at Perry Street
212-647-0668

Tah-Poozie really isn't a toy store, but it sells tons of small kid-friendly toys and accessories. This is the place to pick up goody bag fillers and stocking stuffers.

Target

139 Flatbush Avenue at Atlantic Avenue
Brooklyn
718-290-1109
www.target.com

Centrally located in Brooklyn near most major subway lines, this chain store has a good-size toy section, which includes a section of bikes. This is the type of place where you can pick up commercial toys, DVDs, or a sled. Prices at Target are reasonable and they have a good line of toys sponsored by *Parents* magazine for the younger set. Target also caters to the Gen X parent with a bunch of educational toys and reasonably priced craft/art kits.

Tiny Doll House

1179 Lexington Avenue at 80th Street
212-744-3719
www.tinydollhousenyc.com

I'll admit I spent more time picking out dollhouse furniture for my daughter's dollhouse than I did for my own apartment. Maybe I was drawn to the fact that her dolls have an entire house filled with space while

we live in an apartment. Fans of dollhouses and miniatures should make a trip over to Tiny Doll House to pick out a house and accessories. These homes are divine, with a remarkable amount of attention to detail on even the smallest of home accessories.

Totally Toys

1435 Coney Island Avenue at Avenue K
Brooklyn
718-758-0088

Located in the heart of Orthodox Brooklyn, Totally Toys has an amazing selection of toys and bikes. A neighborhood store, the staff is more than happy to advise you on purchases. They carry a wide variety of toys from educational to those based on TV shows.

Toys "R" Us

1514 Broadway bet. West 44th and 45th streets
646-366-8800
www.toysrustimessquare.com

Upon entering this Manhattan superstore you'll be asked to have your picture taken with their mascot, Geoffrey the Giraffe. These photographs will be available for purchase on your way out. They also have a large Ferris wheel with seats designed after classic kids toys. This Toys "R" Us location hosts various workshops and events like make-your-own-robot and events based on popular TV shows. Check their Web site for the schedule of events.

Toy Space

426 Seventh Avenue bet. 14th and 15th streets
Brooklyn
718-369-9096
www.toyspaceny.com

If you're looking for a toy that is both educational

and fun, this is the place to go. Toy Space seems to cater to the over-four set, having everything from magic sets to lava lamps. It's definitely worth a trip to this South Slope neighborhood favorite and its walls lined with unique board games and good selection of craft projects. The staff is friendly and will recommend suggestions for toy purchases and gift wrap at no additional charge.

Toy Tokyo

21 Second Avenue at 7th Street
212-673-6424
www.theshowroomnyc.com

This East Village shop located on a second floor above lively Second Avenue carries tons of Japanese toys. They have a lot of collectibles, but they also carry kitschy products like bobbleheads and a variety of other toys. The aisles of the shop are filled with interesting finds and parents will enjoy browsing around the shop and may even pick up something for their own office desk.

Train World

751 McDonald Avenue at Ditmas Avenue
Brooklyn
718-436-7072
www.trainworld.com

Although the Web site says the shop is best for the fourteen-and-over set, the large selection of both Thomas trains and model trains tell otherwise. The truth is, these folks take trains seriously, but younger train fans are more than welcome to purchase their first train set here or eye the Hogwarts Express train that is for sale at this amazing Brooklyn store.

West Side Kids

498 Amsterdam Avenue at 84th Street
212-496-7282

This Upper West Side neighborhood favorite, filled with all the toys a city kid could need, carries everything from Playmobil and baseball cards to my daughter's favorite Mad Lib books and art project kits. They have a unique selection of toys and educational gifts. Feeling overwhelmed? Ask one of the friendly folks at the shop to lead you in the right direction. They also offer free gift wrapping in the back of the shop. This store with neighborhood charm also has a bulletin board of ads for local classes and sitters.

Craft Shops and Art Supplies

Arts and crafts projects are as important to kids as their toys. Children love to get out the paints and put on a smock to create artwork. Below are some places to pick up supplies. Just to note, although they not listed below, there are also popular craft chains—A.C. Moore, Jo-Ann Fabrics and Crafts, and Michaels—in Manhattan, Queens, and Staten Island. Check the stores' Web sites for more information.

A.I. Friedman

44 West 18th Street bet. Fifth and Sixth avenues
212-243-9000
www.aifriedman.com

Older kids who want to scrapbook photos from sleepaway camp (if they actually print them off the computer anymore) should visit this NYC shop that has tons of photo albums and materials for scrapbookers. They have a good selection of notebooks and stationery if your child decides to write a letter instead of an e-mail. You can also pick up some standard art supplies here. Additionally, they provide custom framing if you feel your child's artwork is worthy of your living room.

The Artful Place

171 Fifth Avenue at Lincoln Place
Brooklyn
718-399-8199

Located in north Park Slope, this art store also hosts classes and parties. Stop by the shop and pick up everything from beads to craft kits.

Barclays School Supplies

166 Livingston Street at Smith Street
Brooklyn
718-875-2424
www.barclayschoolsupplies.com

Even if you aren't homeschooling your child, it's definitely worth a visit to this downtown Brooklyn shop that is easily accessible from most major subway lines. The shop has tons of craft supplies, so you can create your own art projects at home.

The Craft Studio

1657 Third Avenue at 93rd Street
212-831-6626
www.craftstudionyc.com

Crafty kids can partake in a walk-in craft workshop at this art studio that has been a part of the Upper East Side community for over ten years. If your child doesn't want to engage in painting a pot or other craft project at the shop, choose from a multitude of art supplies and craft kits to work on at home. The shop also carries a wide range of educational toys as well as hosts workshops and birthday parties.

Etsy Inc.

325 Gold Street at Johnson Street, 6th floor
Brooklyn
718-855-7955
www.etsy.com/storque/how-to

Although Etsy isn't a shop, on the last Monday of each month the folks at Etsy Labs offer an open craft night from 4 p.m. until 8 p.m., where kids can use all the craft supplies at the Etsy Lab for free. With boxes of felt, yarn, and other materials, your child's imagination can go wild. If you don't have room to store a sewing machine and have a project that involves sewing, you can use their machines. They also have a shelf of craft books so you can get some ideas for new projects for the kids. On the other Mondays of the month they have instructor-led classes; to see if the sessions' projects are kid-friendly, check the schedule on their Web site.

The Ink Pad

22 Eighth Avenue at West 12th Street
212-463-9876
www.theinkpadnyc.com

Who doesn't like rubber stamps? This West Village shop carries the largest selection of rubber stamps that I've ever seen. You can also special-order personalized rubber stamps. Don't worry if your stamp pads have gone dry, because they have a lot of new ones to choose from at this unique specialty shop.

Lee's Art Shop

220 West 57th Street
212-247-0110
www.leesartshop.com

This art supply store carries a large selection of kids' crafts and art materials, like markers, glitter glue, and all the usual suspects when it comes to kids' art supplies. You could spend hours getting lost in the aisles of this shop and will end up inspired to make an art project with your child.

Little Shop of Crafts

431 East 73rd Street bet. York and First avenues
212-717-6636

711 Amsterdam Avenue bet. 94th and 95th streets
212-531-2723
www.littleshopny.com

Stop by the Little Shop of Crafts and spend the day engaging in craft projects like painting, pottery, beading, making mosaics, and painting Plastercraft pieces. Kids can do their projects leisurely since you aren't charged by the hour at this beloved NYC art shop. They also offer classes and host birthday parties.

Moomah Cafe

161 Hudson Street at Leight Street
212-226-0345
www.moomah.com

Head to the back table of the arts café, where kids can choose from a menu of various craft projects, from making a shadow box to embroidery. There are projects for various ages with instructor-led pointers so there's no need to worry if you're not crafty enough to help. When my daughter and I went, she got to sit with a personal art instructor as she made her shadow box. The instructor explained the project and sat patiently while my daughter put it together and also helped when she wasn't able to do certain parts. For a rare moment, I was able to sit

back with a coffee, happy that my daughter was able to create a project while I took a break. The craft tables are open all day, so you don't have to schedule an appointment.

Pearl Paint

208 Canal Street at Mulberry Street
212-431-7932

Pearl Home and Craft Store

42 Lispenard Street at Church Street
212-226-3717
www.pearlpaint.com

The Lispenard location of Pearl Paint carries craft supplies like the Bedazzler on the upper level. This craft shop doesn't carry craft kits, but sells felt, patches, pipe cleaners, and all the other staples needed to be crafty at home.

Pratt Store

550 Myrtle Avenue bet. Steuben and Emerson streets
Brooklyn
718-789-1105
www.prattstore.net

This large art supply store and bookstore is a part of Pratt Institute, the renowned art college in Clinton Hill, Brooklyn, and has a large selection of arts-and-crafts kits, plus all the other standards like Magic Markers, colored pencils, sketchbooks, and more. Their bookstore upstairs has children's books, and they have a little kids' area on the ground floor.

Spacecraft Brooklyn

255 Bedford Avenue at South 4th Street
Brooklyn

718-599-2718

www.spacecraftbrooklyn.com

This funky craft shop located in Williamsburg, Brooklyn, offers walk-in craft workshops that range from beading a necklace to making a skateboard. They also offer art classes for kids ages three through twelve. If you are simply in search of arts-and-crafts supplies, you'll find it here—from glitter to glue and everything in between. They also host birthday parties. Since the shop is for adults, too, they can host an adult event if you want to plan a party without the kids.

Utrecht Art Supplies

111 Fourth Avenue at East 12th Street

212-777-5353

237 West 23rd Street bet. Seventh and Eighth avenues

212-675-8699

www.utrechtart.com

If your budding artist is in need of a paintbrush or a box of colored pencils, they'll find it at this art supply shop. The store has everything for the professional artist as well as the novice. The staff will help you navigate your way around the shop if you aren't familiar with the world of art supplies.

Design Your Kid's Room:

Guide to City Kids' Furniture

201

Chapter Eleven. Design Your Kid's Room: Guide to City Kids' Furniture

Now that your child has outgrown the nursery, he will need some new digs. It's time to remove the toddler bed from your child's room and enjoy redesigning it with their help. Now that they are older, your kids can assist you in picking out furniture, bedding, and other odds and ends that will give their rooms a personal touch. If your children are sharing a room, try to give them each a space in the room that they feel is their own and can decorate themselves, like a section of the wall where they can display their artwork, or let them choose photos and frames to put on their dressers.

Furniture

Now that the crib is disassembled and stored away, search for new furniture at the following stores with great kids furnishings—from bunk beds to desks and from high-end pieces to discounted items. If you can't make up your mind about how you'd like to decorate the room or simply want to hire a designer, many of the shops below have designers that will work with you in decorating your child's room.

Just to note, if you want to head out of the city to do some shopping on Long Island, you will find a slew of furniture stores right off the Long Island Expressway exit 49S, on Route 110 in Farmingdale.

ABC Carpet & Home
888 Broadway at West 19th Street
212-473-3000

Outlet
1055 Bronx River Avenue at Watson Avenue
Bronx
718 842- 8772
www.abchome.com

This high-end home furnishings shop has gorgeous children's furniture and accessories. From wall hangings to bedroom sets, you'll find a beautiful selection of goods. If you love their merchandise but can't shell out the cash, ABC has an amazing outlet in the Bronx that offers deep discounts on their furniture. The outlet has a kids' section and replenishes stock frequently. ABC also has another outlet in Hackensack, New Jersey.

Bellini Baby Kids & Furniture
1305 Second Avenue at East 69th Street
212-517-9233

363 New Dorp Lane
Staten Island
718-667-0727
www.bellini.com

For over twenty-five years, this children's furniture shop has been a great place to purchase well-made furniture and accessories for your child's room. From bunk beds to dressers, they have a large selection appealing to a variety of tastes.

Bograd Kids

200 Lexington Avenue bet. West 32nd and 33rd streets
212-726-0006
www.bogradkids.com

For over ten years, this kids' furniture company has been selling a large collection of high-quality children's furniture. You can check out the collection by appointment only at the Lexington Avenue showroom or you can purchase furniture from their Web site. If you're in need of an interior designer for your kid's room, the owner Zoya Bograd, is available to provide design services. View samples of her work on the Web site.

Casa Kids

106 Ferris Street at Coffey Street
Brooklyn
718-694-0272
www.casakids.com

Since 1992 furniture designer Roberto Gil has been designing kids' furniture at Casa Kids. They will create custom rooms and made-to-order pieces or you can pick out pieces from their lines of furniture at their shop. They have bunk beds and loft beds available, and work with an assortment of materials from

bamboo to birch plywood. You can visit their showroom in Red Hook, Brooklyn, by appointment only. Their product lines are thoughtfully designed and will enhance any children's room.

Design Within Reach

Check Web site for locations throughout New York City.
www.dwr.com

This modern design store has a large range of furniture and some kids' accessories. Although not especially for kids, they do have furniture that could be used in a child's room. They also have an outlet store in New Jersey.

Giggle

120 Wooster Street at Prince Street
212-334-5817

1033 Lexington Avenue bet. East 74th and 75th streets
212-249-4249
www.giggle.com

Although this shop is for babies and toddlers, they also have a selection of kids' furniture and twin-size bedding.

Ikea

One Beard Street at Otsego Street
Brooklyn
718-246-4532
www.ikea.com/us/en/store/brooklyn

Ikea has a large children's section with a wide range of inexpensive kids' furniture and bedding. The furniture is Swedish designed and is perfectly suited for apartment living since the pieces aren't very bulky.

Katz in the Cradle

2920 Ave L at East 29th Street
Brooklyn
718-258-1990

This well-known Brooklyn-based shop is crammed with furniture and is the best place to pick up cribs and other baby necessities. You can also get a wide range of kids' furniture from bunk beds and twin beds to dressers and desks. The shop closes early on Fridays and is closed on Saturdays.

Kid's Supply Company Junior Home-store

1343 Madison Avenue bet. East 94th and 95th streets
212-426-1200
www.kidssupply.com

This Upper East Side shop has everything you will need to furnish your child's room. Make an appointment with the owner and she will help you pick out the perfect furniture for your kid's room as well as work with you to create custom-designed furniture. The shop also has a service that will come to your home to take measurements and provide a custom design and installation.

Mini Jake

178 North 9th Street at Bedford Avenue
Brooklyn
718-782-2005
www.minijake.com

Mini Jake is a modern children's store located in Williamsburg, Brooklyn. This shop has a selection of twin, full, bunk, and loft beds. They also carry twin bedding and mattresses. Mini Jake is also a great place to pick up some kid-centric accessories like wall hangings and lighting.

Pottery Barn Kids

1311 Second Avenue bet. East 69th and 70th streets
212-879-4746

1451 Second Avenue bet. East 75th and 76th streets
212-879-2513
www.potterybarnkids.com

This chain store supplies a wide variety of simply styled kids furniture that works well for both boys and girls. They also have a large selection of accessories and bedding. If you want to get discounted Pottery Barn Kids furniture and accessories, head to their outlet location at the Tanger Outlet Centers in Riverhead (see p. 165).

Raymour & Flannigan

Check Web site for locations throughout New York City.
www.raymourflanigan.com

This traditional-style furniture retail chain has a selection of kids' room furniture at affordable prices.

Room and Board

105 Wooster Street bet. Prince and Spring streets
212-334-4343
www.roomandboard.com

This furniture shop has a large kids' section with a selection of well-designed beds and dressers. They also sell home accessories like lighting, rugs, bookshelves, and much more.

Schneider's Juvenile Furniture

41 West 25th Street bet. Broadway and Sixth Avenue
212-228-3540
www.schneidersbaby.com

Schneider's has an extensive selection of kids' and teens' furniture. Choose from twin and bunk beds, dressers, desks, and home accessories.

Home Accessories

Accessories are a great way to add some flair to a child's room or give them the opportunity to add their own personal touch. Let your child have fun shopping for accessories for their room at the following shops:

Anthropologie

Check Web site for locations throughout Manhattan.

www.anthropologie.com

Sophisticated kids will enjoy sprucing up their room with some of Anthropologie's shabby-chic home accessories, including mirrors, art, lighting, and rugs. They also sell chairs with upholstery, other furniture, and bedding.

Blue Tree

1283 Madison Avenue bet. East 91st and 92nd avenues

212-369-2583

www.bluetreeny.com

This Upper East Side store owned by actress Phoebe Cates has a great selection of tasteful kids' home accessories. Personal favorites include colorful comforters among a wide range of eclectic items. Parents will find themselves wanting to pick up some goodies for themselves since Blue Tree also stocks nice items for all areas of the home.

Century 21 Home Store

472 86th Street at York Avenue

718-748-3266

www.c21stores.com

The separate home store at this large discount department store has a great selection of bedding for twin beds, along with rugs and other home accessories for your kids' room. If your kids get bored and complain while you're shopping, take them over to the toy section, where you can pick up amazing craft kits at deep discounts. You could even use the finished product to decorate their room.

The Container Store

629 Sixth Avenue at West 19th Street

212-366-4200

725 Lexington Avenue bet. 58th and 59th streets

212-366-4200

www.containerstore.com

This chain store is a godsend for parents because of their wide variety of shelving systems and storage units—good for all the items that your children have accumulated and can't bear to part with. Kids will love picking out fun, colored boxes in assorted sizes to store their toys, books, clothes, and more. On a completely different subject, the Container Store also sells holiday wrapping paper and boxes, and is a great place to pick up containers to organize goody bag gifts for parties.

Exit 9 Gift Emporium

64 Avenue A bet. East 4th and 5th streets

212-228-0145

127 Smith Street bet. Dean and Pacific streets Brooklyn

718-422-7720

www.shopexit9.com

Your child will love sorting through the many fun odds and ends at this gift shop with two locations, in the East Village and Cobble Hill, Brooklyn. From phones that are shaped like hamburgers (just like the one Juno used in the self-titled film) to funky chandeliers, you'll find all of it here. The shop also carries small items that can line your child's shelves or stuff a loot bag for a party.

MoMA Design Store

11 West 53rd Street bet. Fifth and Sixth avenues

212-708-9700

81 Spring Street at Crosby Street

646-613-1367

www.momastore.org

This art museum's design store has an entire section devoted to kids. Have your child decorate their nightstand with a Doodlebook Frame, a picture frame that is also an eighty-page sketchpad, or a cool paper-clip holder. There are tons of other great finds for your child's room, from interesting lighting fixtures to thoughtfully designed stools.

Morning Glory

6 West 32nd Street bet. Fifth Avenue and Broadway

212-736-6606

From cute waste-paper baskets to clocks, this store sells tons of home accessories and even some Hello Kitty merchandise. Pick up a memo board for your kid's wall or coasters for their nightstand. An added

plus: Kids can also stock up on notebooks, pens, and even hair clips at this shop.

Pearl River

477 Broadway at Broome Street

212-431-4770

www.pearlriver.com

Fix up your child's room with straw mats, baskets, and other cool items from this large Chinatown shop that sells everything from toys to kimonos. Kids will love the fountain in the middle of the shop as well as picking through the assortment of cute inexpensive items.

Pier 1 Imports

71 Fifth Avenue at West 15th Street

212-206-1911

1550 3rd Avenue at East 87th Street

212-987-1746

www.pier1.com

I'll be honest with you—I have childhood memories of being annoyed that my mom took me here while she shopped for housewares. I'll also admit that as a kid, I was fascinated by the products at this shop and felt as if we were shopping at a bazaar in another country. I've picked up cute curtains and other products here that are perfect for a kid's room. They also sell inexpensive bed frames and furniture.

Pylones

Check Web site for locations throughout Manhattan.

www.pylones-usa.com

This fun shop, originally founded in France, has tons of kids' accessories such as vacuums shaped like popcorn tins or hamburgers. My kids love picking up accessories like funky staplers and other cool stuff here. This is also a great shop to pick up goody bag items and stocking stuffers.

Sanrio

233 West 42nd Street at Eight Avenue
212-840-6011
www.sanrio.com

Attention Hello Kitty fans! This official Sanrio Store is filled with tons of cool home accessories, from Hello Kitty toasters to stuffed animals. They also have great Hello Kitty pajamas. Basically if you are in need of something with Hello Kitty on it, you'll find it here.

Spencer's Gifts

Check Web site for a list of locations in local area malls.
www.spencersonline.com

This mall chain store is the perfect place to pick up a lava lamp, disco ball, or other kitschy or novelty items to decorate a kid's room.

Target

139 Flatbush Avenue at Atlantic Avenue
Brooklyn
718-290-1109
www.target.com

You can pick up everything from room storage items to cool picture frames at this chain store. New Yorkers gravitate to the shop for their low prices and interesting selection of home goods.

Yoya and Yoya Mart

636 Hudson Street at Horatio Street
646-336-6844

15 Gansevoort Street at Hudson Street
212-242-5511

Despite the baby and toddler focus on this high-end shop, they have a good selection of goods to decorate your little one's pad. You can pick up wall art, cookie jars, and other funky items. They also have a selection of interesting toys, stuffed animals, clothes and bags.

Urban Outfitters

Check Web sites for locations throughout New York City.
www.urbanoutfitters.com

From funky throw pillows that will brighten up your child's space to colorful curtains that will add light even in the darkest area of the home, this shop has tons of cool goods to decorate a kid's room. Tween girls will be drawn to the shop and will probably want to pick up some clothes, too.

Chapter Twelve

What's Happening Today?:
Web Sites, Magazines, and Other Resources for Up-To-Date City Parenting

The city moves at an extremely fast pace and in order to keep up, folks rely on the Internet, magazines, and newspapers. Here are some resources that will help you keep on top of all the kid-friendly happenings around the city:

New York City Parenting Sites, Blogs and Other Resources

www.achildgrowsinbrooklyn.com
Invaluable resource for Brooklyn parents run by Brooklyn mom Karen Connell. The site has a calendar of kid-friendly activities around Brooklyn and offers advice on everything from schools to shops.

www.brooklynbaby.com
The companion Web site for my guidebook *City Baby Brooklyn*.

www.nyc.citymommy.com
The NYC site, part of the National parenting site City Mommy, offers moms a message board where they can post messages on a variety of parenting subjects. There is a list of area happenings. This is a good resource for connecting with other moms.

www.dailycandy.com
Reviews and lists local events and products related to NYC parenting.

www.divamoms.com
Lyss Stern, NYC mom and co-author of *If you Give a Mom a Martini*, runs Divalysscious Moms, a social group for moms that offers tons of fun events from fashion to film screenings. The site is also home to the magazine *Observer Playground*, which is published by the New York *Observer*.

www.hipslopemama.blogspot.com
This webzine for hip mamas run by local Brooklyn mama Melissa Lopata has many articles from local writers and moms.

www.kidcityny.com
An online magazine with lists of NYC kid-friendly events and reviews. There is also a blog that is updated daily run by the creator of Kid City, NYC

Mom and New York expert. Samantha Chapnick. The site offers tons of suggestions and ideas for what to do with your kids in the city. You can also follow Kid City on Twitter.

www.lilaguide.com

The companion Web site for the popular parenting guide *The Lila Guide*, which rates local shops and restaurants in New York City.

www.mamaista.com

Updates parents on the new "must-haves" for child rearing.

www.mommypoppins.com

Run by NYC mom Anna Fader, who is an amazing endless resource for all things related to NYC parenting. Sign up for the mailing list and receive daily updates on the latest happenings. This is truly a wonderful resource for parenting in New York City. You can also follow Mommy Poppins on Twitter. Mommy Poppins and A Child Grows in Brooklyn also have a joint Twitter account called KidBuzzNY.

www.nycmomsblog.com

A bunch of NYC moms who blog about parenting in NYC.

www.nycitymama.com

Local mom that blogs about kids' happenings and the NYC parenting scene.

www.onlytheblogknowsbrooklyn.com

The Web site of Smart Mom, a columnist for the *Brooklyn Paper*, her site often lists kid-friendly happenings around Brooklyn.

www.parentsknow.com

The Web site for two local newspapers, *Big Apple Parent* and *Brooklyn Parent*, that often lists events and articles on parenting issues.

www.parkslopeparents.com

A great resource for parents living in Park Slope, Brooklyn, that features information on parenting-related issues. The site has a message board for both parenting questions and classifieds at Yahoo! Groups, which only costs $25 to join.

www.siparent.com

This Web site for a local Stan Island parenting magazine has a wealth of advice for Staten Island moms.

www.smallbitesonline.com

The Web site for Small Bites, a company that teaches NYC parents and parents-to-be how to make healthy, safe, and sustainable food choices in a way that saves parents time.

www.newyorkkids.timeout.com

The Web site for popular *Time Out New York Kids*.

www.urbanbaby.com

Resources for all urban parents, including listings of baby-friendly events, parenting advice, and a real-time message board for parents, which is extremely addictive.

General NYC Web sites

www.billburg.com
A Web site about the local happenings around Williamsburg, Brooklyn.

www.brooklynonline.com
General information on Brooklyn.

www.brooklyn-usa.org
The official site for the Brooklyn Borough President.

www.flavorpill.com
Cool NYC things to do.

www.freewilliamsburg.com
Lists of local events and reviews of venues in Williamsburg, Brooklyn, and featuring many kid-friendly events.

www.freshdirect.com
An online grocer that is a godsend for all parents who just can't juggle kids and bags of groceries. This service delivers only to some NYC areas, so check the Web site to see if they deliver to your neighborhood.

www.go-brooklyn.com
The Web site for *Brooklyn Paper*.

www.gocitykids.parentsconnect.com
Cool kid-friendly activities in the city.

www.gonyc.about.com
The About.com guide to New York City.

www.gothamist.com
The Web site that dishes out info on the latest happenings in the city.

www.hellobrooklyn.com
Lists of events throughout the borough, from kids' shows to openings of new shops.

www.hopstop.com
The guide to subway directions around New York City.

www.iloveny.com
A NYC tourism site.

www.manhattanusersguide.com
An online guide to city living.

www.mta.info/nyct
Mass Transit Authority information for New York City.

www.newyork.citysearch.com
Activities in New York City.

www.newyorkology.com
A Web site that discusses what is happening in the city.

www.notfortourists.com/newyork.aspx
A tourism site for the city.

www.nyc.gov
The official site for New York City.

www.nycgovparks.org
The Web site for NYC Parks and Recreation.

www.nycvisit.com
Official tourism site for New York City.

www.nymag.com
The Web site for popular *New York* magazine.

www.queens.about.com

The About.com guide to Queens.

www.smalltownbrooklyn.com

A site that breaks down Brooklyn by neighborhood and lists shops in each neighborhood.

www.statenislandusa.com

The official site for the Staten Island Borough President.

www.timeoutny.com

The print edition of this must-have city magazine now publishes a quarterly kids' edition. Check out the Web site for updates on kid-friendly events and activites..

www.visitbrooklyn.org

A Brooklyn tourism site.

General Parenting

www.babble.com

An edgy online magazine from the folks that brought you Nerve.com, which offers honest essays and articles about the realities of modern parenting.

www.parentdish.com

An online parenting magazine run by AOL.com

www.parenthood.com

Tips for parents and great articles on an array of parenting issues.

www.parenting.com

The Web site for *Parenting* magazine.

www.parentsoup.com

Parenting message boards and articles on all stages of parenting run by ivillage.com.

www.tweenparent.com

A parent of a tween runs this interesting blog. You can also follow her adventures on Twitter.

Medical, Nutrition, and Fitness

www.askdrsears.com

A well-respected pediatrician addresses FAQs on many aspects of childcare.

www.autismnetworks.com

A Web site for information on autism and autism groups.

www.webmd.com

Advice on a variety of medical ailments.

Just For Moms

www.hipmama.com

A parenting zine that claims that it's "better than a double Prozac latte" and offers helpful and often witty advice for parents as well as message boards.

www.mamapalooza.com

The site for the annual concert and reading series that runs in New York City and throughout the United States. The Web site has a list of interesting artistic events and also produces a literary journal that is worth a look.

www.momasphere.com

Created by the founder of Hip Slope Mama, Melissa Lopata hosts events for moms that range from literary readings to parties.

www.momlogic.com

Various bloggers discuss parenting.

www.mothering.com

The Web site for *Mothering* magazine with a popular message boards for moms.

www.punkymoms.com

A Web site for hip moms, with great links, such as for clothes, bibs, and other baby-related items handmade and sold by moms.

www.workingmother.com

The Web site for the popular magazine *Working Mother*.

Just For Dads

www.thedadman.com

An organization that promotes better relationships between father and daughters.

www.urbandaddy.com

A site that offers NYC dads info and reviews on where to eat, what to buy and what to do in and around NYC.

Parenting Groups

www.bigcitymoms.com
www.divamoms.com
www.gothambaby.com
www.hrpmamasclubexpress.com
www.metropolitanmoms.com
www.parentzone.com

Index

About the Author

Alison Lowenstein is the author of *City Baby Brooklyn: The Ultimate Guide for Parents, from Pregnancy through Preschool* and *City Weekends: The Greatest Escapes and Weekend Getaways in and Around NYC*. She has written for *The New York Daily News, Newsday, Time Out New York Kids, New York Family Magazine*, Babble.com, among many other publications and Web sites. She lives in Brooklyn with her husband and their two school-aged children.